Who
Killed
SHAKESPEARE?

Who
Killed
SHAKESPEARE?

**What's Happened
to English
since the Radical
Sixties**

PATRICK BRANTLINGER

ROUTLEDGE
New York and London

Published in 2001 by
Routledge
29 West 35th Street
New York, NY 10001

Published in Great Britain by
Routledge
11 New Fetter Lane
London EC4P 4EE

Copyright © 2001 by Routledge
Routledge is an imprint of the Taylor & Francis Group.

Printed in the United States of America on acid-free paper.

10 9 8 7 6 5 4 3 2 1

Library of Congress Cataloging-in-Publication Data

Brantlinger. Patrick, 1941–
    Who killed Shakespeare? : What's happened to English since the radical
       sixties / Patrick Brantlinger.
          p. cm.
    Includes bibliographical references and index.
    ISBN 0-415-93010-3 (acid-free paper)—ISBN 0-415-93011-1 (pbk. :
      acid-free paper)
    1. English literature—Study and teaching (Higher)—United States.
    2. Shakespeare, William, 1564–1616—Study and teaching—United States.
    3. Shakespeare, William, 1564–1616—Study and teaching (Higher). 4. English
literature—History and criticism—Theory, etc. 5. Humanities—Study and
teaching (Higher)—United States. 6. Culture—Study and teaching (Higher)—
United States. 7. Education, Higher—United States—Curricula. 8. Education,
Humanistic—United States. I. Title.

PR51.U5 B73 2001
820'.71'173—dc21
00-051707

For Jerome Buckley

Contents

Acknowledgments

My friends, both faculty and graduate students, at Indiana University and beyond have been, as always, more than supportive. Jim Adams, Todd Avery, Purnima Bose, Ellen Brantlinger, Mary Burgan, Eva Cherniavsky, John Eakin, Jonathan Elmer, Tom Foster, Don Gray, Susan Gubar, Joan Pong Linton, Chris Lohmann, Andrew Miller, Carolyn Mitchell, Jim Naremore, John Reed, Sherri Smith, Janet Sorensen, Bill Thesing, and Steve Watt have all helped in various ways (and whether they know it or not!). I am grateful also to the editors of several journals for permission to include revised versions of articles. An abbreviated version of chapter 2, "Who Killed Shakespeare?" appeared in *College English* in the July, 1999 issue. Chapter 9, "Apocalypse 2001," is a revised version of an article published by *Cultural Critique*, Spring 1998. And chapter 3, "Antitheory and its Antitheses," first appeared in Thomas Rosteck, ed., *At the Intersection: Rhetorical Studies/ Cultural Studies* in 1998. I thank Guilford Press for permission to reprint it with minor alterations. Last but not least, I also thank Bill Germano, the Officer Friendly of the publishing industry, who not only encouraged me to deliver this book over to Routledge but also came up with the idea for the cover.

Introduction

A View from the Ruins

Bare ruined choirs, where late the sweet birds sang.
—Shakespeare, *Sonnets*

Who Killed Shakespeare? is tangentially about Shakespeare; it is primarily about the current and future situations of English, cultural studies, the university, and society at large. Despite its title, it is not a mystery novel. I can, therefore, eliminate the suspense right away: no one, least of all any teacher of English literature, has killed Shakespeare. The Bard is not so central to higher education as he was thirty or forty years ago, but that is not because of neglect, rejection, or homicide by English professors. It is instead because English is being marginalized, along with the other humanities disciplines. And the marginalization (not murder) is occurring mainly through competition from such career-oriented fields as business, computer science, fashion design, sports medicine, and, at least at some universities, hotel and casino management. These mostly new fields are symptomatic of the increasing (but not new) corporatization of academia, as also are the supposedly higher educational offerings of such corporations as IBM, McDonald's, and Disney.

As Plato's critique of the Sophists suggests, competition among educational subjects and disciplines is not new. Often such competition takes the form of a struggle over money and power, with little or no constructive interdisciplinary dialogue. But at least among related disciplines, dialogue can and does occur, generating the emergence of new subjects and disciplines. Thus, cultural studies has developed over the last several decades as one site of constructive dialogue among various humanities and social science disciplines. Its development does not necessarily mean that English, as the most capacious and, perhaps, least well defined of academic disciplines, is evolving into cultural studies, although such a metamorphosis has occurred at some institutions.

How disciplines and universities evolve cannot be understood in isolation from cultural and societal change. According to some apocalyptic claims, not just Shakespeare, or English, or the liberal arts, but higher education in general is on the wane. Over the last couple of decades, neoconservative doomsters such as Allan Bloom (*The Closing of the American Mind*) and Dinesh D'Souza (*Illiberal Education*) have made the decline and fall of higher education and of Western civilization their theme, and the mass media have turned their arguments into incessant, repetitive headlines. Although I do not agree with many of the neoconservatives' arguments, I am attracted to what I take to be more responsible accounts of the current plight of English, the humanities, and the university. On October 31, 1994, an American Eagle flight from Indianapolis to Chicago crashed near Roselawn, Illinois. Among the casualties was Bill Readings, a young associate professor of comparative literature at the University of Montreal. At the time of his tragic death, Bill had almost completed his second book, *The University in Ruins*, in which he argues that the national-cultural basis of higher education as it emerged in the nineteenth century is being eroded by transnational capitalism and "the decline of the nation-state as the primary instance of capitalism's self-reproduction." These have "effectively voided the social mission of the modern University." The traditional goal of liberal arts education, the training of citizens through their inculcation into nation-based cultures—languages, literatures, and histories—is losing its centrality. According to Readings, "The strong idea of culture arises with the nation-state, and we now face its disappearance as the locus of social meaning" (89).

New configurations are vying to fill the increasingly vacuous center of the university. Readings contends that it is precisely at the moment when nation-based cultures are losing significance that both multiculturalism and cultural studies emerge as alternatives to traditional curricular fare. In contrast to neoconservative jeremiads about the decline and fall of both academia and civilization, Readings does not accuse these alternatives of causing that ruination (much less of bardicide). On the contrary, social, economic, and political transformations are necessarily changing the ways universities do business. These transformations are also key issues for cultural studies, among other academic disciplines or interdisciplines. According to Readings, however, a major weakness of cultural studies is that, like the discourse of academic "excellence" he wryly dissects in his second chapter, it "dereferentializes" culture, turning it into a hollow "general equivalent" similar to money. "Cultural Studies presents a vision of culture that is appropriate for the age of excellence," Readings declares (17). Cultural studies strives to fulfill "the redemptive claims of cultural criticism, while expanding those claims to cover everything" (103). Much the same is true, Readings believes, of multiculturalism, which installs ethnic, linguistic, religious, cultural "difference" as general equivalent: what we share with others just is difference, and according to liberal, democratic ideology, all differences are equal, or at least equally different:

> In general, the effect of multiculturalism is necessarily to homogenize differences as equivalently deviant from a norm. This is why multiculturalism replaces national cultural policy for a global economy, whether in the sensitivity training of transnational corporations or in the federal policy of super-states such as Canada or the European Union, which are attempting to align themselves in the global economy. (113)

Instead of alternatives to business as usual in what Readings calls "the posthistorical university," both multiculturalism and cultural studies turn out to be more business as usual or, perhaps, better business as usual—an argument calculated, of course, to upset both academic conservatives and the advocates of new, supposedly "redemptive" or radical developments in higher education.

Who Killed Shakespeare? is not an attempt to defend either cultural studies or multiculturalism against Readings's argument. I admire the intelligence and daring of that argument, and I partly agree with it. At the same time, I explore cultural studies with Readings's critique in mind: are "culture" and "difference" mere empty placeholders, frames for contents they cannot supply? Or do cultural studies and multiculturalism have something more positive to offer? If so, what exactly is it that they offer? Along the way, I consider the impact of cultural studies and multiculturalism on English departments. As a member of an English department for the past thirty years, and as one of the creators of the cultural studies graduate program at Indiana University, I am keenly interested in the evolving relations between these academic units and projects. They have both been crucial to my understanding of higher education and, more generally, of modern and postmodern or even, perhaps, "posthistorical" society.

Who Killed Shakespeare? is a sequel to two earlier books, *Bread and Circuses* (1983) and *Crusoe's Footprints* (1990). The first was a genealogy, as the subtitle has it, of "theories of mass culture as social decay," back to the ancient Greeks and forward to the twentieth century. That genealogy ended with the Frankfurt School and trends in the study of television and the mass media following World War II; I did not pursue it into postmodernity and some of the other "posts" that have emerged since the 1960s: poststructuralism, postindustrialism, postcolonialism, and so forth. In reflecting on the fate of English, cultural studies, and the university after 2000, however, these are unavoidable categories, as are also two other "posts" that I examine here especially in the last two chapters: "posthistory" and "posthumanity."

I wrote *Crusoe's Footprints* as an introductory textbook for the graduate courses in cultural studies that I started to teach in the 1980s. While I deal briefly in it with poststructuralism, postmodernism, postindustrialism, and postcolonialism, I do not engage posthistory and posthumanity, and my current—post-2000—understanding of all of these post-isms is significantly different from what it was a decade ago. One of my reasons for according Readings's *The University in Ruins* as much attention and respect as I do is that I am now less optimistic than I was in 1990 about the future of higher education: I am both leery of and compelled by arguments that, within a very short time (the next decade or two), many of the processes and functions now undertaken in college and university settings

4

will be both corporatized and virtualized (that is, computerized). I hope that won't be the case, but the prognosis isn't rosy.

From one perspective, all of the post-isms I have mentioned are signs of ruination—or just *are* the ruins of the more traditional and substantive formations that preceded them (modernity as a haven from postmodernity, structuralism as a more rational theory than deconstruction, and history and humanity as more positive, secure, and sensible than whatever threatens to succeed them). As has often been noted, however, the "post" in, say, "postmodern" does not necessarily mean the abolition of whatever is being posted, but can just as easily mean more of the same, only under new conditions: the postmodern as a new phase of modernity; the posthuman as a new version of being human. If "post" prefixes "Shakespeare," Shakespeare doesn't disappear, and it isn't that he has been superceded by debased forms of mass culture. He *is* mass culture: witness Lawrence Levine's account of the popular meanings and uses of Shakespeare in nineteenth-century America, or the more recent popularity of such films as *Romeo and Juliet*, *Prospero's Books*, and *Shakespeare in Love*. It seems just as likely that post-Shakespeare in any of its guises is merely and necessarily an inferior performance of the original (the trouble is, of course, that all we have to go by are such performances, including our own readings and interpretations).

Nevertheless, all of the "post" terms I've mentioned are to greater or lesser degree apocalyptic, or at any rate are open to apocalyptic interpretations. So, too, is the title of Readings's book, and yet the apocalypse in higher education (if it is even reasonable to use such a term instead of, for example, the more frequently used "crisis") has been gradual, is ongoing, and perhaps is even as ancient as the university itself. The tendency of all the academic disciplines to convert discoveries and new knowledges into traditions and orthodoxies means that part of their function has always been the production and reification of intellectual ruins—that is, of orthodoxies waiting to be deconstructed and cleared away by new heterodoxies such as cultural studies.

In any event, the "posthistorical university," according to Readings, "is a *ruined institution*" (169, his emphasis), though that doesn't mean it is about to disappear. "Ruins" persist, and therefore Readings argues that administrators, professors, and students alike must pragmatically make the best of the situation:

> Such a pragmatism...requires that we accept that the modern University is a *ruined* institution. Those ruins must not be the object of a romantic nostalgia for a lost wholeness but the site of an attempt to transvalue the fact that the University no longer inhabits a continuous history of progress, of the progressive revelation of a unifying idea [such as culture]. (129)

Part of the solution, Readings thinks, is to accept that the university is no longer a community of consensus, but instead "a community of dissensus," one "structured by a constitutive incompleteness" (185). Or in other words, in place of Central U, now we have Decentral U.

The University in Ruins is one of numerous accounts of the transformations that higher education has been undergoing since the 1960s. Many of these accounts have come from neoconservatives such as Bloom and D'Souza, and have called for an impossible restoration, often in nationalist terms, of coherence or consensus or recentering. But I wonder—and here I may be parting company from Readings—has the university ever had such coherence or consensus? Even though he warns against it, Readings knows that the very thought of ruins evokes nostalgia for what came before; in this case, the grand, original edifice of Central U. But perhaps no Central U has ever existed? Perhaps all that there has ever been is Decentral U or various "communities of dissensus"?

According to Charles Homer Haskins, "Historically, the word university has no connection with the universe or the universality of learning; it denotes only the totality of a group, whether of barbers, carpenters, or students did not matter" (9). In his old but learned and entertaining *The Rise of Universities*, Haskins writes that the classical revival of "the renaissance of the twelfth century" was, "though brilliant...short-lived, crushed in its early youth by the triumph of logic and the more practical studies of law and rhetoric" (29). Haskins continues:

> In the later twelfth century John of Salisbury inveighs against the logicians of his day, with their superficial knowledge of literature; in the university curriculum of the thirteenth century, literary studies have quite disappeared. (29)

Today, if "literary studies" including Shakespeare are again on the wane, that is, I believe, less because of theory, cultural studies, and multicultural- ism than of parks and recreation, accounting, and informatics. In any event, versions of "dissensus" or of what Kant called "the conflict of the fac- ulties" have characterized the university's organization of knowledges and disciplines from the outset. Of course literature, law, rhetoric, and logic are still categories of knowledge today, and these are reflected in various ways in various academic disciplines. But the content and configuration of these categories are very different from what they were in the twelfth century.

If John of Salisbury's remark about the logicians' devaluation of litera- ture sounds like Alvin Kernan's *The Death of Literature*, two caveats are in order. First, the meaning of literature has changed and is always changing. And second, both of these alleged deaths of literature, one medieval and one modern, are signs of border disputes among disciplines of knowledge—disputes that have been and will continue to be interminable, precisely because they are the structuring process of the disciplines.[1] Remember how rapidly, contentiously, but also recently the classical cur- riculum was replaced between the 1880s and World War II by training in modern literatures and languages, including English (Parker, Graff). In the nineteenth century as today, even though the idea of unified, nation-based cultures was then more powerful, the parameters and contents of the disci- plines were evolving, unsettled, and under constant debate. Was history an "art" or a "science" (see, for instance, Hughes)? Should modern languages and literatures be taught alongside or in place of "the classics"? Were the natural sciences valid subjects for higher education? The famous debate between Matthew Arnold and Thomas Henry Huxley over this last question suggests that the conflict between "the two cultures," as C. P. Snow called them, is itself not a modern or postmodern phenomenon, or the result of the rise of "science studies." This prompts the further question of whether it makes sense to think in terms of a conflict between many cultures, a dis- sensual multiculturalism as the very (torn) fabric of history?

"No sooner are totalities closed in on themselves than they start crack- ing all over," writes Bruno Latour. "The end of history is followed by history no matter what" (57). This is certainly true of the "totalities" that get defined as academic disciplines. But while Readings's very invocation of "ruins" evokes nostalgia for a unified organization of knowledge or a consensus that has never existed, he raises the question of whether the "posthistorical university" is becoming *more* dissensual and "ruined" than ever, mainly through the transformative power of transnational capitalism? What does it mean, moreover, to be "posthistorical," especially if, as Latour says, history continues "no matter what"? Does it mean, for one thing, the ultimate vacuity if not evacuation of history departments? I am a cultural and intellectual historian, so for me such an evacuation would be a sad state of affairs indeed. But historical understanding and the historical organization of knowledges and disciplines, at least within the humanities and social sciences, is not about to disappear. For English departments, where versions of poststructuralist theory have challenged historical understanding, the new historicism has had its day in the perhaps twilit ruins, and in some ways it hasn't been much different from older historicisms. Meanwhile, many historians seem impervious to the antihistorical logic of poststructuralism—at least, they have gone on doing pretty much what they have always done, though with new infusions from the subdisciplines of social, cultural, and intellectual history (but see Bonnell and Hunt).

Ruins are always history's signatures or symptoms—history has been here, and done such and such, leading to these ruins—so perhaps one reassuring thought to extract from Readings is that "the ruined university" reinstalls what has always been at the heart of the university: namely, history (or historiography, the study and writing-up of history's ruinous deeds). We—humanities and social science professors of many dissensual sorts—do history differently from our predecessors of fifty years ago, but we are still doing it. So at least there may still be a consensus of sorts in the midst of dissensus. Perhaps, too, this means that today's university, albeit in many ways ruinous, is not "posthistorical." (So long as at least one historian remains at her post, the university will never be posthistorical... perhaps.)

And yet there is much skepticism today—in my opinion, largely healthy skepticism—about both the course of history and courses in history, or in other words about what was once understood as "universal" or "world" history and about the epistemological status and stability of historiography, as well as about what the contents of history courses should be. Instead of one, linear history for everybody and for all time, now there are many histories going in numerous directions. For as Lyotard says, to be postmodern is to disbelieve in "metanarratives"; at best, it is only possible to defend and accept "micronarratives." Anyone with a stake in some version of a single, totalizing "universal history" will be disappointed; anyone with a stake in multiplicity, difference, and individual and social particularity will find this postmodern news encouraging. Universal history may have arrived at the end of its tether, one version of posthistory; but many less grandiose histories are flourishing and multiplying.

Nevertheless, the metanarrative or universal history of "the postmodern condition" is precisely the one that Readings identifies as the ruination of the (traditional, historical) university, namely the triumph of transnational capitalism. Aren't all of the ramifying, multiplying microhistories the products of this totalizing, global metanarrative? It's no news that the ends of centuries and millennia inspire endgame ideas, including the recent proliferation of postisms. Perhaps by 2010 or 2020, vanguard universities will be offering courses in postology or postography. My university has just hatched an entire new school (apparently, a metadiscipline) of "informatics," and I suspect that this category may prove to be a postology. Anyway, in the final chapter, I focus on "posthistory" in ways that, I think, make it a fitting sequel to *Bread and Circuses*, to several of the themes in *Crusoe's Footprints*, and also to the other chapters in *Who Killed Shakespeare?*

The title chapter originally appeared, in abbreviated form, in *College English*, as part of a "symposium" on "English 1999." Its gist is that no one, least of all English professors, has committed bardicide, and yet English professors are the leading suspects as this particular murder story is played out in the media. Many scholars including Readings have noted that Shakespeare—or his name, at any rate—gets used and abused for all sorts of purposes. This is one way, however, in which he or his specter persists. In the neoconservative attack on English departments, one abuse has been to claim that English professors have murdered the Bard.

Chapter 3, "English Departments as Heterotopias," takes up some of the themes, especially about "dissensus," broached in this introduction. I argue that English departments have both utopian and dystopian features, but that they are above all heterotopian. Heterotopias are "third spaces" or places of "*différance*" in a quite literal as well as theoretical sense. The notion that English departments once had a consensus and a unified canon (with Shakespeare at the center of that canon, of course) is no longer tenable, if it ever was; and the necessary dissensus within English departments mirrors the larger dissensus of the university.

"Antitheory and Its Antitheses: Rhetoric versus Ideology," chapter 4, examines literary theory in relation to cultural studies, English, and neopragmatist "antitheory." Theory as such, I contend, is always self-deconstructive. Its self-underminings lead either to rhetoric (Terry Eagleton) or to ideology (Paul de Man) or both. I consider the meanings of theory, rhetoric, and ideology for English and also cultural studies. Resorting to the old antithesis between ideology and utopia, I argue that theory always has a utopian dimension, even as it self-deconstructs, and that one thing needful is a theory of hope.

The fifth chapter, "How the New Historicism Grew Old (and Gained Its Tale)," examines the quick rise to fame and almost instantaneous fall into academic oblivion of the new historicism. I contend that in trying so hard to be an anti-theoretical avant-garde, the new historicism was from the outset a lot like the old historicism (or familiar versions of cultural, intellectual, and literary history). This is a point made with some frequency by so-called new historicists themselves, including Stephen Greenblatt and Brook Thomas; Thomas's *The New Historicism and Other Old-Fashioned Topics* announced the oldness of this new academic trend more than a decade ago. Along the way, I consider the relations among the new historicism, poststructuralism, cultural studies, and neopragmatism.

I explore one source of hope and renewal for both English and cultural studies in the sixth chapter, "Postcolonialism and Its Discontents." But as postcolonialists acknowledge, the term for their field of study is a misnomer, because even if Europe's formal political empires have been dismantled, transnational capitalism means economic imperialism. And the demographic and cultural effects of the old imperial formations are everywhere evident in today's cultures and societies. I also examine the relationships between postcolonialism and multiculturalism. These emergent forms of academic discourse I take to be highly significant for the future of the humanities and social sciences, in the midst of the ruins.

The seventh chapter, "Between Liberalism and Marxism: The Populism of Cultural Studies," examines the old question of the politics of cultural studies. I argue that issues of social class must continue to be addressed, for social justice reasons of course, but also to understand how, despite postmodern flattening or "deliberate superficiality," value hierarchies based on social class continue to organize all of our perceptions about culture (in short, the high/low "great divide" that Andreas Huyssen, for one, insists characterized modernity hasn't disappeared). Pierre Bourdieu's massive demonstration, in *Distinction*, of the class determinants of taste hierarchies supports my argument, as does Peter Stallybrass and Allon White's *Politics and Poetics of Transgression*. And then there are the numerous studies of poverty in postmodern America, such as Ken Auletta's *The Underclass*. Cultural studies, I contend, must continue to focus on social class, even as other categories—race, gender, sexual preference, religion—add to the complexity of that focus.

Chapter 8, "Informania U," deals with the emergence of "informatics" both at my university and around the world as a new sort of interdisciplinary project, one likely to become more central to a corporatized academy than either English or cultural studies. Readings hoped to see "Thought" reinstalled at the not-so-still center of "the ruined university," and many others who do not necessarily share the view that the university is "ruined" continue to believe that "knowledge" or "culture" or "the liberal arts" still holds the center. But the new "general equivalent" at the heart of the university is "information," as Readings himself recognized. One of my main exhibits is the recently approved School of Informatics that will be in operation at Indiana University by the time this book is published. I also discuss information theory, the apocalyptic "crash theories" of Jean Baudrillard, Arthur Kroker, and Paul Virilio, and how (following Katherine Hayles's argument) cybernetics and computers have rendered us "posthuman."

"Posthuman," perhaps, but not yet "posthistorical." In the final chapter, I critique Francis Fukuyama's "end of history" thesis, while also considering the "posthistoire" tradition analyzed by Lutz Niethammer. This older tradition of theorizing about the "end of history" was, in contrast to Fukuyama's optimism about the globally transforming effects of capitalism and liberalism, mainly dystopian, though it had a more or less positive offshoot in the early economists' speculations about progress ending in a "stationary state." Readings's claim that "the ruined university" is also "posthistorical" is, of course, dystopian rather than the reverse. Along with the global versions of "posthistory," both negative and positive, I reject Readings's more specialized use of the term, even while agreeing with him that the university as we have known it is coming to an end through both corporatization and computerization.

Despite these gloomy thoughts, postcolonialism, cultural studies, and multiculturalism—and Shakespeare—will have much to say about the future shapes of the humanities and social sciences. I take it as hopeful that much that had been excluded from academic canons and contexts is now being included. In various ways, postcolonial, cultural, and race and ethnic studies are mutually reinforcing, and can be expected to gain strength in higher education. Together with feminism and "queer theory," the political goals of all of these studies are democratic and broadly emancipatory. Even as the university threatens to dissolve, through its electronic virtualization, into a simulacrum of itself, not everything that it contains is ruined or part of the ruins. As Dick Hebdige eloquently declares: "There are many good things to be grown in the autumn of the patriarch, many good things to be found in the ruins, in the collapse of the older explanatory systems, in the splintering of the masterly overview and the totalising aspiration" (225). The new, interdisciplinary forms of theory and study I have mentioned are, I believe, among those good things.

Who Killed Shakespeare?

What's Happened to English since the Radical Sixties

Not marble, nor the gilded monuments
Of princes, shall outlive this powerful rime.
—Shakespeare, *Sonnets*

A specter is haunting English departments, the specter of Shakespeare. It also haunts the university, the stage, movies, television, advertising, music, politics, and everyday language. Hence, as long as there are English departments, there will be Shakespeare courses. I am not a Shakespearean, but occasionally I get to teach some of his plays—for example, *Hamlet* in a freshman course on mysteries. Once a student complained that *Hamlet* is not a mystery, because "I knew from the start who the killer was." I asked him how he could be so sure, since Hamlet himself is not at first sure? He replied that the Ghost tells Hamlet "up front, so there isn't any mystery." Besides, he added, "I knew the story even before I read it. It's just one of those stories everybody knows, like *Moby Dick*."

I don't remember whether he knew *Hamlet* well enough to answer the questions about it on the exam, but his claim to know it without reading it wasn't entirely far-fetched. He also claimed to know *Romeo and Juliet* in the same proleptic manner (well, maybe he'd seen the movie). He admitted, however, that it was a good idea to read *Hamlet* "for the details." He earned a respectable "B" in the course, but just how much of that outcome was based on his foreknowledge of literary works that he did not read, I cannot say.

I thought about mentioning this student's remarkable acquaintance with Shakespeare at a recent faculty meeting. We were discussing revising our undergraduate requirements for majors, part of which used to be a three-semester survey, Beowulf to Virginia Woolf. The proposed revision called for creating four survey courses, and for the nineteenth- and twentieth-century courses to reflect the emergence of world literatures in English. Students could substitute more specific courses in the periods covered by the surveys. So, for example, instead of taking the first survey course, Beowulf through Shakespeare, a student might take Elizabethan poetry.

The meeting was supposed to end at 5 o'clock, and by 5:15, several people had left to pick up their kids or mix their first martinis. As we were winding up, our very precise Miltonist shot his hand into the air. "I approve of the new requirements, with one exception," he said; "Our majors should *not* be allowed to substitute a Shakespeare course for the first survey course. A course in Chaucer or Spenser would be fine, but we shouldn't let them take Shakespeare." The Miltonist then made a motion to exclude Shakespeare from fulfilling our new requirements.

5:25 P.M. Nobody left. The motion to exclude Shakespeare evoked much consternation, jawing, and guffawing, until two things became clear: first, the Miltonist was serious; and second, the other teachers of medieval and Renaissance literature, including the Shakespeareans, agreed with him. Shakespeare, they pointed out, can take care of himself. If you allow students to take Shakespeare to fulfill the requirement of one course dealing with English literature before 1620, then most of them will take Shakespeare, and never read Chaucer or Spenser or Marlowe. "The demand for Shakespeare is so great," someone said, "that if we offered six or seven Shakespeare courses every year instead of three or four, they would all fill." Another colleague added: "It's a fetish thing. Bardolatry. You can deconstruct other authors into oblivion, but Shakespeare really is immortal."

"What will happen," said a young Americanist, "if we exclude Shakespeare from our requirements and then the parents of our students—or, God forbid, our board of trustees—find out about it?" And suddenly, there it was, for all of us to dread, the nightmare of headlines in the Indianapolis *Star*: PROFESSORS STRIKE SHAKESPEARE FROM REQUIREMENTS, or even FACULTY DECONSTRUCT SHAKESPEARE. Such headlines might very well provoke an inquisition by our benevolent but meddlesome trustees, who would not appreciate that "it's a fetish thing," and who might rule that every undergraduate be required to take Shakespeare.

5:45 P.M. Only two more colleagues left. The rest of us stayed riveted to our chairs, the fate of Shakespeare hanging in the balance. I imagined state Representative Woody Burton, Republican fundamentalist, descending upon us with his usual cartloads of Hoosier wisdom. The last time Woody visited our campus, it was to object to the establishment of our new Gay-Lesbian Student Center.[1] Woody declared that he was no "homophobe," but still, he told us, homosexuality is not something we should teach in our tax-supported universities. We tried to explain that the center would not be for teaching, but it didn't matter. Woody informed us that, while it may be OK to have support facilities for blacks or Jews, homosexuals are not a minority because you can tell a black or a Jew just by looking at one, but you can't necessarily tell a homosexual. "Homosexuality is a lifestyle," not a minority, Woody told us, adding: "What about overweight people? Are we going to spend state tax dollars for a center for overweight people?" Public outrage over his remarks caused Woody partially to retract them, but not to back down from his stand against the Gay-Lesbian Center. So our administration funded the center through private donations rather than through state tax money (for this and other recent examples of homophobia affecting colleges and universities, see Wilson, 43–49). Anyway, you can just imagine what Woody will say if he learns that we have excluded Shakespeare from our requirements. To Woody, it won't matter a bit if we tell him that Shakespeare can fend for himself. Woody won't believe anything we tell him; after all, we're just English professors.

6 o'clock. The chair called the meeting to an end, the ultimate disposal of Shakespeare left to a future faculty meeting. The next day, however, the discussion continued informally. One colleague suggested, "Perhaps we

should establish a completely separate Shakespeare department? The required courses for majors in Shakespeare would then consist entirely of Shakespeare courses. The trustees would love it." Another offered: "Let's just have one requirement—a single Shakespeare course; make everything else elective." Overhearing these wisecracks, a somewhat morose Chaucerian chimed in: "If you require Shakespeare, then you should require Chaucer." "Don't leave out James Whitcomb Riley," I added as I escaped into my office.

The final upshot is that we voted for our new set of requirements, including a policy that allows students to substitute courses with broad historical resonance for the surveys. But courses in single authors will ordinarily not count—Shakespeare for one, but also Chaucer, Milton, Wordsworth, Joyce, and so on. But just imagine what bloody grist these additional exclusions may become for the publicity mills that love to grind up English departments these days! Headlines about our deconstructing Shakespeare would have been bad enough; however, we appear to have added Chaucer, Milton, Wordsworth, and every other single great author to our hit list! (I mean "hit list" in the *Godfather,* not the MTV, sense.) Anyway, in a conservative state like ours, with legislators who, even if not all of them are Republican fundamentalists, seem to believe that faculty in general are high-paid loafers who don't teach enough classes, clearly we are living dangerously by excluding every single, great, canonical author from our requirements! IU ENGLISH DEPARTMENT REJECTS THE CANON, the headlines may blare; or THE DEATH OF THE AUTHOR AT INDIANA UNIVERSITY. And Woody and other educationally challenged politicians may hold news conferences, saying things like, "Look what they've done to Shakespeare, not to mention every single other great author who ever lived! Why are we supporting a department like that with our hard-earned tax dollars?"

At least, we are not alone: other English departments have faced the same Shakespearean dilemma. When in 1997 the English department at Kent State, for reasons similar to ours, deleted a Shakespeare course from its requirements, headlines across Ohio ranted: "SHAKESPEARE GONE FROM KENT" and "KSU BUMPS THE BARD," while English professors at that institution were pilloried either as sinister bardicides or as blithering idiots who, according to the *Toledo Blade,* "fall prey to every academic charlatan with a stupid idea" (14 January 1997). More evenhandedly, perhaps, the *Blade* also opined that "education is too important to be left in the hands" not only of nutty English professors, but also "of university presidents, provosts, [and] academic deans." So, why not chuck the whole kit and caboodle of higher education and simply have those in need of true wisdom subscribe to the *Blade*? The chair of English at Kent State informed me that he was accused of bard murder by a member of another department, so bardolatry of the hothouse, headline variety is not restricted to nutty journalists. As at Indiana, however, the only item deleted from the Kent State curriculum was a required Shakespeare course *for English majors.* The vast majority of Kent State undergraduates have never had to take Shakespeare, though numerous Shakespeare courses, in high demand, continue to be offered.

Similarly, the National Alumni Forum recently accused the English department at Georgetown University of striking Shakespeare from its requirements. This news did not cause a huge uproar, unlike the famous deconstruction of Western civilization at Stanford, when—so William Bennett and other neoconservative educational experts claimed—the Rev. Jesse Jackson led hordes of radical students in the chant, "Hey hey ho ho, Western civ has got to go!" It didn't matter that Jackson had done no such thing and even explained to the press that what the students were opposing was a course named "Western Culture," not Western civilization in general. The neoconservative gang believed what they chose, and the press believed the neoconservatives (on the Stanford "Western Culture" episode, see Wilson, 64–69). So, too, when Georgetown officials pointed out that Shakespeare had never been required at their university, it didn't matter— the damage had already been done. For the William Bennetts and *Toledo Blades* of the world, the defense offered by the Georgetown officials was no defense at all. "*WHAT? Shakespeare Has Never Been Required at Georgetown? What Kind of University is That?*"

When I became chair of my department in 1990, I naively thought that we were insulated from the attacks by the neoconservatives and their allies in the press, but my four-year term taught me otherwise. I found myself, for instance, corresponding with the elderly widow of a deceased colleague. She had generously given us $12,000 to start a graduate fellowship in his honor. But after she'd signed over the money, something she read—perhaps in Dinesh D'Souza's *Illiberal Education,* or maybe in Roger Kimball's *Tenured Radicals*—convinced her that she had made a huge mistake. "I didn't realize," she wrote to me, "that I was giving my money to a *Marxist* department," one that her husband would hardly have recognized as his own. I wrote back to her—several times—explaining that we have not become a "Marxist department"; that some of us use concepts drawn from the various Marxist traditions, but so did earlier faculty; and that even her husband—I quoted from several of his publications—had respected Marx as a great intellectual and social critic. I'm afraid this approach did nothing to mollify her. She may even have believed that I was accusing her revered husband of being a Marxist. However, the money was legally ours; she could not retrieve it.

More worrisomely, I found myself in frequent dialogue with the then-president of Indiana University, Thomas Ehrlich, a legal scholar who took a keen interest in what faculty in all disciplines were doing. About English, he worried that we were slipping away from canonical literature—Shakespeare and company—toward so-called literary theory. "Why are people in English writing books about Foucault and Bakhtin," Ehrlich wondered, "instead of about Chaucer and Shakespeare?" I replied that people were still writing books about Chaucer and Shakespeare, though sometimes from a Foulcauldian or Bakhtinian perspective. But that didn't explain—not to his satisfaction—the books about Foucault and Bakhtin. He was much too savvy to believe the more defamatory versions of English and humanities bashing in the press. On the other hand, he was drawn to the more intelligent arguments about the decline and fall of the humanities—books like Kernan's *The Death of Literature.* On one occasion, Ehrlich gave me a copy of David Lehman's *Signs of the Times: Deconstruction and the Fall of Paul de Man,* and asked what I thought of it. I replied that it is an intellectual hatchet job—an intelligent one, but nevertheless a hatchet job—and I tried to show him why. Whether I convinced him or not, I do not know.

I did point out to our president that, though many of us—myself included—use ideas drawn from de Man and Derrida, as also from Foucault and Bakhtin, none of us is an orthodox poststructuralist or anything else so far as I know. Moreover, I told him, "literary theory" does not mean one unified thing, and certainly not one malign thing aiming at the deconstruction of literature or "the death of the author." "You don't imagine that we want to put ourselves out of business?" I asked him. "Contrary to popular superstition, the Yale critics who first adopted the ideas and methods known as 'deconstruction'—Geoffrey Hartman, J. Hillis Miller, Paul de Man—revered great literature. Their version of deconstruction did not aim to dismember great books, but to enhance our understanding of them. The phrase 'literary theory,' moreover, covers a wide range of *theories*, plural, including Marxist, feminist, psychoanalytic, semiotic, and so forth. True, all of these theories lead us to understand literature as a historically constructed category, and in some instances to view it as ideological. But even viewing literature as ideological does not turn it into chopped liver. If these competing theories have one or two things in common, it may be the aspiration to answer a couple of questions that have always been central to English: first, how literature fits into the larger culture—that is, what functions does it perform? And second, just what is the process of interpretation? What exactly happens when we interpret, say, *Othello*?"

I also found myself saying to our president (as if he didn't already know this) that English, like every other discipline, is always changing, and that one function of so-called literary theory is to understand and perhaps control such change. There are objective, historical factors affecting every English department, I said. Given the proliferation of new literatures written in English around the world, English departments must choose either to adapt or to restrict ourselves to the literature of England. But long ago, English departments began to teach American literature. And now we are confronted with new writing from India, Jamaica, Nigeria, and so forth. These new writers and literatures in English also change the English language. Read Michelle Cliff's *No Telephone from Heaven*, for instance, and note its Jamaican Creole glossary. We can either stand still, or we can open up the canon to these new literatures in English, which are also reshaping our language. Whether we like it or not, we are necessarily becoming "multicultural" and "postcolonial."

The opening up of the canon—or, better, its pluralization, *canons*—has also resulted from causes internal to American culture. A major aspect of work by feminists and African Americanists, I pointed out, has involved the rediscovery, or in some cases discovery, of major literary works by women and writers of color. It's not reasonable to teach these works only in African-American and women's studies programs. The Harlem Renaissance, for instance, was a major aspect of American literary modernism. And what about the claim, made by Theodore Parker in 1849, that the only American literature that was homegrown rather than just imitative of European models was "the Lives of Fugitive Slaves"? "All the original romance of America is in them," Parker declared, "not in the white man's novels" (qtd. in Baker, 12–13). And no one, I added, would seriously contend today that rediscovered works by Kate Chopin or Charlotte Perkins Gilmore should not be included in American literature courses.

Our president agreed with me about canons, plural, and new literatures in English. He remained, however, suspicious of literary theory. And why not? A number of my colleagues remain suspicious of it. A former chair of my department has been known to ask the president's question: Why are younger faculty in English writing about Foucault and Bakhtin, instead of about Chaucer and Shakespeare? The cause of literary theory is hardly helped, moreover, when an ex-theorist like Frank Lentricchia recants (see *Lingua Franca*, September/October, 1996). Lentricchia apparently now believes that literary theory is the English department version of "the God that failed." For the rest of his career, he says, he will be a "rhapsode" and "anarchist" instead of a theorist. I gather that he thinks a theorist is somebody who denigrates literature, whereas a rhapsodic anarchist appreciates it. But if the intellectual analysis of literary texts interferes with appreciating them, then literary scholarship and criticism in general—and not just literary theory—ought to be scrapped. To me, Lentricchia's back-sliding seems perversely anti-intellectual, and not just antitheoretical (on the "back to literature" movement, or sentiment, see Bruce Robbins).

Then there is the question of cultural studies. When I started my term as chair, I knew that some of my colleagues either hoped or feared that I would transform our department from literary into cultural studies. I did help to establish the small graduate program in cultural studies now offered outside the department, and my research and teaching have always involved cultural history and cultural studies. Moreover, there is the now-familiar claim that English departments are, for better or worse, evolving or devolving into cultural studies (see Easthope, and also the *PMLA* forum on cultural studies, March 1997).

Several years ago, I helped evaluate an English department at another university. In the early 1970s, two-thirds of its faculty specialized in traditional literary periods. At the time of the evaluation, this department included just one medievalist and two Renaissance scholars. Only one-third of its faculty concentrated in traditional areas. Half a dozen were in creative writing; another half-dozen, in composition; another half-dozen, in film studies; five or six focused on theory or cultural studies; four were linguists; three were African Americanists; and there was also a lone folklorist. I suspect that the stories have been similar at many universities. I do not think that this means that English is inevitably evolving into cultural studies, but at least three powerful factors have been moving departments away from historical, literary fields toward contemporary culture. One I have already mentioned: when we attend to new literatures in English, something has to give—and usually that means the older, traditional areas, like medieval literature. Also, when we attend increasingly to both composition and creative writing, there is again a historical foreshortening, a movement away from the early literary periods toward such contemporary phenomena as new poetry and fiction, the standard reading fare in creative writing courses. While the increasing attention to writing may be healthy, the growth of composition and creative writing programs has its costs. Suppose a trade-off confronting a department was composition *or* Shakespeare? Which should it choose?

At many universities, a related but very real trade-off is eroding the teaching of literature. When administrators hire part-timers to replace full-time faculty, the part-timers aren't expected to be the new generation of experts on Shakespeare or Chaucer. Instead, they are expected to teach basic composition, and little else. In many cases, moreover, the part-timers have even less status, lower pay, and fewer benefits than graduate assistants. A decade ago, the average wage for a section of composition taught by a part-timer was about $2,000 with no benefits, whereas the average per-section pay for a graduate assistant at the Big Ten universities was about $3,000 plus tuition, fees, and low-cost health insurance. Many part-timers are, of course, former graduate students, either ABDs or new Ph.D.s, struggling to make their way in a downsizing academic marketplace (Nelson and Watt, 197–211). The curricular outcome of the administrative push to replace full-time faculty with part-timers is obvious: once again,

21

what is being downsized, this time through no fault of English departments, is the teaching of literature, whether canonical or otherwise.

Downsizing, the expansion of writing programs, and the pressure from new literatures in English are all causing English departments to mutate toward contemporary culture, if not exactly toward cultural studies. But when we also attend to the mass media—film, television—then cultural studies may indeed be the outcome of this mutation. It's arguable that English faculty should stick to literature and writing, and not stray into media studies, which should have their separate academic units. But at many schools, because of our general interest in narrative, aesthetics, and culture, English departments have been the logical starting place for teaching film in particular. Nationally, how far the evolution of English into cultural studies has gone, I do not know. However, this evolution is not caused or forced upon us by literary or cultural theory. It is instead driven by cultural, institutional, and economic forces that neither traditionalists nor theorists nor the neoconservative gang seem able to slow down, much less control.

Meanwhile, during the neoconservative backlash against higher education, it's been absurdly easy to pick on English departments. Millions of people including trustees, journalists, and Woody speak English, or some version of it. Many think they are experts, perhaps especially if they remember that beloved Shakespeare course they once took. In contrast, while millions of us can do basic arithmetic, we can't do higher mathematics, and few of us remember nostalgically that beloved calculus course we once took. The Woodys of the world treat English professors with groveling respect when we correct their grammar. But tell them an English department contains Marxists, deconstructionists, feminists, or gay/lesbian theorists, and they are ready to call up the military. For all I know, the biologists are cloning human beings at this very moment on my campus, and nobody will be the wiser unless either the biologists or the clones hold a press conference. But just let us English professors exclude Shakespeare from our requirements for our majors, and watch the media, the trustees, and Woody go ballistic.[2]

What I find more disturbing than the bad press we've been getting are the misunderstandings of English department work that many faculty from other disciplines express. At my institution, a distinguished fractologist has for years tried to tell us—or the administration, rather—what's wrong with our department, because his wife got her bachelor's degree in English from a prestigious university back in the 1950s, and wrote her honors thesis on Jane Austen. This formidable background empowers her to tell him to tell us how to conduct our business, even though no one in English would ever be rash enough to tell the fractology department how to conduct its business. (*Fractology*: the hard science devoted to tracking down the fractiles, fragments, and factoids about what is allegedly wrong with other disciplines.) The fractologist, believing his wife, believes that we in English no longer teach the appreciation of great literature; today we only teach radical feminism, Marxism, and extreme forms of cultural relativism. I'm not sure what the fractologist would think of Lentricchia's advanced rhapsodic anarchism, but I'm not going to ask. I've found that there is little to be gained from arguing with people like the fractologist; after all, his wife has memorized most of Shakespeare, not to mention Jane Austen.

The fractologist illustrates the Kantian problem noted by Bruce Robbins: "Which faculty has the right to interpret the conflict of the faculties?" ("Return," 26). In my opinion, the answer must be all the faculties, provided we make good-faith efforts to inform ourselves about the other disciplines. Even in the largest universities, members of all disciplines are expected to serve on campuswide tenure and promotion committees. As a member of such committees, I have learned a great deal about the teaching, service, and research expectations in many disciplines besides my own. I have reported on the work of colleagues in other humanities disciplines; and I have read the files, letters, and statements about colleagues from many of the science disciplines. I cannot pretend to be an expert on any discipline besides my own; but I have some sense of what it takes to be an informed observer and sometimes critic of other disciplines. I would never dream, however, of uttering a full-scale condemnation of, say, chemistry or mathematics. And yet people with no expertise in the discipline of English write broadside condemnations of what we do, because they think they know English, and Shakespeare, and Jane Austen, just as well or better than us.

What do you say, though, to a microbiologist who tells you that most of the research English professors do is just bullshit—that apart from facts like Shakespeare was born in 1564, all we can say about literature is mere opinion? This guy doesn't accuse us of teaching cultural relativism; he says that that is all we *can* teach—that anybody's interpretation of a poem is as good as anybody else's. If he knew about it, he would probably agree with Lentricchia's rhapsodic anarchism. "Unless you run experiments on people's aesthetic responses to *Hamlet* and *King Lear,* then who's to say that *Hamlet* is better than *King Lear,* or vice versa?" he argues. "Just give your students some good books to read, and let it go at that." You can see why I would rather talk to him about the weather or the genetic code of the fruit fly than about Shakespeare. I just keep on drinking my coffee until I get a chance to say something like, "But what about the ethics of cloning human beings?"

Shortly after our faculty meeting, I got on the elevator with another friendly acquaintance, a retired sociologist. He greeted me jokingly, "How are things going in the Deconstruction department—I mean, the English department?" I responded: "Things are going fine, though there's still a lot to deconstruct—we have only just started to deconstruct Western civilization." I thought the sociologist would accept this exchange of jokes and leave it at that, but instead he replied with another barbed question: "Have you read any good articles lately in that journal of yours, *Social Text?*" I realized that he was thinking of the Sokal hoax—the fake article on science studies that physicist Allan Sokal published in that journal, in order to debunk science studies, cultural studies, and *Social Text* itself. "What makes you think *Social Text* is *my* journal?" I replied, somewhat testily. "It isn't even an English literature journal." The sociologist looked vaguely embarrassed. "It isn't?" he said. "I thought it was an English journal, literary theory or something like that." "Well," I said, "of course it's written in English; but *Social Text* is an interdisciplinary journal, and its editorial board includes at least one well-known sociologist." "Oh," he asked, "who is that?" And I, a quaver of triumph in my voice, announced: "Stanley Aronowitz. For all I know, there may be several dozen sociologists on its board."

When I saw the sociologist a few days later, he apologized, saying: "I had told a couple of my colleagues about the Sokal hoax and said it had appeared in an English literature journal, and now I've had to correct myself." (Of course, there *are* English professors on the editorial board of

Social Text, but I did not mention this to the sociologist—let him find that out for himself!) I came away from this exchange thinking that if all the nutty articles published in the English language, including hoaxes by physicists, get blamed on English professors, and indeed if every interdisciplinary journal, whether nutty or otherwise, published in English also gets attributed to English departments, then we really are in trouble. The sociologist, moreover, isn't a Republican fundamentalist or the *Toledo Blade*, but an intelligent, responsible scholar who can separate fact from fiction and history from headlines. These admirable qualities account for his apology.

Nevertheless, this was not the first time that *Social Text*, the Sokal hoax, and the bugbear of deconstruction had been laid at my doorstep by a colleague from another discipline. At a New Year's Eve party, a distinguished professor of economics had collared me in exactly the same way: "What do you think of the Sokal hoax," he asked, "and of that journal of yours, *Social Text*?" Well, I'm not actually sure that he said "that journal of yours," but he did identify it as an English literature journal that publishes articles on what he considers to be the nutty subject of "literary theory." As I would later do with the sociologist, I pointed out that *Social Text* is an interdisciplinary journal, Marxist in orientation; that Sokal had aimed his hoax at science studies, and more broadly at cultural studies, and not at English or even literary theory; and so forth.

The economist seemed to accept these points, but he still wanted to talk about literary theory. He is more an intellectual historian than an economist, and many of his publications deal with economic and political theory from the Enlightenment forward. So he is used to theories of various sorts and knows how to approach them historically. Nevertheless, the economist told me, he had recently read "an anthology of literary theory," and he'd found many of its essays "jargonish, illogical, and absurd." I asked him what anthology, and when he couldn't remember its title, I resisted the temptation to suggest that he hadn't read it very attentively. Instead, I said that I sometimes also find literary theory difficult and jargonish, and that I don't always agree with it. "When I disagree, however," I added, "I don't necessarily conclude that it is illogical or absurd. Besides, the phrase 'literary theory' is a misnomer. There are many theories that get lumped under the single rubric 'literary theory.' This gives the erroneous impression that there is a consensus in English studies today, whereas in reality there is

25

very little consensus, not only about what sorts of theories are necessary or even interesting to us, but even about what constitutes a theory."

The economist started to define "theory" for my edification, but just then our host walked up, and the focus of our conversation shifted. I found myself saying something like, "Jacques Derrida is often identified as a 'literary theorist,' and he is indeed someone I find interesting, though I don't always either understand or agree with him. But he's not first and foremost a 'literary theorist'; he's a philosopher." "That's as it may be," said the economist, playing Socrates to my Phaedrus; "but is Derrida a *good* philosopher? And if he is *not* a good philosopher, then why should you English professors allow him to addle your brains?" "But I think that Derrida *is* a good philosopher," I replied. "At least, I am certain that he is an *important* one." And I went on to cite no less an authority than Richard Rorty. In my one and only conversation with that philosophical luminary, I asked Rorty what he thought of Derrida, and Rorty replied: "Derrida is one of the most important philosophers of our time." "Yes, yes," said my economical inquisitor, "but is Richard Rorty a *good* philosopher?"

Besides, he went on, "even if you tell me that Derrida has a lot to say about language and interpretation that is interesting to you and your colleagues, why is it that faculty in English are so keen on resurrecting Marx and Freud? What's the attraction to you of those moribund thinkers, with their unscientific theories? You won't find any reputable economist who teaches Marx these days. And as to psychoanalysis, go ask the chair of our psychology department just how many courses they offer on that equally passé topic! Yet there seem to be many English professors who call themselves Marxists or psychoanalytic critics."

I said something like, "Marx and Freud—Nietzsche, too—were *major* thinkers. They were the agenda setters for our time. They raised questions that we are still struggling to answer. Moreover, you can't begin to understand modernist literature—Yeats, Pound, Lawrence—without knowing something about Marx, Nietzsche, and Freud." The economist agreed with this last remark and had just started to tell me why he disagreed with all my other remarks when I was saved by the bell. It struck midnight, we started celebrating, and soon the party ended.

During the next week, I worried that my responses to the economist had been inadequate. I wanted to tell him that one of the most eloquent recent defenses of Marx that I have read is Derrida's *Specters of Marx*, which conjures up the ghost of Hamlet's father to show why Marx's ghost will continue to haunt us until we finally deal with the social injustices that Marx so eloquently anatomized. Shakespeare, Marx, and Derrida! What a powerful, almost canonical combination to help me make my case! Anyway, I also worried that, if English professors can't explain ourselves to intelligent colleagues in other disciplines, then they won't defend us at the trials to which the Woody Burtons and *Toledo Blades* of the world would like to arraign us, especially when they discover that we have excluded Shakespeare from our requirements. So I decided to write a fuller, more considered response to the Economist:

Dear Lord Keynes [that's not really his name, of course; I've changed it to protect the innocent and also to express my great, albeit undereducated, regard for the noble discipline of economics]:

Later this semester I'll be speaking to the English Association of Ohio on the topic, "How to respond to people who think that something is rotten in the state of the English Department?" Because our conversation on New Year's Eve was an instance of the sort of situation I encountered frequently when I was chair (and still do encounter), I am writing my talk partly as a letter to you. Of course our conversation was a collegial and, I trust, intelligent one, which is more than I can say of some of the encounters I've had with people over the last decade who think, for instance, that we've deconstructed literature, or that we've guillotined the author, or that we've jettisoned Shakespeare in favor of Donald Duck.

In our conversation, I tried to make several points:(1) The Sokal hoax has little or nothing to do with English departments.

(2) I don't know what anthology of literary theory you've read and found impenetrable and jargonish. Some of what passes for research, whether theoretical or not, in English today *is* impenetrable and jargonish, but that's probably always been true, and anyway it is also true, so far as I can tell, in every discipline. I am sure that you could direct me to recent publications in economics that I, at least, would find impenetrable and jargonish.[3] Also, I have read enough about current debates between Keynesians and monetarists to know that economists don't have any consensus about some of the most basic questions, like how to deal with unemployment or the national debt.

(3) Perhaps you economists have managed to exorcise the specter of Marx from your discipline. Yet there are a number of self-proclaimed Marxist

economists teaching in U.S. colleges and universities—including some of the editors and contributors to *Rethinking Marxism* and *Monthly Review*—though I suppose you don't find them interesting or important. But perhaps that is because, as feminist economist Dianne Strassman declares, "dissent" in today's economics departments "is labeled not economics and is suppressed" (qtd. in Wilson, 40). True, the communist regimes in eastern Europe have collapsed, and many commentators have—foolishly, I think—declared that Marx and Marxism have therefore been proven wrong. As Shaw once remarked, however, this is like saying that Christianity has been proven wrong because nobody has ever tried it. In any event, there are many humanists and social scientists who continue to think that the questions arising from the various modern versions of Marxist historical and cultural theory—the Frankfurt School, for example—are important. You may not like or use the term "ideology," but for me it evokes a whole range of issues that I consider when I read, say, a Dickens novel. Nor am I led thereby to any such reductive, dismissive conclusion as, "*Pickwick Papers* is just bourgeois ideology." Some of Marx's ideas may be defunct; few Marxists today, for example, believe that a revolution of the proletariat will overthrow transnational capitalism. But by the same token, isn't Adam Smith also defunct? Or does *his* "invisible hand" stretch somehow all the way from 1776 down to the present, still influencing how economists think?

(4) Ditto for Freud. I don't know anybody, in English or any other field, who treats Freud as gospel. But, just as Michel Foucault says that all historians operate "within a horizon of thought...defined and described by Marx" (*Power/Knowledge*, 53), so we—especially, perhaps, those of us engaged in trying to understand complex linguistic, narrative, interpretive processes—operate within a horizon of thought defined and described by Freud. As W. H. Auden puts it:

> *if often he was wrong and, at times, absurd,*
> * to us he is no more a person*
> *now but a whole climate of opinion*
> *under whom we conduct our different lives....*
> ("In Memory of Sigmund Freud")

I think I pointed out to you that it would be impossible to understand modern literature without knowing Freud. You agreed, but responded that Freud and psychoanalysis aren't taught in our psychology department, which is behaviorist in orientation. So much the worse, I say, for our psychology department. But if anyone in psychology believes that B. F. Skinner is a more interesting and influential thinker than Freud, I'd be surprised. I once heard a talk on game theory by a famous mathematician who made the distinction between *interesting* and *uninteresting* psychology. The latter he associated with behaviorism and bean counting. The former he associated with Dostoevsky. Not all of the important, interesting questions about the human condition can be squeezed through the wringer named science. And even in the most scientific of fields, the answers to many of the most basic questions—the makeup of the atom, for instance—are under constant revision.

In regard to dreams and their interpretation, Freud's *Interpretation of Dreams* is not the last word. I'm aware of laboratory research on patterns of behavior during sleep—the different phases of sleep and their neurological connection to dreaming. While such research may be both scientific and important, however, it doesn't tell us anything about whether and how dreams are meaningful. For understanding dreams as forms of narrative or communication, Freud was asking the right questions, and it would be sad if these questions were undreamt of by our psychology department. After Freud, the best, most sensible book on dreams that I've read is Charles Ryecroft's *The Innocence of Dreams*. Though acknowledging Freud's seminal importance, Ryecroft, a practicing psychiatrist, is not an orthodox Freudian. One chapter in his book, moreover, analyzes Kafka's *The Trial*. The connection between literature and dreaming is a traditional one, in part because poems and novels so often take their inspiration from dreams—besides Kafka, Shakespeare's *A Midsummer Night's Dream*, for example.

I won't say much about Jacques Lacan, a favorite theorist among some of my younger colleagues, except to point out that his revision of (or, as he puts it, "return to") Freud, works through the "linguistic turn" that has influenced all of the human sciences—well, maybe not economics—since the 1930s. My own reading of Lacan, I confess, is limited, because I often find his writing impenetrable. However, I don't necessarily mean "impenetrable" as a criticism of Lacan, but of myself. I accept as a given that deep, complex problems may require deep, complex responses, or in other words that not everything that is published in a field—even one so supposedly accessible as English—can or should be clear, free of ambiguity and difficulty. I also accept that I may not be patient or smart enough to fathom everything that Lacan (shall I add Derrida, Freud, Marx, Nietzsche, and even Shakespeare?) has authored. If I have world enough and time, I may try again, and maybe succeed, or maybe conclude that I'm just not smart enough. But I'm also aware that Lacan is something of a con artist or great actor. He plays with ideas and plays upon his audiences. He says in various places: "in listening to my discourse, you are listening to the voice of the unconscious." This is, of course, a deliberate, provocative contradiction:

how can one analyze the unconscious, when the analysis one utters is the voice of the unconscious? But, then, if Freud and Lacan are right, and the unconscious (whatever *that* may be) affects everything we do and are, Lacan's deliberate contradiction can be read as an almost self-evident description of the human condition. Or as Shakespeare put it:

> *We are such stuff*
> *As dreams are made on, and our little life*
> *Is rounded with a sleep.*

After I sent him this letter, the economist responded with a thoughtful one of his own, and we continued our dialogue. As I've indicated, not all of my attempts to defend what goes on in English departments have been thoughtfully received. I wish that the economist were typical of the people who wonder what we're doing, and who are so often—on the basis of little or no evidence—critical of our work. I wish at least that people would believe us when we tell them that Shakespeare really is alive and well—so much so that we don't need to require English majors to take Shakespeare. I will tell the Honorable Woody, when he comes to our campus to investigate allegations of bardicide, that we hired two and a half Shakespeareans in the 1990s. I will also tell him that, when our youngest Shakespearean publishes his first book, it is likely to be received as one of the most innovative, exciting studies of the Bard and his era to appear in the last several years.[4] Think of the headlines this news might generate: YOUNG FACULTY RESURRECT SHAKESPEARE, or SHAKESPEARE IS ALIVE AND WELL AGAIN ON IU CAMPUS. This sounds almost as good as spotting Elvis or Bigfoot in your local shopping mall. But how will I tell Woody that the main critical approach of this outstanding young Shakespearean of ours is what is called, in the arcane jargon so often used by obscurantist English professors these days, "queer theory"?

English Departments as Heterotopias

3

Chaos is come again.
—Shakespeare, *Othello*

A map of the world that does not include Utopia is not worth even glancing at, for it leaves out the one country at which Humanity is always landing. And when Humanity lands there, it looks out, and, seeing a better country, sets sail. Progress is the realisation of Utopias.
—Oscar Wilde, "The Soul of Man under Socialism"

The Trouble with Paradise

For one of the first lecture courses I taught, I chose "Utopias and Dystopias" as the topic and assigned *The Republic*, bits of the Bible, *Utopia*, Rabelais's Abbey of Thélême, *The Tempest*, poems by Blake and Eliot, and a science fiction novel. The last item varied from semester to semester: *The Time Machine*, *1984*, Clarke's *Childhood's End*, and Le Guin's *Lathe of Heaven*. I thought this was an exciting topic that would pry open the political imaginations of my students. Yet, with the exceptions of Clarke and Le Guin, the readings were quite canonical; and Le Guin was both the only woman and the lone American whom I included. It didn't occur to me that I was dishing up classical, Western, male literature in a manner Allan Bloom would have applauded.[1]

The results never matched my utopian expectations,[2] so I moved on to other topics ("Dreams," "Mysteries"). For one thing, there was nothing utopian about the fact that the course enrolled 250 freshmen and sophomores (I had teaching assistants, fortunately). For another, as the students pointed out, something is wrong with paradise, because life in most utopias is boring. It is just very hard and very dull to be virtuous all the time. This helps to explain why modern utopias so often turn out to be dystopias.

Also, that Plato excludes poets from his Republic should give any literature teacher pause. Many utopias are structured around repression. Most of them don't ban poetry, but do ban self-indulgence and sin in all their colorful varieties. More's *Utopia* operates on this deprivation model, and so does Shakespeare's parody of that model. I have in mind Gonzalo's speech in *The Tempest:*

> I' th' commonwealth I would by contraries
> Execute all things; for no kind of traffic
> Would I admit; no name of magistrate;
> Letters should not be known; riches, poverty,
> And use of service, none....
> No occupation; all men idle, all;
> And women too, but innocent and pure;
> No sovereignty— (II, i, 143–152)

"No sovereignty?" Sebastian says: "Yet he would be king on't." The courtiers' cynical mockery of Gonzalo's utopianism matches, I'm afraid, the typical reactions of my students: "'No letters'? They wouldn't even be able to read Shakespeare!"

Cynicism about utopia is widespread also among faculty. I doubt that English professors are different in this respect from deans and provosts: we all think of ourselves as hardheaded, pragmatic realists who know better than to credit Gonzalo's sort of wishful thinking as anything more than that. The trouble is, however, that such realism makes it difficult to think of *The Tempest* as anything more than that. Shakespeare's own realistic bent encourages this result: the play is a "romance" or a "dream," and the utopian power of forgiveness is "magic"—that is, not real.

The difficulty of imagining ideal social conditions underscores the poverty of our realism. Fredric Jameson claims that "the Utopian text...hold[s] out for us the vivid lesson of what we cannot imagine" (*Seeds of Time*, 75), which may explain why the iconography of heaven is mostly clouds. "The vocation of Utopia," Jameson contends, is "failure," including above all the failure to know exactly what it is that we collectively want. The "epistemological value" of utopia, Jameson continues,

> lies in the walls it allows us to feel around our minds...the miring of our imagi-
> nations in the mode of production...the mud of the present age in which the
> winged Utopian shoes stick, imagining that to be the force of gravity. (75)

Perhaps as a result of this "vocation" of "failure," the numerous utopian experiments over the last two centuries, such as New Harmony in southern Indiana, have had very high dropout rates—maybe even as high as the attrition rate among freshmen at my university (I just hope that my utopian enthusiasms did not contribute to their attrition).

In any event, my students clearly preferred dystopias to utopias. With its satanic aliens and UFOs, *Childhood's End* seemed closer to their anxieties and anticipations than did Prospero's magic. Common sense told them that individual perfection is hard enough to achieve, a fact that greatly diminishes any chance of social perfection. Further, the dystopias told them that the world they were living in could be a lot worse.

Most undergraduates have a basic, if underexamined, faith in social progress—at least, progress for the United States. After all, their lives have been pretty good—privileged, even—and it's easy for them to see that America's general history of freedom and prosperity has a lot to do with their good fortunes. But why does faith in social progress involve the odd corollary of skepticism about that progress ending in the utopian perfection that seems logically to be its telos? My students were much readier to believe that progress might end in dystopia—through nuclear holocaust, or ecological collapse, or an invasion from outer space.

I have not taught a course on utopias and dystopias since the early 1970s. Today, many students seem not to believe so automatically in social progress, which might make it even more difficult for them to take utopias seriously. But I suspect there is an inverse, dialectical relationship between increasing skepticism about social progress and the kindling of an at least subliminal utopianism. Or perhaps what is being kindled, as we enter the new millennium, is heterotopianism. This is an awkward, unfamiliar word, and I don't think I will try to add it as a third category in a new course on utopias. But the concept of heterotopia has come into play in recent discussions of postmodernism, and it may help in thinking in some new ways about English departments. Of course English departments are neither utopias nor dystopias, although they have features of both. But they are heterotopias. Before indicating what I mean by this, it seems useful to consider what features of English departments are utopian and dystopian.

Utopia

After thirty years of teaching in an English department, I can say that very little about it is utopian.[3] Still, there are several ways that faculty in English belong to what Jameson calls the "underground party" of utopia. He notes that during a time when utopian thinking is supposedly waning, it is making a surprising comeback. Just as utopias often turn into dystopias, so a dystopian era seems to evoke its opposite, at least in imagination. This isn't to say that postmodernity is a completely dystopian condition in which there are no longer any alternatives to transnational capitalism.[4] But the significance of utopian thinking today is related to the degree to which, at least from the perspective that celebrates the global triumph of "the market" and the supposed "end of history," it seems to have been rendered irrelevant.[5] Jameson contends that "in our time, where claims of the officially political seem extraordinarily enfeebled and where the taking of older kinds of political positions...inspire[s] widespread embarrassment...one finds everywhere...not least among artists and writers...an unacknowledged 'party of Utopia': an underground party," to which Jameson himself apparently belongs (*Postmodernism*, 180).

Whether we acknowledge it or not, all members of English departments belong perforce to the "underground party" of utopia, because literature privileges the imagination of alternative lives, societies, and worlds, including utopias and dystopias. The romance genre of *The Tempest* is inherently utopian; Northrop Frye's claim that "romance is the structural core of all fiction" (15) points toward the underlying identity between utopianism and literature, while Ernst Bloch contends that "the utopian function" is basic to all aesthetic experience (105).[6]

Contra Walter Benn Michaels, even works of narrative realism are as apt to criticize as to celebrate reality.[7] A realist novel like *Robinson Crusoe* may valorize empiricism and insist that there is no point in hankering after what is out of reach. But in rendering the stoic moral that Crusoe must limit himself to what he is given, his tale inexorably demonstrates that reality *is* limiting—that it is a realm of scarcity, hardship, and struggle. The great nineteenth-century realist novels—*Vanity Fair, Madame Bovary, Middlemarch*—are also both obedient to and even more explicitly critical of "the reality principle." They render the limitations of reality in thematic ways that make them legible as the dialectical antitheses rather than simple opposites of utopian discourse.

That the discipline of English promotes the utopianism of "the aesthetic dimension" is a point most often made, at least by English professors, in terms of Arnoldian humanism with its stress on the supposed power of literature to humanize the individual into her "best self." It is less often made in terms of the *promesse de bonheur* inherent in the experience of the beautiful. This second approach is both more radical and more utopian than liberal humanism, because it suggests that the aesthetic can be experienced without any mediation—that is, for one thing, without professors—which is perhaps why professors are more attracted to Arnold than to versions of avant-gardist immediacy. For professors, by and large, the *promesse de bonheur* approach smacks of instant gratification, as in "commercially prepackaged masturbational fantasy," which is what Allan Bloom called rock music (75). Ironically, the advocates of abandoning literary theory and going "back to literature" often sound like they are also abandoning Arnoldian humanism for instant gratification, as in Frank Lentricchia's conversion to "rhapsodic anarchism."

Whether Arnoldian or rhapsodic, the goal of aesthetic appreciation produces institutional symptoms that are at least pseudo-utopian. The aesthetic has traditionally been associated with freedom from work—that

35

is, with leisure—and at least tenured full professors sometimes behave as if they are particularly free and leisured. Take, for instance, this "back to literature" formulation by Helen Vendler:

> We owe it to ourselves to teach what we love in our first, decisive encounter with our students and to insist that the freedom to write is based on a freedom of reading. (25)

I wonder if Vendler's students fathom what "freedom" of reading and writing she is "insisting" upon? For her, it seems, the hard work of reading and writing isn't work at all, but is instead "love" and "freedom." I suspect she does not mean that the study of literature is as rhapsodic as watching MTV, nor am I about to suggest that English departments are places where "all men [are] idle, all; and women too...." Nevertheless, English departments maintain a certain fiction of leisure or cultured "freedom," at least for those at the top of the hierarchy—I mean for tenured full professors like Helen Vendler.[8]

Nontenured faculty have to work double overtime if they hope to earn tenure, so they may be less inclined than Vendler to figure their work in terms of "love" and "freedom." That many tenured professors keep right on being workaholics is also true. Still, tenure, sabbaticals, long vacations, high salaries, good fringe benefits, and academic freedom help make being a professor in any field "the last good job in America," as Stanley Aronowitz puts it (qtd. in Nelson and Watt, 58). And academic freedom sometimes does turn out to be, at least for some tenured faculty, the freedom to stop doing the hard work of research and writing, if not of reading and teaching.

The pseudo-utopian notion that what English professors do isn't really work can be traced back to Arnold and other nineteenth-century exponents of "liberal education" such as Cardinal Newman, who declared that the aim of a "liberal education" is to produce "gentlemen"—that is, men of leisure with all the right values, including good taste. As Jerry Herron notes, one outcome of this tradition of thinking about liberal education "is that academic professionals have yet to develop a coherent notion of work, except as something that *other* people do" (59–61). Indeed, many faculty prefer to ignore the fact that the work we do has a direct bearing on the work our students will one day do. Of course, there is widespread agreement that the teaching of writing, of "critical thinking," and of literary and cultural appreciation can help students lead fuller, happier, wiser lives. There is less willingness to recognize that a key economic good that professors produce is evaluations including grades, which means that we play a major role in "sorting out student abilities" (Watkins, 108). In *Work Time: English Departments and the Circulation of Cultural Value*, Evan Watkins notes that "English is . . . a primary distributive force in . . . constructing race and gender [and] in the formation of [social] class boundaries" (26).[9]

Fortunately for us professors, the hardcore cases—the kids who don't graduate from high school or who graduate with low grades and, if they take the SATs at all, low SAT scores—are presorted into the working- and underclasses. Yet nearly half of the U.S. population now receives some higher education, and the process of evaluating students and sifting them into slots in the great socioeconomic machine grinds on. If this sounds dystopian, nevertheless tenured English professors, with our profession of aesthetic appreciation and our various academic freedoms, are a privileged lot. Which may be one reason why we can be so hard to get along with (a cliché among chairs of English departments: chairing is like "herding cats" or, on a bad day, "snakes").

Dystopia

Our obfuscation of the work that we do as nonwork makes it difficult to convince anyone else that we actually do work. Surveys show that most professors of English are working furiously, putting in fifty-, sixty-, and sometimes seventy-hour weeks.[10] As one of the rewards, we have the satisfaction of knowing that we are members of a profession, and a highly intellectual one at that—one far removed from any of the forms of manual labor. No fetching in firewood for us. But this in turn—our professional status—makes it difficult for faculty unions and collective bargaining to develop.[11]

Even to mention unionizing is to admit that English and other departments have their dystopian aspects. Most faculty in most of the English departments that I know anything about are far readier to describe their workplaces as dystopian than utopian. One quality that English departments share with other disciplines is that they are seldom so collegial as they pretend. The hilarious account of a committee meeting in Richard Russo's *Straight Man* suggests as much. The committee is charged with hiring a new chair, but the present chair has his doubts: "our department is so deeply divided... we have grown so contemptuous of each other... that the sole purpose of bringing in a new chair from the outside [is] to prevent any of us from assuming the reigns of power. We're looking not so much for a chair as for a blood sacrifice" (17).[12]

Many English departments today are more like shark tanks than like gentlemen's clubs where the old boys chat amicably over glasses of sherry about their latest canonical favorites. Supposedly after decades of agreement about the one and only canon, the curriculum is a hodgepodge of competing aims and interests. As Cary Nelson and Steve Watt put it in *Academic Keywords*, "many departments maintain relative peace only by avoiding large-scale curricular planning" (20).[13] Although Gerald Graff demonstrates that English has evolved around conflicts, and although he recommends "teaching the conflicts" as a solution to disciplinary disharmony, conflict hardly sounds utopian. Graff also has a rather high-minded, Arnoldian notion of debating issues of interpretation, theory, and the canon. But there is usually a running battle over salaries, and there is always too little money for everything from travel to paper clips. The classrooms and faculty offices are not conducive to aesthetic appreciation. At least a couple of the old boys are chronic alcoholics or sexual harassers who see their vices as virtues. If there happens to be a disputed tenure case, then everyone is miserable, especially the candidate. According to Nelson and Watt:

> In extreme cases departments become unable to perform key functions. They cannot agree on who should be head or who should be hired. Warring camps try to demolish every one of each other's tenure cases. Fluctuating enemies lists shape basic decisions like teaching schedules and travel awards. At some point... receivership may be the only option: someone from another department has to come in and run things. The department may have to be virtually mothballed until retirements make it possible to rebuild. (18–19)

One hopes that such clearly dystopian departments are the exception, but the rule is not idyllic. For one thing, English departments are hierar-

chized bureaucracies for organizing educational work. This leads to conflict if too many faculty imagine themselves and their work in terms of the
nonwork of "love" and "freedom" and refuse to chair committees or help
with recruitment. Like the university as a whole, the English department is
a class system—no pun intended—in part because the classes we teach
serve the socioeconomic function of sorting students into social classes.[14]
The class hierarchy in English has its apex in the penthouse, with the old
boys' network, and descends through the ranks past nontenured assistant
professors to graduate student teaching assistants, professional staff, secretaries, and on to the lowly part-time faculty, who occupy the basement.

Notice what this hierarchy says about the value given to undergraduate teaching by many English departments, especially those that rely most
heavily on part-timers to teach their courses. Part-time faculty are in the
basement—lower even than secretaries—because they get paid less, have
no fringe benefits, and no permanent employment. Nationally the per-sec-
tion pay for a part-timer hovers around $2,000. As Nelson and Watt indi-
cate, many get even less, so that "Some part-timers calculate their average
pay at *under* $1 per hour" (58).

> Full-time college teaching in a research institution may be . . . the last good job
> in America, but part-time teachers have the worst salaries of any employment
> category in the country. (58)

As an aspect of the "corporatization of the university," the increasing
reliance on part-timers especially for teaching basic writing courses (ah,
for that "freedom" of writing whereof Vendler writes!) makes English
departments especially dystopian.[15] English has become, Nelson and Watt
conclude, "America's fast-food discipline" (55–58), doling out composition
courses like so many Happy Meals.

The plight of the part-timers, however, bolsters the sense of pseudo-
utopian privilege among the tenured faculty. That sense of privilege gets
passed down the fast-food chain even to the part-timers, many of whom
keep at it for the paltry pay and killer course overloads not just because
they must eat, but because they still aspire to become tenured professors. A
bit further up the fast-food chain, graduate students tolerate overwork and
underpay not only because they are better paid and treated than the

part-timers, but because they too aspire to become professors and are encouraged to think in those pseudo-utopian terms by their professors. It matters not that their professors once encouraged the part-timers in just the same way. Meanwhile, without improving their Morlocklike underworld status, the part-timers collectively threaten to cannibalize the false paradise of the tenured Elois. As Nelson notes, increasing reliance on part-timers is how tenure is being gradually eliminated, "not with a bang but a whimper" (*Manifesto,* 4).

Whether we worry about the class hierarchies within English departments and the larger society or not, many faculty—myself included—like to think that by teaching literature critically we are helping our students to think critically. But the general, insitutional pull is in a contrary direction. As Richard Ohmann puts it:

> I used to wonder why it is that society pays English teachers so much money to do what by and large is fun: teaching fine literature. I now think that our function is extremely valuable: namely, to ensure the harmlessness of all culture; to make it serve and preserve the status quo. (63)[16]

Still, in surveys conducted at Indiana, most of my colleagues say that the main goal of their teaching is to get their students to be "critical thinkers." "Critical" about what is not always apparent, however. It's a common ailment of a number of disciplines these days to offer professionally spruced up versions of "critical thinking." There are courses, conferences, and textbooks on this trendy topic. Mostly what is meant by that phrase, though, seems to be trivial-pursuits problem solving on the order of how many critical thinkers does it take to screw in a lightbulb?

Even if we do sometimes raise the level of critical thinking among our students, from either end of the political spectrum one can think critically of English departments, and more generally of universities, in Althusser's dystopian terms as "ideological state apparatuses." For leftists, it is a given that educational institutions "interpellate" students into conformist values, beliefs, and behaviors. For the neoconservative critics of today's supposedly left-tilting universities, higher education performs much the same dystopian function, though with the ideological valences switched:

tenured radicals are interpellating—that is, brainwashing—students in Marxism, feminism, gayism, Afrocentrism, deconstructionism, cultural relativism, and general all-around victimism. According to this view, English departments with all our radical "theories" and "critical thinking" are especially nefarious.[17]

It does not take much critical thinking to recognize that both sides are correct about the "interpellative" functions of higher education, but also that the leftists are more realistic (or just honest) about actual outcomes than are their right-wing parrots. Of course universities are in the business of "interpellating"—that is, educating—students. Of course, too, most students don't become Marxists or other sorts of fire-breathing radicals. But student cultures have always fostered ethical and political idealisms—a phenomenon that some neoconservatives find both surprising and terrifying—and faculty have often, through the ages, defended and encouraged such idealism. I hope that continues to be the case. Student idealism is a version of critical thinking and of utopianism. Still, most undergraduates do not become critical thinkers in any consistently radical sense. Although many students think critically about social and political issues, that is not necessarily because of what we teach them.[18]

Heterotopia

As models of possible worlds, both utopias and dystopias falsely unify the heterogeneity of social experience. Dystopias bring this imaginative failure to the fore by illustrating the totalitarian implications of utopian simplifications and communal harmonies. Dystopian authors such as Zamyatin, Huxley, and Margaret Atwood in *The Handmaid's Tale*, writes Laurence Davies, "propose . . . that variety can triumph over uniformity, [and] alterity, over the contemptuous refusal of difference." Paradoxically, they thus also "take part . . . in a utopian enterprise" (207). I would suggest, however, that the covert utopianism of most dystopias is heterotopian. In contrast to both utopias and dystopias, heterotopias are places of difference and diversity; optimally, they are places of "equality in difference."

According to Tobin Siebers, postmodernist theory invokes heterotopias, because it stresses freedom and desire rather than unification and deprivation.[19] Siebers's anthology, *Heterotopia: Postmodern Utopia and the Body Politic*, echoes other recent considerations of heterotopias as postmodern places or spaces. These include Gianni Vattimo's *The Transparent Society* and Edward Soja's *Thirdspace: Journeys to Los Angeles and Other Real-and-Imagined Places*. Both "transparent" and "real-and-imagined" offer clues to another distinction between heterotopias and utopias/dystopias. The latter, even if they have very real symptomatic significance for actual social formations, are unreal. In contrast, heterotopias are "real-and-imagined," paradoxically positioned between these epistemological extremes: they are real places or spaces of imagined play and possibility. They are places, therefore, where the ideas of theatricality and of the performable aspects of identity come to the fore, and thus where an individual can achieve a certain distance and difference not only from others, but from her past, present, and future selves. Such real-and-imagined places include cities, theaters, cinemas, amusement parks, museums, concerts, universities, tourist sights, shopping malls, the MLA, and English departments.

This is *not* to suggest that these are all the same, or that an English department or even the MLA is no different from a department store. Vattimo, however, links the postmodern proliferation of heterotopias to the mass media, consumerism, and "the market," but also to "aesthetic experience" in a way that again fits English departments.[20] His contention that capitalism spawns heterotopias, including such performative, commercially based phenomena as "lifestyles" and "subcultures," prompts the question, "To what extent are today's English departments market driven?" Depending on your politics, you may be tempted to single out those aspects of the discipline that you least approve of—whether it's theory, technical writing, or film studies—as market driven. But all academic disciplines have always been shaped by economic forces both within and beyond the university. Further, heterotopian or, if you prefer, "schizoid" though English departments have grown, they have distinct disciplinary protocols, including pedagogical aims and evaluative standards for research, that are not mere knee-jerk responses to student demand and the larger urgings of the market.[21] I take "schizoid" from Dominick LaCapra, who contends that "the contemporary academy is based on a systemic

schizoid division between a market model and a model of [collegial] solidarity and . . . responsibility." But when since the advent of capitalism or
perhaps even before has the university *not* been "schizoid"—or, as I prefer
to think of it, heterotopian—divided between practice and theory, between
economic expediency and the pursuit of knowledge for its own sake, and
between what Kant called the "higher" and "lower" faculties? The disciplines are also internally divided in similar ways.

Within today's "transparent society," according to Vattimo, approaches
to utopian unification through aesthetic experience do not unify. They lead
instead to the recognition and experience of difference, and again this is a
major aspect of what happens in today's English departments—and not
just through poststructuralist and postcolonial emphases on *différance*
and otherness, though that is part of the picture. Imaginative literature has
always functioned as a powerful scripting of heterotopian possibilities.
Echoing Kant, Vattimo declares that "The beautiful is the experience of
community," but he adds that "community, when realized as 'universal,' is
multiplied and undergoes pluralization." This leads to the rule: "Aesthetic
utopia comes about only through its articulation as *heterotopia*. Our experience of the beautiful in the recognition of models that make world and
community is restricted to the moment when these worlds and communities present themselves explicitly as plural" (69). For Vattimo, the general
effect of mass-mediated culture isn't the "one-dimensional society" of
dystopian imagining. It is instead the increasing proliferation and fragmentation of aesthetic experiences and possibilities, including possibilities for what the new historicists have called "self-fashioning." Just such
aesthetic experiences and performative possibilities are what English
departments promote, when they aren't simply processing and pigeonhol-
ing students through evaluating their work. Of course English departments
do both, which only reinforces the fact that they are heterotopian, because,
as Foucault points out, heterotopias are "reversible."

In "Of Other Spaces," Foucault says that a mirror "functions as a heterotopia" because "it makes this place that I occupy . . . at once absolutely
real, connected with all the space that surrounds it, and absolutely unreal,
since in order to be perceived it has to pass through this virtual point which
is over there" (24). As a heterotopian object, the mirror is in a sense

reversible—simultaneously real and unreal, transparent and opaque, a "me" and a "not-me." This liminal "thirdspace" quality characterizes all heterotopias, including English departments.

Foucault sets forth five principles of heterotopias, all of which are applicable to today's English departments. After noting that a heterotopia is a "simultaneously mythic and real contestation of the space in which we live," Foucault says that the "first principle" is that "there is probably not a single culture in the world that fails to constitute heterotopias" (7). But certain societies—primitive ones, on Foucault's account—try to control, limit, or shut them down. In contrast, fewer taboos mean greater heterotopian freedom, until we arrive at postmodern "heterotopias of deviation" (25).

The second principle is that heterotopias are "reversible"; they can be made to "function in a very different fashion." Foucault's example is cemeteries. I won't go into what he says about them, but insofar as English departments are not cemeteries, that is partly because they have their own mode of heterotopian reversibility. Thus, English departments function just as Watkins and Ohmann suggest, as cogs in the great people-sorting machine and as ideological reinforcers of the status quo. Nevertheless, they also promote critical thinking, the utopianism of literature and "the aesthetic dimension," and heterotopian difference, pluralization, fragmentation, possibility, and multiculturalism.[22] Further, English departments are hierarchical scholarly communities based on rules of governance and a disciplinary unity of interests, even though those interests, it seems, are often running in reverse. The harder English faculty try to harmonize around course requirements, for instance, the more we produce the "conflicts" that Graff talks about. English departments are unruly rule bound workplaces where both the expected and the unexpected are, as it were, expected.

Foucault's third principle is that a "heterotopia is capable of juxtaposing in a single real place several spaces, several sites that are in themselves incompatible." His examples are theater and the cinema, which like the mirror offer presence and absence, the real and the imaginary in a single, physical site. This is the case also with the literature classroom and even with the main English department office, center of decision making about the curriculum and about the futures of both students and faculty.

Moreover, the teaching of literature by historical periods corresponds to Foucault's fourth principle, which is that "Heterotopias are most often linked to slices in time...they open onto what might be termed, for the sake of symmetry, heterochronies" (26). Through imagination, students taking Shakespeare courses, for instance, enter Shakespeare's real-and-imagined times, at least for a time.

Foucault's fifth and final principle is that "[H]eterotopias always pre-suppose a system of opening and closing that both isolates them and makes them penetrable," which is probably true of all human institutions, and certainly true of all educational ones. You are admitted as a student or hired as a faculty member; you graduate or retire, and so on.[23]

This quick tour of some of the current discourse about heterotopias should make it clear that English departments have always been hetero-topian, in part because they have always valorized the mirror-like aspects of the aesthetic dimension. Literature as such, both real and imagined and always and obviously about difference (no, Mme. Bovary is not me, but I imagine myself in her place), is perhaps more heterotopian than utopian, though I believe it is both. But English departments are more obviously heterotopian today than they were thirty years ago, and it is no longer pos-sible—if it ever was—to insist that one out of their many tasks and respon-sibilities is more central than others.

Usually this one thing is "literary criticism," as in Stanley Fish's *Professional Correctness.* While I agree with Fish that there is such a thing as literary criticism with its own disciplinary distinctiveness, I do not agree that it is the main, defining feature of what does or should go on in today's English departments. Literary and cultural history, composition, creative writing, linguistics, and often folklore and film studies are among the legit-imate or, as some would argue, illegitimate activities that fall within the purview of English departments. Further, if English departments are now more heterotopian than ever, that is partly because of the explosive trans-formation of "English literature," formerly understood as the literature of England and maybe North America, into postcolonial, multicultural litera-tures written in English in many parts of the world. And the burgeoning of often conflicting literary and cultural theories, no one of which serves as a unifying orthodoxy as the New Criticism perhaps did for a while, is clearly heterotopian, especially given that many of the theories stress difference, performativity, and the postmodern fragmentation and pluralization of experience both real and imagined.

This does not mean that an English department—or any heterotopia, for that matter—is all things to all people. Nor does it mean that all theories are equal, let alone commensurate with each other. I do not think that "teaching the conflicts" will resolve the differences generated by our quite appropriate interests in and theories about teaching and research, language and interpretation, reading and writing, ideology and identity, culture and society, representation and the unrepresentable, and so forth. "The conflicts" are instead one of the inevitable outcomes of our pluralistic, heterotopian condition. From this perspective, perhaps the most publicized of the conflicts—between traditionalists and theorists, which is too often viewed by the media as a "culture war" between neoconservatives and "tenured radicals"—strikes me as beside the point. For if indeed English departments are structurally, intrinsically heterotopian, then the production and recognition of theoretical, literary, cultural, and social differences are precisely among the differences that they make.

Foucault ends his essay on "other spaces" with the familiar yet strange example of "the ship," which he calls "the heterotopia *par excellence.*" "In civilizations without boats," he says, "dreams dry up, espionage takes the place of adventure, and the police take the place of pirates" (27). But just as he claims that there are no societies without heterotopias, I doubt that he believes there has ever been a civilization without boats. However, applying the analogy of "the ship" to English departments, one can ask not only where we are sailing and expect the answer today to be to many different ports, but also where we would be if our "ship" were not heterotopian? If English departments were instead tidy, canonical never-neverlands devoted to the teaching of English and maybe American literature following some critical orthodoxy—let's say, the New Criticism—whose educational needs would they possibly serve in today's postmodern, multicultural world? Some may still feel that a return to such a nostalgically utopian model would at least get rid of "the pirates" who've swarmed on board since the radical '60s, but a lot of us are now tenured pirates, and besides, the orthodoxy could only be maintained by "espionage" and "the police"—a distinctly dystopian prospect, if you ask me.

Antitheory and Its Antitheses

Rhetoric versus Ideology

What's in a name? that which we call a rose
By any other name would smell as sweet.
—Shakespeare, *Romeo and Juliet*

Various trends and "isms" contributed to the heady mix that, in the late 1960s or early '70s, came to be called simply "theory," in the singular, and to dominate the anxieties, if not always the practices, of scholars in humanities and sometimes social science disciplines.[1] Diverse though these trends and -isms are, all have been commonly identified as one hegemonic rough beast, slouching (depending on one's politics, academic or otherwise) either toward Bethlehem or toward Bedlam. Just how and when *theories* became *theory* is uncertain, but a plausible answer is the 1966 conference at Johns Hopkins University on "the languages of criticism and the sciences of man," which inaugurated on this side of the Atlantic both "the structuralist controversy" and poststructuralism. Aspirations toward a "general *theory* of signs and language systems" are expressed throughout the conference proceedings (Macksey and Donato, xvi; my emphasis). Evident in all the papers is the "linguistic turn" that had deeply affected European philosophy and that, for literary scholars, shifted attention from literature to language.

According to the standard theory story, what preceded its hegemony was the New Criticism, often figured as the untheorized practice of close reading. But the New Criticism was not theory innocent; it was intensely, combatively theoretical (see Wellek and Warren, *The Theory of Literature*) even while it functioned as practical and as practice (see Brooks and Warren, *Understanding Poetry*). A practical theory or theoretical practice of how to read and evaluate a poem or any other literary text, the New Criticism was also a theory (*the* theory, according to Wellek and Warren's title) of what constituted literature. After World War II, the New Criticism offered literary scholars a united front, an intellectual hegemony with distinct disciplinary boundaries. Ironically, the more recent theory regime has involved the dissolution of those boundaries through conflicting claims and methodologies. Where there was once (apparent) unity, now there is disunity.[2]

One meaning of "theory" is just the intellectual arena, mostly academic, where conflicts over literature, culture, and interpretation now occur. In the midst of these conflicts, the main object of *literary* scholarship—literature—has been dethroned or at least somewhat marginalized. A corollary of the linguistic turn was a widening of focus from literature to textuality, including the writ-large texts of culture, society, and history. Literary theory transgresses the boundaries of both literature and nonliterary disciplines because it is "a discourse about discourses" (Cohen, xv). In short, literary theory either ignores literature or treats it as the mere offshoot or effect of some larger category: textuality, communication, discourse, culture, or rhetoric. For theorists as different as Paul de Man and Terry Eagleton, theory's ultimate object proves to be "rhetoric," a category that overlaps with or is closely related to—perhaps indistinguishable from—"ideology" (de Man, 11; Eagleton, *Literary Theory*, 206–210).

For de Man, rhetoric takes precedence over ideology, which he defines as the tendency to overlook rhetoric—to treat it as transparent and nonmetaphoric. Ideology is rhetoric that persuades its audience that it is not rhetoric. The deconstruction of rhetoric, the revealing of its secret workings where it claims not to be working, is therefore ideological critique. In contrast, for Eagleton, ideology is the main category; rhetoric is just the set of linguistic conventions, tropes, and so forth that convey those aspects of ideology that get translated into discourse. From Eagleton's Marxist perspective, however, the distinction is minor, because whether one calls it "rhetoric" or "ideology," the discourse of a given social formation is the product of that social formation, and more specifically of its economic mode of production. Every social formation produces the discourse—the rhetoric or ideology—that rationalizes it. But for Eagleton it isn't rhetoric that ideology occludes; rather, the rhetoric of ideology occludes social exploitation and injustice.

Over the past three decades, literary theory has produced many variations upon these two positions. The Marxist position, informing much of the work that identifies itself as cultural studies, privileges ideology over rhetoric. The poststructuralist position privileges discourse or rhetoric over ideology. In both cases, however, theory itself proves to be a sort of mirage. Theory becomes antitheory whenever it recognizes itself as the product of either ideology or rhetoric or both. Perhaps the most notorious theoretical case against theory is Steven Knapp and Walter Benn Michaels's "Against Theory." For Knapp and Michaels, it doesn't make any difference whether the target of theory is rhetoric or ideology, because both of these terms are just alternative labels for theory's inconsequential identity with practice—that is, for its identity with either rhetoric or ideology. But Knapp and Michaels's essay is only symptomatic of the general tendency whereby rhetoric and ideology become alternative names for theory's impossibility.

For Marx and Engels, ideology primarily meant the set of mystifications—false consciousness, a pre-Freudian version of the unconscious—that caused people to tolerate intolerable social conditions. Rhetoric was the main medium through which ideology was conveyed, but it was not for them a primary consideration. How rhetoric has come into focus as either a synonym for or a category that sometimes takes precedence over ideology concerns the much more recent, academic story of theory, and especially of antitheoretical literary and cultural theory.

When literary theory reaches the conclusion that its object is either rhetoric or ideology, it both ceases to be literary and in a sense ceases to be theory. Much—perhaps most—literary and cultural theory, certainly since the poststructuralist turn of the late 1960s, has been relentlessly antitheo-retical. Another way of stating this paradox is that theory uses the tools of philosophy to deconstruct philosophy; theory thereby aligns itself with the traditional antithesis of philosophy—namely, with rhetoric.[3]

The antiphilosophical tendency of theory is manifest in Derridean deconstructions of metaphysics and of all forms of essentialism; but it is also manifest in much modern so-called philosophy, from logical posi-tivism to neopragmatism. Philosophy originally aspired to discover the general, absolute truths about existence. In contrast, theory, though it also asks fundamental questions, declares philosophy's main aspiration to be unattainable. Theory's simultaneously more modest and more radical aim is to understand how both knowledge and illusion are socially constructed, if only because necessarily expressed through language. This pared-down object of analysis—language or discourse rather than existence—in turn generates a series of subcategories, the most important of which have been rhetoric and ideology.[4] Moreover, theory undermines philosophy by imply-ing or declaring *itself* to be, in common with all forms of culture, socially constructed, and hence either rhetorical or ideological.

The shift from literature to discourse, culture, or rhetoric has been par-alleled by the also conflictual process of canon revision. But while it is often attributed to theory, canon revision has not been dependent on theory. As even T. S. Eliot recognized, the literary canon is constructed in history rather than heaven, and revising it is a main ongoing function of literary criticism, whether theorized or not. Like the New Critics, however, Eliot understood the literary canon to be based on a stable set of aesthetic crite-ria and also to be straightforwardly incremental. In contrast, just as its neo-conservative opponents charge, recent canon revision has been based as much on a politics of democratic representation as on formalist literary criteria.[5]

Both canon revision and the shift from literature to rhetoric raise polit-ical as well as aesthetic questions. But why? As the opponents of theory often ask, doesn't the transformation of literary into cultural and social criticism involve a categorical error?[6] This question might be a theory stop-per if it weren't that literature is made out of language (and therefore rhetoric), that language is what binds people together in cultures and soci-eties, and that—from even the most traditional perspective—literature plays or should play a significant educational and, hence, social role. Further, the category of the aesthetic is inherently political. In order to answer basic questions about literature, even the most traditional versions of literary criticism must operate as cultural and social theory some of the time. Just what kind of social theory the study of literature needs to be is a main source of controversy, to which the key terms *rhetoric* and *ideology* insistently point.[7] In common with philosophy, theory raises fundamental questions not just about the interpretation of works of literature, but about culture and society, language and identity, history and knowledge. Repeatedly, rhetoric and ideology, though not the answers to these questions, prove to be the medium within which, it is hoped, the answers can be found.

The spate of recent reference books focused on theory suggests that its hegemony is far from weakening. Those published between 1991 and 1994 include *A Dictionary of Critical Theory* (Orr), *Encyclopedia of Contemporary Literary Theory* (Makaryk), *A Glossary of Contemporary Literary Theory* (Hawthorn), and *The Johns Hopkins Guide to Literary Theory and Criticism* (Groden and Kreisworth). All of these books recognize the diversity of theory or, rather, theories—the very idea that there needs to be a dictionary or guide suggests as much—and their prefaces all emphasize this diversity.[8] But not only do all of these tomes use "theory" in the singular—perhaps equally symptomatic is that three out of the four do not even provide an entry for this singular term, suggesting, albeit by default, the taken-for-grantedness of "theory." It seems that theory is just all of the items for which entries are supplied.[9]

But the appearance of such reference works may also be symptomatic of theory's decline. Like the *Blue Guide* demythologized by Roland Barthes (*Mythologies*, 74–77), guides to theory express a touristic nostalgia for history's monuments. Theory itself has been theorized as intellectual mourning for a lost or impossible coherence.[10] If these reference books are any guide, theory does not trail after practice, it has gone before—it has always already transpired—and it is the misfortune of those who come in its wake to be able only to catch a glimpse of its traces, its dawning spurs, its winged and shining heels, through the gaps and absences of monumental volumes like these. Theory, in other words, from the reference-book standpoint, is a codifiable *fait accompli*, even though theory is forever in the vanguard: it is the future, or the promise of one. It's just that theory, like everything else, can never be in the present or fully self-present. All that we have in theory's absence is rhetoric, or ideology, or both. At least these guides signal that much of what has occurred under the theory rubric has been absorbed into academic routine.

In contrast to the other three, Orr's *Dictionary* offers an entry labeled "theory, theoretical":

> a coherent set of hypothetical, pragmatic, or conceptual principles forming the general frame of reference for a field of studies...; abstract knowledge; a hypo-thetical entity... explaining...a set of facts; a working hypothesis giving proba-bility by experimentation or by conceptual analysis.... Theory is generally the opposite of practice or application (but in Marxist terminology, "praxis" is practice informed by theory). (415)

Much could be said about this entry, starting with the observation that it isn't directly relevant even to such standard critical practices as interpret-ing literary texts. Also, whatever else literary theory may be, its diversity suggests the opposite of "a coherent set of... principles forming the gen-eral frame of reference for a field of studies."

Moreover, a great deal of theory has been, like Knapp and Michaels's tour-de-polemic, "against theory." Insofar as much literary theory has been antitheory, Orr's definition does not match its object. In any event, the gen-eral spectacle has been one in which the philosophers—the theorists, that is—turn over the keys of the kingdom to the rhetoricians: theory tells us that rhetoric and/or ideology is all we can expect. This is not to say that the theorists, once they have reached their antitheoretical conclusion, stop theorizing. To conclude, as do Knapp and Michaels, on the basis of a lengthy theoretical argument, that theory as such is an impossibility only generates more theory. Allegations of the death or decline of theory are often just the latest versions of theory taking its licks out on itself.[11]

Some of the participants in the 1966 Hopkins conference were more intent on deconstructing than on expressing the aspiration toward a "gen-eral theory" of semiosis. Such a deconstruction is implicit in the title of Jacques Lacan's contribution, "Of Structure as an Inmixing of an Otherness

Prerequisite to Any Subject Whatsoever," while Derrida's "Structure, Sign, and Play in the Discourse of the Human Sciences," by decentering the necessarily centered concept of structure, subverts the goal of establishing a set of first principles or a central, unifying theory for any of "the human sciences."[12] Derridean deconstruction has been a potent antitheory theory, in part because the main object of its critique is the "logocentrism" of the Western metaphysical tradition, that highly influential canon of theories. "Deconstruction resists theory...because it demonstrates the impossibility of...the closure of an ensemble or totality on an organized network of theorems, laws, rules, methods" (Derrida, "Some Statements," 86). What we are left with is, for Derrida, just what all theories are made of: metaphors, language, rhetoric. But theory has higher aspirations than merely to recognize its entrapment within rhetoric or ideology, and therefore theory, according to Derrida, is productive of "monsters"; he suggests a theory of theory as "teratology," although "this teratology is our normality" ("Some Statements," 67).

The antitheoretical arguments of what is sometimes viewed as the most radical sort of theory (deconstruction) have not prevented its frequent identification as *the* vanguard theory among theories. Nor have these arguments prevented "theory" from being used in the singular, perhaps because the aspiration toward a grand, totalizing *Summa Theoretica* motivates deconstruction even while it emphasizes the inevitable frustration of that motivation, and even while other varieties of poststructuralism, neopragmatism, and postmodernism also emphasize (totalistically, theoretically) the nullity of all theoretically totalizing ambitions. So Jean-François Lyotard's claim that "postmodern" means "incredulity toward metanarratives" would seem to spell an end to aspirations toward grand or ultimate theories in any field (Lyotard, *Postmodern,* xxiv). But of course Lyotard's claim is both metanarrational and another instance of antitheory theory.

According to de Man's influential *Resistance to Theory,* one result of literary theory's "self-resistance" (19) is the production of a "universal theory of the impossibility of theory" (18). De Man is less concerned with theory's external enemies than with its internal evasions of "its own project," which includes de Man's project.

Nothing can overcome the resistance to theory since theory *is* itself this resistance. The loftier the aims and the better the methods of literary theory, the less possible it becomes. Yet literary theory is not in danger of going under; it cannot help but flourish, and the more it is resisted, the more it flourishes, since the language it speaks is the language of self-resistance. What remains impossible to decide is whether this flourishing is a triumph or a fall. (19–20)

For de Man, what literary theory "resists" is specifically "the rhetorical or tropological dimension of language" (17), the constant temptation being to keep rhetoric under the sway of grammar and logic, and hence to reinforce "the claims of the *trivium* (and by extension, of language) to be an epistemologically stable construct" (17). By revealing the ways rhetoric always already overrides grammar and logic, theory becomes "a powerful and indispensable tool in the unmasking of ideological aberrations" (11), including its own aberrations. Accordingly, literary theory approximates Marxist ideological critique. "What we call ideology is precisely the confusion of linguistic with natural reality, of reference with phenomenalism" (11). There are, of course, different, more obviously political definitions of ideology in Marx, Gramsci, Barthes, and Althusser (among others); nevertheless, de Man insists that "literary theory" comes under frequent attack because "it upsets rooted ideologies by revealing the mechanisms of their workings" (11).

For de Man, "ideologies" work by occluding "rhetoric"; ideological critique, identical with deconstructive literary theory, entails the rigorous analysis of "the rhetorical and tropological dimension of language" against the claims of grammar and logic as well as of transparency, naturalness, and objectivity. Eagleton has no problem with de Man's perspective, so far as it goes; but it does not go far enough, because the rhetorical expression of ideology is only the tip of the iceberg.[13] In *Criticism and Ideology* and elsewhere, Eagleton models his conception of ideology on that of Althusser, for whom it is a structuring and causal principle that, if not exactly equivalent to the social totality, informs all aspects of that totality. "Ideology represents the imaginary relationship of individuals to their real conditions of existence," Althusser writes, but it is also more than just simple illusion or false consciousness; it is the very principle or power that creates individual

ANTITHEORY AND ITS ANTITHESES

identity in the first place: "ideology interpellates individuals as subjects" (162, 170). This proposition situates ideology beyond individual control while also granting it a positive force similar to an economic mode of production. Later elaborations of Althusser's theory—for instance, Slavoj Žižek's—come almost full circle to something like Foucault's theory of discourse: ideology doesn't produce illusions about social reality; it produces social reality.[14] In any event, from an Althusserian perspective, rhetoric and subjectivity (or individual identity) are both mere reflexes of ideology.

Poststructuralists, however, have developed powerful theories—or antitheories—that prioritize rhetoric and that are at least suspicious of the entire category of ideology. Foucault, for instance, gives three reasons why the "notion of ideology... cannot be used without circumspection": first, to identify ideology one must be able to identify its antithesis, "something else which is supposed to count as truth"; second, ideology "refers...to something of the order of a subject," that is, of a presumably reasoning or, at least, rationalizing mind that produces it in place of truth; and third, ideology "stands in a secondary position relative to something which functions as its infrastructure, as its material, economic determinant" (*Power/Knowledge*, 118). In contrast, for Foucault there is no outside to discourse that can be identified as truth, or as the integrated mind that produces it instead of the other way around, or as a nondiscursive mode of economic production. If one accepts the poststructuralist proposition that all that is available to analysis is discourse, then ideology cannot be understood as existing outside rhetoric, much less as somehow shaping or determining rhetoric as, say, the political unconscious to what appears within the conscious but illusionary frame of rhetoric. It then only makes sense to avoid using the term "ideology," as does Foucault, or else to restrict it to overtly politicized forms of discourse and propaganda.[15]

Both ideology and rhetoric ordinarily signify the untruths, partial truths, or relative truths that are perhaps, as theory in its various guises suggests, the only forms of enlightenment (or illusion) attainable. Those theorists who privilege ideology also insist that all forms of consciousness are socially constructed, which may or may not mean socially determined.[16] Those who privilege rhetoric are less inclined to see everything in sociological, historical, or political terms, and more inclined to an at least quasi-Foucauldian pragmatism that treats the surfaces of discourse—rhetoric—as all that there is to analyze, or all that can be analyzed.

Despite the different meanings that various theorists attach to rhetoric and ideology, both rhetorical and ideological critique have as their goal enlightenment or emancipation from the illusions generated by rhetoric and ideology. Eagleton ties his version of theory as ideological critique to an "emancipatory" politics (both Marxism and feminism) that is not part of de Man's agenda of theorized reading. Charges that de Man's version of theory is an evasion of history are surely correct to the extent that he insists on the literariness of what literary theory can and should deal with. Literary theory that becomes socially critical is necessarily, from de Man's perspective, itself an evasion of the main difficulty that properly literary theory struggles within and against. For de Man, any move away from literariness—that is, from the focus on rhetoric—expresses the very "resistance to theory" that he claims to be resisting.

The critique of those illusions with which all individuals set forth in life has always been a principal aim of humanistic education. From this very general perspective, it perhaps hardly matters whether one calls these illusions rhetoric or ideology. In contrast, much current antitheory theory, speaking "the language of self-resistance" and repeatedly demonstrating its own impossibility, seems harmlessly self-deconstructive and also far too abstruse to have any effect on most individuals, much less on politics. The only way it can be held to threaten the subversion of Western civilization is if it is also held to have a central, influential place in Western civilization. This centrality the opponents of theory regularly deny, even while simultaneously accusing it of unhinging Western civilization. The belief that theory, in its persistent forms of ideological and rhetorical critique, is radical or subversive of the status quo also raises the question: just what is the ideology of theory? But if theory seeks to undo ideology by revealing its rhetorical construction, then how can theory be said to have an ideology or to be itself ideological and, hence, "radical"?

In "Against Theory," Knapp and Michaels contend that theory can have "no consequences"; it is just the illusory "attempt to escape practice" (30). On their account, all of the potential ways in which theory might oppose practice appear to be not just "resistance" to its own insights, but willful perversity: theory should know that it can't "escape practice," and should therefore stop theorizing. But like de Man, Knapp and Michaels depend on a definition of theory that narrows it to the question of literary interpretation, even while they attribute to it the impossible aspiration for some ultimate, grand theory that would settle all questions of interpretation. They blame theory both for its inability to stabilize the proliferation of meanings even within single literary texts *and* for its inability to be grandly totalizing and politically efficacious. As Jonathan Crewe notes in his response to "Against Theory": "Practice [according to Knapp and Michaels] is always institutionally or otherwise given, always encompasses us, and belated attempts to seize control in the name of principle are consequently foredoomed. 'Doing' theory accordingly becomes a mode of impotent presumption equivalent to doing nothing" (53). But if this is so, then isn't the kind of antitheory theory that Knapp and Michaels practice also just "impotent presumption equivalent to doing nothing"? At least they have the good faith (or is it irony?) to acknowledge, echoing Stanley Fish, that their argument (like theory in general, according to them) can have no "practical consequences whatsoever" (26).

Despite—or because of—arguments like those in "Against Theory," the antitheoretical adventures of theory are bound to continue, in part because theory sophistication is now an aspect of the professionalization of most academics in literary and cultural fields. According to John Guillory, theory has emerged alongside literature as a distinct, in some ways rival "theory-canon" (xii). Guillory argues that the rise of the theory-canon has been a response to "the technobureaucratic restructuring of the university," itself a response to the rise of the new "professional-managerial class" for which "literature" is no longer a significant form of "cultural capital." As a discourse distinct from earlier forms of literary history and criticism, theory expresses the "technobureaucratic" values of the "professional-managerial class," though if this is the case it is difficult to understand why both academic and nonacademic members of that class so often find even antitheory theory threatening. But from Guillory's perspective, "the emergence of theory is the symptom of a problem which theory itself could not solve" (xii).

Revising de Man's title, Mas'ud Zavarzadeh and Donald Morton, in *Theory as Resistance*, contend that "the dominant academy's antitheory theorists" are in effect all defenders of liberal pluralism and pragmatism, or the rationalizers "of (post)modern capitalism as an apparatus of crisis management" (3). What is being resisted is "new theoretical knowledge of the social totality"; but it turns out to be not exactly "new," because for Zavarzadeh and Morton, the only sort of theory that counts is orthodox Marxism. Whether or not one agrees that theory as such, by definition, means socioeconomic critique of a sort that offers a "global understanding of capitalism" (3), the authors of *Theory as Resistance* are surely correct that much antitheory theory has been either apolitical or nonradical at least in its consequences. From their perspective, antitheory theory is mere academic collusion with "late capitalism": it is its intellectual superstructure and "alibi" (4).

Bruce Robbins also notes that "the history of literary criticism in its received versions [has been] a narrative of professionalization" ("Oppositional Professionals," 1) and hence of collaboration with capitalism, but he contends that "literature" in one direction and "theory" in another both function as "anti-professional" discourses. If the New Criticism saw itself as professionalizing literary studies by displacing the old-style belletrism of the "gentleman-amateur," theory today has claimed a similar professionalizing function against the New Criticism. But much theory is not only antitheoretical, it is also antiprofessional, Robbins contends, in the sense of being both antidisciplinary and politically oppositional (as, for instance, both Marxists and feminists are oppositional), which also means critical of the very institutions, including those of higher education, that employ and authorize professionals (that is, professors). For Robbins, being a professional and being an oppositional critic are not antithetical roles. Robbins suggests that one way to understand theory in humanities fields today is precisely as the discourse of socially critical or oppositional professionals.[17]

Robbins's argument will hardly reassure the neoconservative opponents of theory, for whom political radicalism in the academy is at least as threatening as the antitheory tendencies of theory. Those antitheory tendencies themselves add up to forms of relativism or antifoundationalism that, as Zavarzadeh and Morton believe, are disabling to Marxists, feminists, or African-American theorists, while more logically supportive of varieties of neopragmatism which, in turn, are more consonant with liberal pluralism than with forms of political radicalism. But antifoundationalism in the case of Marxism reinforces the tendency to treat the interpretation of texts as ideological demystification. And antifoundationalism for feminists, queer theorists, and theorists of race and ethnicity reinforces the critique of biological determinism and essentialism in favor of, for example, Judith Butler's theory of gender as performative.

Antifoundationalism is the main way that much current theory is antitheoretical. Theorists who argue that there is no ultimate grounding for understanding—that the knowledges generated by the "human sciences" are partial, relative, unscientific, and always socially constructed—must resist the temptation to believe that they themselves are approaching some ultimate truth or developing the Final Grand Theory. But such a position is very different from the claim that theory as such is impossible, or even that it is inconsequential. While the most compelling evidence of theory's failure comes from theorists, failure is not the same either as having no consequences or as decline or demise.

To return to Orr's definition, his familiar though strange claim that "theory is generally the opposite of practice" can be understood in at least three different ways. First, theory opposes practice as its critique, whether practice means literary interpretation or culture, heterosexism, capitalism, history. Second, theory is a completely different enterprise from practice: it has no bearing on practice and, therefore, as Knapp and Michaels theorize, no practical consequences. A third meaning of "opposite," related to this second one, stems from the notion that theory always comes after practice (the owl of Minerva, Hegel declared, flies only at dusk). In this third sense, theory is not necessarily either irrelevant to practice (incapable of commenting on it at all) or critical of practice: it just comments on practice after the fact. Both the second and third meanings undermine the first meaning: theory as critically opposed to practice in ways capable of changing it.

A lot of antitheory theories, including Knapp and Michaels's neopragmatist manifesto, utilize disabling versions of the second and third meanings of "opposite" (irrelevant, belated). "The resistance to theory" from this perspective is also, as Zavarzadeh and Morton contend, a resistance to political radicalism (and not merely, following de Man, to the full recognition of "rhetoric"). In Knapp and Michaels's *reductio ad absurdum*, "theory...is taken preemptively to be an illegitimate imposition *on* practice, never a term dialectically paired with practice or the product of a theoretical moment that need not forever preclude the moment of practice" (Crewe, 55). Orr's definition itself seems to restrict theory as critique to Marxism, because it concludes with the parenthetical remark that "in Marxist terminology, 'praxis' is practice informed by theory." So one inference would seem to be that only Marxists worry about "praxis"; other forms of theory either cannot or do not try to "inform" or change practice.

Even though it identifies "praxis" with the Marxist tradition, Orr's definition does not explicitly preclude other critical relationships between theory and practice. If that definition is problematic, it is so mainly by being highly general (or theoretical) and more oriented toward the sciences than toward literary or cultural fields. On its basis, it is possible to conclude that anyone who does any intellectual work whatsoever is theorizing: theory either is "abstract knowledge" or is a condition for the production of such knowledge. Similarly, in *The Significance of Theory* Eagleton says that "all social life is in some sense theoretical: even such apparently concrete, unimpeachable statements as 'pass the salt'... engage theoretical propositions of a kind, controvertible statements about the nature of the world" (24). This is no more helpful than Orr's definition, obviously in part because it fails to discriminate theory from any of its possible antitheses such as rhetoric or ideology. But, for Eagleton, "the significance of theory" resides in its ability to make such discriminations.

Perhaps the most widely read text on theory has been Eagleton's *Literary Theory: An Introduction* (1983). In his survey, Eagleton describes and critiques a number of the more prominent sorts of literary theory: phenomenology, hermeneutics, and reception theory; structuralism and semiotics; poststructuralism; and psychoanalysis. But his central purpose is to demonstrate that "literary theory... is really no more than a branch of social ideologies, utterly without any unity or identity which would adequately distinguish it from philosophy, linguistics, psychology, cultural and sociological thought" (204). Literary theory is "a chimera," because the object of its study is a chimera: "Literature, in the sense of a set of works of assured and unalterable value, distinguished by certain shared inherent properties, does not exist" (11). As a result, Eagleton declares that his book "is less an introduction than an obituary" for literary theory (204).

Eagleton's move from the literary text to rhetoric and the social text does not mean, however, that he is "against theory" in general. "Many valuable concepts" can be retrieved from literary theory "for a different kind of discursive practice altogether" (206). The recognition that literary theory is a form of ideology opens the way to social theory; merely literary criticism is or should become "political criticism" (194–217), which for Eagleton means rhetorical/ideological critique and both Marxist and feminist theory. How is this different from de Man's move from "literature" to "rhetoric" and "ideology"? De Man himself resists theory insofar as he accepts the idea that, once the theorist has identified "rhetoric" as the medium of all meanings and values, there is no definitive way to frame even relative truths as opposed to confronting the abyss of rhetoric (hence, there is no beyond to literary theory once it has deconstructed the distinction between literature and rhetoric). In contrast, Eagleton believes that the theoretical ability to identify rhetoric or ideology entails moving beyond their orbits, and therefore moving from literary into social theory. But of course arguments to the effect that theory as such is illusory or impossible do not stop with "literary theory"; they often also proclaim that social theory, at least in any grand or totalizing manner, is an impossibility. Eagleton himself contends, echoing Lyotard, that the ultimate object of theory-in-general is history, not literature, but since theory is also a product of history, constructing a "Grand Global" or "meta-theory" is "impossible" (*Significance*, 28).

Nevertheless, Eagleton thinks, theory is inevitable, because "all social life is . . . theoretical" (*Significance*, 24). Since this argument merges theory with its usual antitheses (practice, rhetoric, ideology), Eagleton proceeds to speak of "emancipatory theory," by which he mainly means ideological critique in the Marxist tradition and which he sets over against other forms of theory that have been co-opted or "incorporated" by "late capitalism" and its well-paid professionals (including academics). "Theory can be seen as providing a flagging literary critical industry with a much-needed boost of spiritual plant and capital, largely imported" from Europe (*Significance*, 31). But Marxism is also, for Americans and Britons alike, an import, and it also helps to give "a flagging literary critical industry . . . a . . . boost," as Eagleton's version of it has done. However, Eagleton rightly suggests that the theory hegemony can be understood *both* as an "incorporated" product of late capitalism *and* as resistance to its domination. As with Robbins, being professional and being oppositional are not necessarily antithetical. Further, theory begins precisely with the recognition of the socially situated and constructed nature of all discourse (including its own discourse). The sea of everyday life in which everyone swims consists of either rhetoric, or ideology, or both; if theory means anything (if it has any consequences), it means alertness to this condition, the human condition. But insofar as understanding anything is the necessary first step toward fixing it or letting it alone, theory also proffers the hope, at least, of opting for social change. Literary theory paradoxically becomes social theory via the linguistic turn, which means, as it does for both de Man and Eagleton, that it identifies, at least as a first stage, literature and all other discourse as rhetoric or ideology rather than either absolute truth or transcendent aesthetic value. But this opening onto rhetoric is necessarily also the opening onto the historical terrain of relative truths.

Perhaps the main antithesis of ideology is not theory, and certainly not science or truth of some absolute variety, but versions of critical utopianism, including works of literature and art, that express the political, moral, and aesthetic claims to social justice and "the good life" mystified by ideology.[18] If theory is the space or moment in which literary criticism, on the hinge of linguistics, turns into social critique, it is also the case that an emancipatory politics has always already been simultaneously if unevenly expressed and repressed in literature. This politics is both the ideology and the utopianism of the aesthetic, whose contradictory duality Eagleton has explored as fully as anyone since Adorno. "The construction of the modern notion of the aesthetic artefact is...inseparable from the construction of the dominant ideological forms of modern class-society"; nevertheless, "the aesthetic...provides an unusually powerful challenge and alternative to these dominant ideological forms" (Eagleton, *Ideology of the Aesthetic*, 3). In other words, aesthetic ideology is also a theory of hope, which needs to be disencumbered from its parasites, such as elitist politics. The logic here is similar to that informing the idea of critic-theorists as oppositional professionals, except that now the critical "challenge and alternative" to the status quo is understood to reside within "the aesthetic artefact," or more specifically that literature already implies, albeit in rhetorical or ideological forms, the social criticism that literary theory aspires to become.

The various metamorphoses of literary theory into social critique by way of rhetoric and ideology are not arbitrary, but as John Brenkman says, are instead responses to the "clash between the legitimation and the contestation of domination" that is "internal to expressive forms themselves" (54). As "aesthetic artefact," literature may still be just as ideological as Eagleton declares it to be in *Literary Theory*, but it is simultaneously a "challenge and alternative" to the very social reality that produces it. Quite apart from those moments when works of literature explicitly voice social criticism, literature as such is a domain of the imagination antithetical to reality, and in this sense resistant also to the categories of rhetoric and ideology insofar as these work to reduce both theory and "the aesthetic dimension" to that reality.[19]

If Eagleton is right that the goals of a genuinely critical, emancipatory theory are, first, ideological demystification and, second, the undoing or subversion of capitalism, then everything else, from saying "pass the salt" to teaching deconstructive reading practices in graduate seminars (mere undoings of rhetoric), must be false theory or some form of ideology. But Marxism is not the only theory that claims to be politically oppositional: so do Derridean deconstruction, feminism, queer theory, African-American antiracist theory, postcolonialism, and some versions of postmodernism. In some measure, these forms of emancipatory theory draw much of their critical energy from the works of literature that each form valorizes or seeks to canonize. Emancipation from what? Logocentrism, racism, patriarchy, homophobia, and imperialism can today all be grouped under the rubric of late capitalism, which both reinforces and is reinforced by these other types of domination. But none of these types or, rather, modes of domination can be said to be the product of late capitalism, in the same way that "the postmodern condition" is, according to Fredric Jameson, "the cultural logic of late capitalism." Each of these modes of domination has a history older than that of capitalism. Comparing "modes of domination" to Marx's "modes of production" makes theoretical sense, both because Marx's historical analyses of main economic configurations demonstrated that these have always also involved domination, and because, as Foucault contends, power-in-general is productive: the modes of domination are

63

also ideological modes of production (symbolic or rhetorical capital) that are historically earlier but contributory to capitalism, the modern and modernizing economic mode of production through class, race, and gender domination.

Granted that social theory (literary theory may be a different, limited or even illusory case, as Eagleton contends) should be emancipatory, which of the modes of domination should it challenge first? That there are multiple, interactive modes of domination should surprise no one except the most Panglossian believer in the status quo. That it is now possible to name, analyze, and seek to undo the common, historical modes of domination is one of the more hopeful signs of the times. Theory is one source of this hopefulness; like literature, theory speaks a language of possibility. Emancipatory theory is above all an expression of social, collective hope. It is the spark, the necessary intellectual beginning, if any of the many hopes for emancipation that both divide and unite people, societies, and cultures can be fulfilled.

Will the elimination of one mode of domination eliminate any or all of the others? Or will reaction set in and reinforce the others, as is now happening in the United States and Britain? Also, just how much (if any) domination is necessary for there to be any social formation whatever? How much emancipation is possible? No matter how pessimistically anyone answers these questions, and while anyone is free to believe that culture and literature are hopelessly ideological, culture is the site of struggle between dominant and resistant or emergent (hopefully progressive) forces, between power and (hopefully) emancipation.

Even to mention hope in this age of postmodern cynicisms, including cynical antitheory theories, is to risk being deemed hopelessly naive and untheoretical. Perhaps therefore what is needed is a theory of hope (which would also be a theory of mourning) in relation to the quite old-fashioned, yet utopian, ideals of liberty, equality, and social justice.[20] Despite cynicism, postmodernism itself can be understood in terms of utopianism (strongly laced with dystopianism). In the introduction to *Heterotopia*, Tobin Siebers writes: "It is no accident that the idea of utopia has emerged in the work of Donna Haraway, Fredric Jameson, and many others as the high concept of postmodernism" (3). So perhaps there is hope in and for the postmodern condition after all. Further, perhaps heterotopias (plural) are new sorts of theoretical constructs to set over against the modes of domination: a multiplicity of places or prospects for freedom, based on equality-in-difference, or "a togetherness of diversity" beyond both "identity" and "contradiction" (Adorno, *Negative Dialectic*, 150). Yet, given the collapse of the communist regimes in eastern Europe, reinforcing the global domination of a transnational capitalism to which there are currently no effective alternatives, going for rides on "the flying carpet of utopia" may seem merely fantastic, merely theoretical game playing and despair (Enzensberger, 20). Given the New World Disorder since 1989, such antiutopian, antitheoretical pessimism is understandable; nevertheless, it implies its opposite—the need for radical alternatives to the status quo.

Does each mode of domination necessitate a separate form of emancipatory theory (feminist for patriarchy, postcolonial for imperialism, etc.)? Is it really the case that, as Zavarzadeh and Morton believe, orthodox Marxism can adequately deal with the plurality of modes of domination? Even if Marxism still offers the most "global" emancipatory theory, the plurality itself—giving rise to a plurality of emancipatory theories—is not reducible to liberal pluralism. The mistake Zavarzadeh and Morton make is to conflate all versions of social critique (feminism, etc.) that are not self-evidently Marxist with capitulation to capitalism, so that only Marxism escapes being just more of the same: grist for the mill of the ruling class, under the twin complicit headings of "bourgeois literary and cultural studies" (167). Quite apart from whether the plurality of modes of domination require different emancipatory theories or forms of critique, that there can be effective but different degrees of critical enlightenment and opposition (even neopragmatism is politically preferable to neoconservatism) Zavarzadeh and Morton do not appear to fathom.

Perhaps Derrida is right that a priority for any emancipatory theory should be the deconstruction of logocentrism. If there is a hierarchy of ideologies, then logocentrism (philosophy) may be at the apex, because it poses as pure theory, knowledge, truth disencumbered from common sense and practice, and from rhetoric and ideology. In one of their first collaborations, Marx and Engels attacked philosophical idealism as "the German ideology." Thus emancipatory theory must also be antitheory, because it deconstructs those logocentric illusions that pose as philosophy. Emancipatory theory, therefore, cannot be either an all-encompassing explanatory system or a methodology for cracking every rhetorical ploy or ideological code. It comes closer to being an intellectual stance toward both the social and the ideological status quo—one that combines critique with utopian aspiration. Certainly deconstruction can be an exemplary method of ideological critique, at least for those patient enough to follow its subtle maneuvers of discursive subversion. Every mode of domination is obfuscated or rationalized by rhetoric and ideology, so emancipatory theory must involve rhetorical and ideological critique.[21] But to experience domination and to be aware of that experience is to begin to theorize in an emancipatory direction. Whether one calls it emancipation or enlightenment, the aim of all theory is in part the thoroughly classical one inscribed in both the Socratic and the Sophistic traditions. Even in its most apparently anti-Enlightenment forms, theory's utopianism—its desire for or goal of "noncoercive knowledge produced in the interests of human freedom" (Said, *World*, 29)—aligns it with the much-embattled Enlightenment ideals of democratic reason, liberty, equality, and community.

While it is possible to declare that all theory is mere rhetoric or ideology, or in other words that all theory is an inconsequential waste of time, such cynicism cannot begin to account for politics and history as common (communal but also everyday) struggles against modes of domination. While it is also possible to attribute such theorization to *ressentiment*, according to Nietzsche the obverse of a successful will-to-power, it makes equally good theoretical sense to attribute it to a will-to-emancipation. Moreover, the difficulty of distinguishing between theory and either rhetoric or ideology only increases the urgency to construct an adequately emancipatory theory (or theories). Given this urgency—indeed, given the current global domination of transnational capitalism—there does not seem to be any end to theory in sight. Where there is either rhetoric or ideology (which is everywhere), there will be theory—that is, "theory as resistance" to rhetoric and ideology—for just the same reason that de Man understood theory as the resistant (in two senses) recognition of rhetoric.

Among many possible heterotopias, one can imagine an emancipatory university (or institution of critical theory), perhaps like the "free universities" of the 1960s or the "hobo colleges" of earlier decades (see Brundage), in which each discipline or, better, antidiscipline, though in no sense rigidly separated from the others, would theorize and seek to dismantle a mode of domination through ideological and rhetorical critique. Women's and African-American studies programs are already doing so. Also, some departments of English have, tentatively, moved toward becoming departments of literary theory—poststructuralist, Marxist, feminist, gay and lesbian, postcolonial. When they haven't arisen simply as newfangled media studies with a critical edge, cultural studies programs have also encompassed several or all of these emancipatory trends. In any event, it is possible to construct, with the aid of one or more emancipatory theories, images of collective experience free of domination. It is the task of emancipatory theory to enable the construction of such images and to encourage the hope that they can be realized in practices both locally and globally, both among individuals and among all cultures and societies.

If nothing comes after theory except more rhetoric and ideology, that won't be because theory has no possible consequences, but because the central ideals of the Enlightenment remain unfulfilled—or in other words because, as Jürgen Habermas has famously put it, "the project of modernity" remains "unfinished." In one direction, theory is the critique of Enlightenment; in another, it is its expression. "If we can and must be severe critics of the Enlightenment, it is Enlightenment which has empowered us to be so" (Eagleton, *Ideology of the Aesthetic*, 8). Or as Adorno and Horkheimer declared, "the Enlightenment *must consider itself*" if humanity is "not to be wholly betrayed. The task to be accomplished is not the conservation of the past, but the redemption of the hopes of the past" (xv). From this perspective, the answer to the question of what theory seeks, beyond mere rhetorical and ideological critique, becomes clear. When it isn't just cynical antitheory pointing to more of the same under the rubrics of rhetoric and ideology, theory seeks to understand and bring to practical realization the "concrete utopias" and emancipatory aspirations expressed in the aesthetic forms of all cultures and societies.

How the New Historicism Grew Old (And Gained Its Tale)

5

Last scene of all,
That ends this strange eventful history,
Is second childishness, and mere oblivion,
Sans teeth, sans eyes, sans taste, sans everything.
—Shakespeare, *As You Like It*

The short answer is that the new historicism was old—or over—to begin with. This was already one of the main theses in new historicist Brook Thomas's 1991 book, *The New Historicism and Other Old-Fashioned Topics*.[1] For one thing, the new historicism was over, because not long after providing this vanguard movement in literary studies with its name, Stephen Greenblatt announced that he preferred the phrase "cultural poetics" and that if there was some sort of movement he wasn't aware of it, or wasn't its leader, or both (Greenblatt, "Towards," 1).[2] At the same time, that sense of uncertainty—"giddiness," even (1)—in response to the notion that he might have started something hasn't prevented Greenblatt from more or less defining that something and even serving as its spokesman: "I shall try if not to define the new historicism, at least to situate it as a practice—a practice rather than a doctrine, since as far as I can tell (and I should be the one to know) it's no doctrine at all" ("Towards," 1).

Greenblatt repeats his "giddy" hesitancy or perhaps coyness most recently in *Practicing New Historicism*, coauthored with Catherine Gallagher. The two authors now seem willing enough to accept the phrase "new historicism" and even to claim it as their own, while insisting that it isn't an orthodoxy, nor a theory, nor even susceptible to theorization; it is, rather, an interpretive practice or assortment of practices. The coyness is matched by others who have been identified or who are self-identified with the new historicism, including Brook Thomas, and that very coyness, it seems to me, has been one of its central features: the new historicism is neither this nor that; it isn't Marxism, and it isn't poststructuralism; it isn't a theory, but it is "open" to theory ("Towards," 1); it isn't formalist literary criticism, but neither is it merely an American version of cultural studies; and so on. The coyness has contributed mightily to the success of what David Simpson has called "the most fashionable literary-critical movement since feminism" (*Subject*, 12). What will its next move be? which has some-times amounted to, what will Stephen Greenblatt say next?

If the new historicism isn't a theory, a doctrine, or even clearly a move-ment, it is nevertheless a "practice," says Greenblatt. But what sort of prac-tice, and how new is it? Further, because it has often been compared to and even identified with cultural studies, to what extent is the new historicism a version of this other, older, more encompassing movement?[3] I believe that not much is really new about the new historicism, either as a historio-graphical or as a literary-critical "practice," and that there are several sig-nificant differences between it and cultural studies or, to be more precise (because there are many practices that now go on under that rubric), cul-tural materialism.

The new historicism has been treated as theory, doctrine, movement, and practice, despite Greenblatt's disclaimers about all but the fourth term, by H. Aram Veeser in his two anthologies. Sometimes, as has frequently been noted, all it takes to produce and reify a canon is an anthology or two. More than Greenblatt, Gallagher, or anyone else, Veeser has sought to codify what Greenblatt and Gallagher insist cannot be codified. Both the codification and new historicism's resistance to that codification contribute to what might be called the theory-effect of the (non)movement. In his introduction to his 1989 anthology, *The New Historicism*, Veeser lists five "key assumptions [that] continually reappear and bind together the avowed practitioners and even some of their critics." These five assumptions are:

1. that every expressive act is embedded in a network of material practices;
2. that every act of unmasking, critique, and opposition uses the tools it condemns and risks falling prey to the practice it exposes;
3. that literary and non-literary "texts" circulate inseparably;
4. that no discourse, imaginative or archival, gives access to unchanging truths nor expresses inalterable human nature;
5. finally... that a critical method and a language adequate to describe culture under capitalism participate in the economy they describe. (xi)

It would be easy to show that none of these assumptions is new: each is a variation upon themes deriving either from versions of older historicisms, including Marxist historical materialism, or from poststructuralist theory. The first assumption is obviously a version of historical materialism, but with the deterministic hard edges associated with orthodox Marxism fuzzed up by "embedded," "network," and "practices." It isn't at all clear from Veeser's statement (or from new historicist works such as Greenblatt's *Marvelous Possessions*) if "every expressive act" is in any way determined or caused by the "network" of "material practices" within which it circulates. Further, the statement leaves it unclear as to whether such an "act" is itself a "material practice," partly "embedding" and in some very general way helping to determine or at least shape all the other "expressive acts" that make up the "network" of culture, although that is implicit. At the same time, the statement sounds very much like the assertions of "reciprocity" between the economic base and the cultural or ideological superstructure in, say, Raymond Williams's "Base and Superstructure in Marxist Cultural Theory," and that is certainly one way in which the new historicism is at least aligned with cultural studies.

If Veeser's second statement, that demystification and critique use "the tools" of their opposites, also sounds familiar, that is because it registers a certain poststructuralist and especially Foucauldian skepticism and even

71

cynicism about ever getting outside the whale of ideology (or rhetoric, or culture, or discourse, or textuality—take your pick). Such skepticism is also, of course, registered in some versions of cultural studies and Western Marxism—those that do not purport to be "scientific" or to find an Archimedean point of objectivity from which to judge the ideology of others, but that instead understand culture or hegemony in terms of competing ideologies. Veeser's fifth statement, moreover, seems only to be a repetition of his second one, but with the more specific phrase "culture under capitalism" added to the mix: critiques of capitalism "participate in the economy they describe," just as "every act of . . . critique . . . uses the tools it condemns."

Veeser's third statement, "that literary and nonliterary texts circulate inseparably," will surprise no one who has ever been in a bookstore or a library. Even that whipping boy of the new historicist Shakespeareans, E. M. W. Tillyard, sought in *The Elizabethan World Picture* to illuminate literary texts by showing their relationships to nonliterary texts. The New Critics, moreover, operated sometimes as historians and never claimed that literary texts couldn't or shouldn't be contextualized in relation to the nonliterary texts among which they "circulated" (what they did claim was that the "extrinsic" and nonliterary should not be mistaken for the "intrinsic" in the interpretation of a literary text). Perhaps the only novelty in Veeser's third point is the suggestion that the new historicism does not privilege the literary over the nonliterary, which is not the same as saying, with Terry Eagleton in *Literary Theory*, that the literary is nonexistent or that there are only different forms of rhetoric or ideology.

Finally, the fourth proposition in Veeser's list seems merely to be a version of poststructuralist cultural relativism: "truth" changes historically, and so does "human nature." While poststructuralist assertions of such relativism have themselves often seemed both novel and radical, poststructuralists have been quick to point out their indebtedness to Nietzsche and Nietzschean "genealogy" (as in Foucault's essay, "Nietzsche, Genealogy, History") if not to more traditional versions—perhaps including Marxist versions—of historicism. So, at least in relation to Veeser's account, what is new about the new historicism isn't the five key assumptions taken by themselves, but must instead derive from the combination and/or practice of them (assuming they constitute a methodology for interpreting both literary and nonliterary texts).

As itself an instance of the new historicism, Thomas's book can be read as a genealogy in the Foucauldian/Nietzschean sense of an antihistory or "countermemory." After pledging his own coy allegiance to the new historicism, Thomas offers a nonprogressive narrative that leads back to John Dewey, William James, and Charles Peirce as much as to Foucault and Nietzsche. What is most distinctive about the new historicists, according to Thomas, is their at least covert relationship to American pragmatism, instead of to French poststructuralism, neo-Marxism, or British cultural studies. Or rather, when the poststructuralist, neo-Marxist, and culturalist tendencies in such studies as Greenblatt's *Renaissance Self-Fashioning* and Walter Benn Michaels's *The Gold Standard and the Logic of Naturalism* are added up, the sum is a neopragmatist inflection or set of implications that, while not new, has the appearance of novelty in the context of current literary and cultural studies.

Thomas contends that, in James Harvey Robinson's 1912 *The New History*, as well as in the works of other American progressive, pragmatist historians such as Charles and Mary Beard, several of the epistemological and methodological assumptions of the new historicists were already at work. William James's "Will to Believe" was an American, pragmatist version of Foucault's "Will to Knowledge," which Foucault adapted from Nietzsche's "Will to Power." And Thomas aligns James's concept with Charles Beard's essay, "Written History as an Act of Faith" (94). If the new historicists, Thomas suggests, turn to Foucault and Nietzsche more readily than to Dewey, James, and Peirce, it is perhaps because they are reluctant to acknowledge debts to an American progressivism or liberalism that has run aground in "Watergate, Vietnam, and the Reagan era" (Thomas, 95).

Greenblatt's emphasis on practice as opposed to theory is one way he can be understood as a neopragmatist rather than a Foucauldian, a neo-Marxist, or anything else that one can easily pin a label to, perhaps including the label "new historicist." Neopragmatism is explicitly thematized in Walter Benn Michaels and Stephen Knapp's manifesto "Against Theory," in which theory turns out to be only another kind of practice (or according to which there are only practices of different sorts, without any overarching epistemological vantage point or method). New historicist works such as Michaels's *Gold Standard* and D. A. Miller's *The Novel and the Police* suggest an affinity if not an exact identity between Foucauldianism and pragmatism, such that Foucault's more theoretical claims are just the way of his practice.

Thomas thinks that part of the appeal of the new historicism has been its temporizing, ambivalent stance toward the more radical implications of both poststructuralism and Marxism. It is at once a weak Foucauldianism and a weak Marxism, marked as much by doubts about these two isms as by any synthesis of them. Greenblatt himself has been the first to concede that the new historicism is not systematic, which is partly why the phrase "cultural poetics" suits him. But a lot of other isms, theories, and methods, according to Greenblatt, are also not really systematic, at least "in American universities," where "critical affiliations like new historicism or deconstruction or now even Marxism are not linked to systematic thought" (*Learning*, 3).

Reading that assertion, one wonders whether Greenblatt thinks that "systematic thought" of any sort is possible or even a goal to be striven for, but he doesn't explicitly confront that question. He does, however, add, "It is possible in the United States to describe oneself... as a Marxist literary critic without believing in the class struggle as the principal motor force in history; without believing in the theory of surplus value; without believing in the determining power of economic base over ideological superstructure; without believing in the inevitability... of capitalism's collapse" (*Learning*, 3). No doubt, Greenblatt is here referring to the state of his own quasi-Marxist sentiments.[4] He suggests that his version of new historicism is a form of Marxist literary criticism minus belief in any of the ideas that could still make it recognizably Marxist. He also suggests that in American academic life today, even the Marxists have learned how to commodify and sell their theories, without offending too many of the powers-that-be—a point that is also true of the new historicists, of course.

According to Catherine Gallagher, "The new historicist, unlike the Marxist, is under no nominal compulsion to achieve consistency" ("Marxism," 46). But if that is the case, then the new historicism must either be very much like the old historicism, in the broad sense of liberal historiography and literary history, or else it must, through adopting Foucault's genealogical procedures and philosophical nominalism, undertake the impossible (or self-contradicting) task of rejecting historicism altogether.[5] The new historicism seeks to evade this problem in part by stressing the contingent in history, and therefore the very impossibility of systematizing it.

Veeser's five key but rather coy assumptions and Greenblatt's and Gallagher's claims about the unsystematic quality of the new historicism betray, as Stanley Fish has noted, an anxiety about becoming "entrapped" in theories or systems of thought—an anxiety, however, that Fish himself also betrays. According to Fish, "anxiety, of a particularly self-righteous kind, is what" the new historicists "do for a living" (*Professional*, 2), although Fish himself turns out to be anxious about both the new historicism and cultural studies. In *Professional Correctness* and elsewhere, Fish tries, in the name of professionalism, to shed self-righteousness, which he identifies with what he sees as the radical "political agenda" of both the new historicism and cultural studies. But if Thomas is correct and the new historicism is really a version of neopragmatism decked out in Foulcauldian-Marxist garb, it is puzzling to find Fish attacking it from his own neopragmatist position.

Fish thinks that both the new historicism and cultural studies represent a straying from the disciplinary fold of literary criticism. But just how central has literary criticism ever been to the "discipline" of English? As Graff shows in *Professing Literature*, perhaps only during the two or three decades of the New Criticism's hegemony was literary criticism in Fish's sense the defining center of what professors of English did. Fish's own examples of supposedly nonliterary (and therefore unprofessional) work include G. Wilson Knight and Douglas Bush, which suggests that strayings from the fold have always been just as central to what English professors do as literary exegesis of the sort that Fish models through his "professionally correct" reading of "Lycidas." "Many years ago Douglas Bush and Cleanth Brooks engaged in a celebrated debate," Fish writes, "with Bush representing the historical method and Brooks representing what was then, in fact, the New Criticism" (83). Fish is well aware, of course, that literary and cultural history are old and quite professional practices, ones that "complement" literary criticism. But he sides with Brooks against Bush in contending that historical studies cannot and should not replace criticism,

75

and also that there is an intrinsic literariness to a poem such as "Lycidas" that only the "professional" critic can properly fathom. Just how Fish's reading of "Lycidas" enhances the literary-aesthetic appreciation of that poem for anyone besides Fish is, however, unclear.

Of course history, even literary history, isn't the same as literary criticism. Besides assuming that a lot of other perfectly intelligent people can't or won't make this distinction, Fish insistently conflates any and all versions of literary and cultural history—even Douglas Bush's old and politically quite conservative version—with the radical politics he attributes to both the new historicism and cultural studies. Fish also lumps together both of these interdisciplinary movements in his opposition to "the claims and hopes of those who believe that literary criticism can be made to engage directly and effectively with the project of restructuring the whole of modern society" (41). Because I don't know anyone so naive as to think that literary criticism can march out of the academy and change the world—a preposterous scenario quite different from the proposition that academic work of all sorts matters in and can help to change the world for the better—I can't tell what Fish means (he must have a lot of naive colleagues).

Furthermore, it is just such "claims and hopes" that some new historicist works—Michaels's *The Gold Standard and the Logic of Naturalism*, for instance—also deny. Michaels's central thesis is that naturalist novels such as Frank Norris's *McTeague*, while seeming to criticize capitalism, cannot really do so because they are themselves the commodified products of capitalism. And Michaels and Knapp's "Against Theory," which takes a neopragmatist position close to Fish's, might have suggested to him that the new historicism isn't either as insistent on theory or as politically radical as he makes it out to be.[6] The one time in *Professional Correctness* that Fish cites Michaels comes in the appendix, "The Folger Papers," where he writes:

> You can choose to do interpretive work, to try and get at the truth about texts or events or cultures (although, as Walter Michaels observes, you can't choose your interpretations), or you can choose to do political work; but you can't do intepretive work (at least not in the humanities) with the intention of doing political work because once you decide to do political work...you will be

responsive and responsible to criteria that do not respect or even recognize the criteria of the academy. (133)

Fish hastens to add that there is nothing wrong with doing "political work," but insists that it isn't "academic" and has no bearing on the "professional" practice of literary interpretation and criticism, and vice versa. He cites Michaels only to support a parenthetical point, and without identifying him as a new historicist (the new historicist whom Fish cites most frequently in *Professional Correctness* is Louis Montrose).

Quite apart from whether Fish would be willing to count the "political work" that goes on in laws schools or in, say, Harvard's Kennedy School of Government as legitimately academic, his categorical separation of "politics" from "literary interpretation" makes no sense, in part because, even from the standpoint of neopragmatism, every interpretive and communicative action carries with it ideological, political valences or implications of some sort or other. Fish understands that everything, even literary-critical readings of "Lycidas," can be viewed as political or at least as having political (ideological) significance. His response, however, is to treat this counterargument as irrelevant, in part because the claim that everything is political is logically no different from other totalizing claims such as that everything is cultural or that "there is nothing outside the text." To all such claims Fish says, in effect, "so what?" But he also says that if you lump literature into culture or ideology or politics or history, it loses its "distinctiveness." This is true, however, only if you actively erase or deny that distinctiveness, as Eagleton does (literature doesn't have a "distinctive" existence, only an illusory one; it is just one sort of rhetoric or ideology). But every "distinctive" category and entity in the world swims in many larger contexts. And every professionally demarcated "interpretive community," to borrow Fish's phrase, swims in the larger interpretive community of "public opinion," for instance, which has greater or lesser influence over the more specific interpretive community. Thus, an English department in an elite, private university such as Harvard or Duke is likely to be somewhat more insulated from public opinion than is a state university such as Illinois.

Contexts do not swallow up texts, as Fish seems to think. As I noted in chapter 1, even treating literature as ideological does not turn it into chopped liver: a poem is a poem is a poem, as Gertrude Stein might have put it, although it can also be understood as ideological, rhetorical, a piece of historical evidence, part of the context for understanding another poem, and so forth. Further, I doubt that there is any complex, "professionally correct" interpretation of a complex literary work such as "Lycidas" that refers *only* to the strictly literary, "intrinsic" qualities of the work. Fish's reading of "Lycidas" at the outset of *Professional Correctness* in fact does just the opposite. Fish interprets Milton's elegy in relation to a series of contexts, ranging from Milton's other writings to the development and various definitions of pastoral back to Theocritus. These contexts are necessarily both "extrinsic" to the text and historical. "I could go on for ever in this vein," Fish declares, "adding to the contexts I have already introduced the context of Italian verse forms, the context of the myth of Orpheus, even the context of Jungian archetypes" (13), all helping to demonstrate his key point that "Lycidas" is a "poem" and needs to be read as such. But even if Fish could claim that all of these "extrinsic" contexts (and contexts are of course always extrinsic to specific texts) are themselves somehow intrinsically literary,[7] he would still be sinning (professionally) in one of the ways that he believes all interdisciplinary work, including both the new historicism and cultural studies, sins, and that is by reading "Lycidas" within and through the larger "cultural text."

Ignoring his own elaborate contextualization of "Lycidas," Fish cites my *Crusoe's Footprints* as an illustration of interdisciplinary, cultural studies work, and declares that "what Brantlinger calls the cultural text...has no epistemological or ontological superiority over the texts...it displaces." Fish adds:

> The cultural text, if it comes into view, will not provide a deeper apprehension of the literary text or the legal text; rather it will erase them even in the act of referring to them, for the references will always be produced from its angle of interest, not theirs. (79)

Besides the fact that I was myself citing the injunctions of both Gerald Graff and Robert Scholes to teach "the cultural text," I do not fathom Fish's anxiety about contexts "erasing" or swallowing up texts. This anxiety seems especially illogical given Fish's own contextualizing, historicizing reading of "Lycidas." But it is, I suppose, the political significance that I (and others) attach to cultural studies that really worries him, rather than simply the obvious and unavoidable notion of reading texts in relation to contexts. Partly in regard to their political valences, however, cultural studies and the new historicism are not identical or just more of the same old would-be political thing that Fish makes them out to be. In any event, whatever else it may or may not be, the new historicism is a mode of interpretation that necessarily contextualizes texts: history is a name for all of the contexts of the past out of which texts emerge, including such contexts as literary traditions (classical and Italian elegies, for instance), authors' biographies, and past uses and interpretations of texts. Fish's supposedly strictly literary reading of "Lycidas" does not demonstrate that the "literary critic" can avoid the historical or the larger "cultural text," but just the opposite. Besides, few if any "literary critics" have been more politically engaged and controversial throughout their careers, both inside and beyond the academy, than has been the supposedly nonpolitical, "professionally correct" Stanley Fish. But then, who gets the last word in Veeser's first anthology, singing the praises while also criticizing the new historicism for its various logical inconsistencies? Fish there advises the new historicists to "abandon" whatever residual hopes they entertain for political change, and tells them to "sit back and enjoy the fruits of their professional success, wishing neither for more nor for less. In the words of the old Alka-Seltzer commercial, 'try it, you'll like it'" ("Commentary," 315).

Rejecting the new historicism in favor of "Marxist or dialectical materialism," David Simpson writes that only such materialism "consistently offers...ways to explain how both representations and reality are necessary to an account of the production and reproduction of cultural life, without either flattening out the analytical model into a tautological indifference (representation is all there is) or simplifying the relation between cause and effect to the point that it is easily ridiculed by anyone armed with a few apt deconstructive nostrums" (*Subject*, 7–8). Though Simpson treats the new historicism just as dismissively as does Fish, he distinguishes it from "materialism" and, by implication, from cultural studies. Of course, not all versions of cultural studies add up to "Marxist or dialectical materialism." But that cultural studies has at least tended to be more overtly political, more obviously "materialist," and, indeed, more Marxist

79

than has the new historicism is one major difference between them. Again, if Brook Thomas is right, the new historicism is a version of neopragmatism and not of Marxism, though in good pragmatic fashion it makes use of ideas drawn from Marx, as also from Foucault, Derrida, and many other cultural and literary theorists.

A number of recent accounts acknowledge the affinities between the new historicism and cultural studies or cultural materialism, while also insisting on the differences between them. Of course the two movements share several issues, assumptions, and methods, and at least some of the same practitioners. If a certain amount of "theory-hope" (Fish's phrase) clings to both movements, that is partly because both are sometimes seen as the successors to poststructuralism, just as poststructuralism succeeded structuralism. But any claim to newness in the sense of advancing beyond poststructuralism is in both cases problematic, if only because both have been heavily influenced by poststructuralism. Yet in his 1986 essay "What Is Cultural Studies Anyway?" Richard Johnson suggested that it might be a "post-post-structuralist" movement, and the same could be said of the new historicism. In a self-evident way, anything that comes after poststructuralism is either part of that phenomenon, from which it only slightly departs, or a new post-something, though it remains to ask whether this new post-something delivers the mail in such a completely new way as to displace, deconstruct, or even just somewhat disrupt the previous delivery system.[8] The "new" historicism clearly promises novelty, although not necessarily in relation to poststructuralism—perhaps only in relation to an old historicism which, in most of its variants, looks like Hegelian idealism, Whig liberalism, or Marxist materialism. Cultural studies, too, does not always seem especially new or novel: it typically blends Marxist ideological critique, of either an Althusserian or a Gramscian sort, with an "ethnographic" approach to everyday life under capitalism, and it sometimes appears to be completely innocent of poststructuralism. Thus the new mail promised by both cultural studies and the new historicism may be destined never quite to arrive, at least in terms of answering the question, What will come after poststructuralism?

Rather than being advances beyond poststructuralism, the new historicism and cultural studies are either adaptations of it or reactions against its more radical implications (or both). Some of my English department and MLA colleagues have welcomed the new historicism as a retreat from what they see as the ravages of literary-critical deconstruction: let's get back to reality, and history. Ironically, they find a comforting reassurance in the very word *historicism*, which to earlier generations of scholars often signaled an epistemological relativism now identified with poststructuralism (the thought that everything is historically constructed is logically no different from the thought that everything is socially constructed). Simpson makes the same point in criticizing "the kind of 'new historicism' that looks to history as to a safe and approved harbor, a place where one may sleep peacefully, lulled by anecdotal stories, after tossing on the stormy seas of deconstructive and theoretical Marxist uncertainty" ("Raymond Williams," 9).

For my comfort-seeking colleagues, cultural studies, in contrast to the new historicism, usually does not appear to be a solution, but part of the problem, roiling the stormy seas. This is partly because cultural studies stresses contemporary culture instead of the past—often today using that panic-inducing term *postmodernism*—and tends also to deal in mass culture. Cultural studies work is sometimes accompanied by the claim or perhaps disclaimer that, in "the postmodern condition," there is nothing but mass culture. New historicists, however, have continued to focus mostly upon canonical works of literature (Shakespeare looms large, of course), while culturalists such as Stuart Hall and Dick Hebdige have focused on questions of ideology, social class, race, and gender in relation to the contemporary mass media (rock music and youth subcultures, for instance). But, then, what can you expect? Hall and Hebdige were trained as sociologists, not as historians or literary critics.

Although not alternatives to poststructuralism, cultural studies and the new historicism are, I think, its necessary corollaries—two branch post offices established because the Grand Central PO had too much mail to deliver. Poststructuralism had to deliver, especially on the very truth claims it appeared to deny, and so cultural studies and the new historicism have arisen and flourished in part to recall, with qualifications, the forms of truth-claiming representation necessary for any communication whatsoever to take place. Although no longer understood as substitutes for "the real" in any absolute sense, "culture" and "history" are the messy, totalizing terms that reopen the questions of reference and reality by refusing to

81

reduce them entirely to language and textuality. If this is correct, both movements are in some sense retreats from the ultimate poststructuralist abyss—from, as Michael Holquist puts it, "the perpetual elusiveness of meaning as it fades away in the phantom relay of the signifying chain" (165). They are also in different ways responses to the crisis of Marxist historical materialism, a crisis that, on the theoretical level, has itself been partly caused by poststructuralism and the postmodern attack on "metanarratives" (see, for instance, Aronowitz). Or it could be said that both cultural studies and the new historicism are attempts to fuse elements of poststructuralism (especially Foucault) with something like "the best that has been thought and spoken" in Western Marxism (Anderson, Michael Ryan).

In terms of their institutionalization—their accommodation to established disciplines and the powers-that-be of higher education—the two movements cannot be so easily reconciled. In the early 1980s, the new historicism emerged within North American English departments to almost instant celebrity status, while cultural studies began in Britain in the 1960s, first at the Birmingham Centre for Contemporary Cultural Studies and later at the Open University and elsewhere, as an alternative, radical form of higher education. Despite its celebrity status, the new historicism has not been much of a force beyond English and other language and literature departments. With a few notable exceptions such as Lynn Hunt, Dominick LaCapra, and Thomas Laquer, historians lodged in history departments have not paid much attention to it.[9] On the other hand, cultural studies has from the outset attracted malcontents from various academic disciplines (English, history, sociology, and education, for instance), in part because it has offered or at least promised a concerted critique of the present constitution of the academic disciplines.

Cultural studies uses versions of recent Marxist, feminist, poststructuralist, and postcolonial theories to analyze and perhaps influence contemporary cultural, political, and economic formations in progressive, emancipatory ways. Hence, it also focuses on the major modes of domination in the world today: gender, class, race, neoimperialism. The new historicism, on the other hand, circulates around the question of how to do advanced literary criticism and/or cultural history by using insights generated by poststructuralism and recent Marxist and feminist theories. But, granting that the new historicism is more literary, more willingly or complicitly academic, and less overtly out to change the world than is cultural studies, how much of a contrast is there between the basic assumptions of the two movements? Are cultural studies and the new historicism competing methodologies and perhaps theories (insofar as they are not consistently poststructuralist *or* Marxist-materialist, a case could be made that both are untheoretical), or are they, despite superficial differences, one movement with two names? Moreover, in relation to poststructuralism, just what do they deliver?

Some new historicists claim allegiance to cultural studies; it is less clear that most practitioners of cultural studies would or could call themselves new historicists. For one thing, again, culturalists are not always either literary critics or historians; they are just as apt to be sociologists or mass media and film analysts. But Alan Sinfield and Jonathan Dollimore—the British editors of one of the key texts in the emergence of the new historicism, *Political Shakespeare: New Essays on Cultural Materialism*—claim a dual allegiance. Their volume contains perhaps the most frequently cited example of new historicist work, Greenblatt's "Invisible Bullets" essay, and also an afterword by one of the founding fathers of cultural studies, Raymond Williams. Similarly, when in *Learning to Curse* Greenblatt explains how he became a new historicist, he points to the year he spent at Cambridge University as a graduate student and the impact Williams's teaching made upon him. In place of Yale New Criticism, Williams offered a thoughtful version of Marxist literary and cultural analysis: "In Williams's lectures all that had been carefully excluded from the literary criticism in which I had been trained [at Yale]—who controlled access to the printing press, who owned the land and the factories, whose voices were being repressed as well as represented in literary texts, what social strategies were being served by the aesthetic values we constructed—came pressing back in upon the act of interpretation" (*Learning*, 2).

Greenblatt's autobiographical sketch complicates the brief, critical comparison of the two movements offered by Robert Young in *White Mythologies*.[10] Writing about "the tactical use of Foucault...in current forms of criticism," Young spies a difference between the new historicism and "cultural materialism": "The former is identified closely with Foucault, while the latter owes its allegiance to Raymond Williams, and really only amounts to a way of describing British ex-Marxists" (88). For Young as for Stanley Fish, one obvious similarity between the new historicism and cultural studies is that both forms of critical/theoretical practice want also to be versions of radical political practice—to change the world, not just interpret it. His assertion that "the British cultural materialists quickly adopted a name which tactfully removes the suggestion of Marxism as such" (89) is matched, if not exactly balanced, by his claim that the cultural materialists are after all more commonsensical and effective about politics than "the more fastidious" and "more strictly academic new historicists, whose own politics remain more carefully hidden" (90; cf. Easthope, 119–123).

Because one of Young's main targets is the old-style, orthodox Marxist metanarrative of history, he is inconsistent in criticizing perhaps ex- or perhaps post-Marxists for distancing themselves from that very metanarrative. Is post-Marxism less honorable in its postal politics than poststructuralism? Is it a sign of weak-kneed apostasy to arrive at Young's recognition that "Marxism's universalizing narrative of the unfolding of a rational system of world history is simply a negative form of the history of European imperialism" (2)? Indeed, if the new historicism is new, it is so largely through its claim to offer a version of "historicism" while challenging the teleological, imperializing assumptions of nineteenth-century forms of historicism, and especially what Thomas calls "narratives of progressive emergence," including both liberal and Marxist varieties. Historicism in general can be defined as any attempt to theorize or understand history by finding in it a pattern, hidden unity, direction, or goal that gives meaning to the totality of human time and experience. But the new historicism registers skepticism, at least, that there is any pattern or direction to find, and also that the necessarily linguistic tools of the historian can adequately represent that totality. This skepticism is, perhaps, its most distinctly poststructuralist trait.

Given its more clearly radical political orientation, cultural studies often claims to have just the sort of activist "political agenda" that Fish thinks is unprofessional and extra-academic.[11] At the same time, in most cultural studies work, there is nothing coy about at least staking claims to theoretical consistency. In contrast, the new historicism seems to practice a studied avoidance and occasionally explicit rejection of theory. Writing about Greenblatt, Fredric Jameson declares that "self-fashioning" and "the new historicism" are "post-theoretical" (*Postmodernism*, 188). In Greenblatt's *Renaissance Self-Fashioning*, says Jameson,

> There is . . . a remarkable combination of interpretive sophistication, of intense intellection and theoretical energy, with an exclusion of self-consciousness or reflexivity of the classical type, which will then characterize all the most successful productions of the New Historicism. (189)

Jameson suggests that the new historicism has been a success story in the marketplace of academic fashions in part because it has made "resistance to theory" and to "systematic thought" look like systematic thought, with often brilliant but inconsistent theory-effects. "We will therefore formulate the discourse of the New Historicism as a 'montage of historical attractions,' to adapt Eisenstein's famous phrase," writes Jameson, "in which extreme theoretical energy is captured and deployed, but repressed by a valorization of immanence and nominalism that can either look like a return to the 'thing itself' or a 'resistance to theory'" (190).

In Michaels's *The Gold Standard*, according to Jameson, money and capitalism become "respectable" for academic, literary critical discourse, in part because Michaels's "sounding of the economic motif has today shed all of its (once inevitable) Marxist connotations" (193).

> It is not hard to show [as Michaels does] that the force of desire alleged to undermine the rigidities of late capitalism is, in fact, very precisely what keeps the consumer system going in the first place. (Jameson, 202)[12]

Much the same is true, Jameson goes on to suggest, of Greenblatt's "trademark" focus on "travel narrative and imperialism" (193).

Compared to Edward Said's *Orientalism* or *Culture and Imperialism*, Greenblatt's *Marvelous Possessions* is not primarily a political project, in the sense of contesting imperialism and racism as these are represented in literary (and other) texts and also as they persist into the present. Though Greenblatt certainly acknowledges the violence that Columbus and those who came after him visited upon the New World and its first inhabitants, his purpose is less to protest that violence retroactively than to show the many ways that "the performance and production of wonder" reinforced the European invasion and "possession" of the Americas. For better or worse, the discourse of the "marvelous" was, Greenblatt argues, politically and economically productive in all sorts of ways. Moreover, Greenblatt seems uninterested in linking his project to postcolonial theories of race, empire, and exploitation; he does not cite Said's work or that of other post-colonial critics (cf. Brannigan, 126). And the only time Greenblatt mentions Marx it is not to cite Marx's critique of imperialism, but to "adapt" Marx's idea of the circulation of capital to "the reproduction and circulation of mimetic capital" (a phrase that sounds closer to Pierre Bourdieu than to Marx) (*Marvelous*, 6).

Greenblatt's notion of the "circulation of mimetic capital" is one of the ways that a quasi-Marxist economic discourse circulates through his stud-ies, including *Marvelous Possessions*—a quasi-Marxism, again, with few or perhaps none of the defining concepts of Marx himself. For Greenblatt, what circulates isn't money and capital in the brute, materialist sense, but money and capital as forms of discourse. At the same time, Greenblatt's analyses are anti-historicist because they are *both* antitotalizing and anti-imperialist.[13] Greenblatt's work, and the new historicism more gener-ally, is partly a critique of the logocentric, ethnocentric tales called national histories that the European victors have told themselves throughout cen-turies of imperial domination of the rest of the world. But on what grounds is the new historicist critique made? Because the Marxist metanarrative of the past is just as Eurocentric as other versions of historicism, what allows for the narration of different, non-Eurocentric interpretations of the past? One virtue of substituting "cultural poetics" for Marxism or even "historical materialism" may lie in the acknowledgment that, as Derrida says, "there is nothing outside the text." But this virtue is just as readily understood as an intepretive or epistemological cul-de-sac. After poststructuralism, the only materialism possible seems to be a merely discursive or cultural one. "Cultural poetics" is a tautological phrase—culture equals poetics—that expresses the poststructuralist view that language can only refer to other language. It also represents a foreshortening of the Marxist base/super-structure paradigm: the material or economic base has withered away; now there is only superstructure, culture, poetics. What sorts of explanations can a cultural poetics produce except relative, inadequate, poetic ones?

Cut loose from its moorings in some sense both of systematic representation and of historical causality, the ship of the new historicism drifts anywhere and everywhere, from anecdote to anecdote (*Learning*, 5; Gallagher and Greenblatt, 49–74). Anecdotes, Greenblatt says at the outset of *Marvelous Possessions*, "are registers of the singularity of the contingent," and through them his study is "shaped by a . . . *longing* for the effect of the locally real and by a larger historical intention that is *at once evoked and deflected*" (3; my emphasis). This is, to say the least, coy. But the move from metanarratives to anecdotes solves nothing, because most of the same epistemological claims are at stake in both micro and macro forms of narration. Are they rooted in documentable evidence? What do they explain or represent? What explains *them* (why does the new historicist choose to retell them)? And so forth. Arguments around representation are too familiar to rehearse here (but see Thomas, *The New Historicism*, 3–23). In relation to causality, however, Frank Lentricchia (still in his theoretical incarnation) notes that for there to be "historicism" at all there must be some "principle of causality." He quotes Williams: "'A Marxism without some concept of determination is in effect worthless. A Marxism with many of the concepts of determination it now has is quite radically disabled.'" Lentricchia then writes: "Substitute historicism for Marxism and perhaps Stephen Greenblatt for Raymond Williams, and you have a description of the theoretical quandary within which some recent historically minded critics, with strong and problematical relations to Michel Foucault, and who tend to specialize in the English Renaissance, now find themselves" (232).

Greenblatt's efforts to solve this "theoretical quandary" are fascinating, brilliant, and yet ultimately unsatisfactory. The final two essays in *Learning to Curse* are as close to programmatic statements as any new historicist has written, but the first, "Towards a Poetics of Culture," which also appears in Veeser's anthology, involves the rejection of *both* Marxist *and* poststructuralist theory as "eschatological," "utopian," or teleological in the bad old historicist sense. Greenblatt discovers the old Marxist metanarrative in Jameson's *Political Unconscious* and dismisses it as having "the resonance of an allegory of the fall of man" ("Towards," 3).[14] Having rejected Marxism even in its postmodern, Jamesonian guise, Greenblatt turns next to Lyotard's postmodern poststructuralism. Greenblatt finds in Lyotard the mirror opposite of Jameson's "allegory of the fall of man," but with nearly identical results. For both Jameson and Lyotard, "history functions... as a convenient *anecdotal ornament* upon a theoretical structure, and capitalism appears not as a complex social and economic development in the West but as a malign philosophical principle" ("Towards," 5). But it is Greenblatt more than Jameson who treats history in terms of "anecdotal ornaments," while Lyotard is more theoretically consistent, for better or worse, about what he sees as the necessary reliance on anecdotes or micronarratives.

Lumping both Jameson's Marxism and Lyotard's poststructuralism under the falsely unifying term "theory," Greenblatt accuses both of an "effacement of contradiction [which] is not the consequence of an accidental lapse but rather the logical outcome of theory's search for the obstacle that blocks the realization of its eschatological vision" ("Towards," 5). But how is the "cultural poetics" Greenblatt substitutes for an "eschatological" Marxism and, as he sees it, an equally eschatological poststructuralism an improvement? By implication, at least, cultural poetics recognizes the complexity or contradictoriness of capitalism as a world historical process. Capitalism must be viewed, writes Greenblatt, "not as a unitary demonic principle, but as a complex historical movement in a world without paradisal origins or chiliastic expectations" ("Towards," 5). In particular, in understanding the relationship between art and society, "complexity" must be an operative word, and in Greenblatt's essays the nature of that complexity is conveyed especially by quasi-economic terms such as "negotiation" and "circulation": "the work of art is the product of a negotiation between a creator or class of creators... and the institutions and practices of society. In order to achieve the negotiation, artists need to create a currency that is valid for a meaningful, mutually profitable exchange," and so on ("Towards," 12). Greenblatt adds that "the society's dominant currencies, money and prestige, are invariably involved," and also that the "terms 'currency' and 'negotiation' are the signs of our manipulation and adjustment of the relative systems" (12), whatever that means. They are also the signs of, in Greenblatt's antitheoretical theory (or deliberate avoidance of being too theoretical or systematic), a very weak "principle of causality" or determination.

Greenblatt does not privilege the economic as final cause or even outer limit, as in all variants of the Marxist base-superstructure paradigm, but rather treats it merely as the source of metaphors by which "exchanges" take place between a society's institutions and its cultural and artistic creators. These exchanges can be described on a case-by-case, "contingent," or anecdotal basis, rather like Clifford Geertz's ethnographic "thick description" that is also one of the methodologies of cultural studies (see Gallagher and Greenblatt, 20–30), and they can also be ascribed to the vast and vague set of economic developments and processes Greenblatt is still willing to call "capitalism" from the Renaissance forward. However, they cannot be understood more systematically, theoretically, or teleologically as *leading somewhere*—as the inexorable, world-unifying or -massifying march of economic and cultural modernization (and now postmodernism).

A similar rejection of theory, whether Marxist or poststructuralist, occurs in the last essay in *Learning to Curse*, "Resonance and Wonder." Here Greenblatt cites one of the definitions of "historicism" given by the *American Heritage Dictionary*: "The belief that processes are at work in history that man can do little to alter." Greenblatt responds: "New historicism, by contrast, eschews the use of the term 'man'; interest lies not in the abstract universal but in particular, contingent cases, the selves fashioned and acting according to the generative rules and conflicts of a given culture. And these selves, conditioned by the expectations of their class, gender, religion, race and national identity, are constantly effecting changes in the course of history" (*Learning*, 164).[15] That is to say, individuals may be "conditioned" by circumstances, but they have just as much to do with the making of the circumstances as vice versa. This tautological proposition leads Greenblatt next to assert "the new historicism's insistence on the pervasiveness of agency" (165). In other words, everywhere you look in history, there are people—selves or individual "agents"—doing things that affect the course of history. This notion in turn seems to be a variant of Foucault's famous proposition that "power breeds resistance," which means, of course, that there is power (hence, "agency") everywhere in society—it's

89

just that some agents have more of it than others (Columbus, for instance, had more agency than did the Arawaks). According to Althusser, an ideological state apparatus is an "agency" for self-fashioning that the selves fashioned have little or no control over. But Greenblatt's agents seem to be the selves or unit-individuals that make up the stock and trade of American individualism. Then again, Greenblatt's agent-selves, as Jameson suggests, may be more postmodern than the unified, "rugged" individuals of the early economists: Greenblatt's, Jameson thinks, are "selves capable of modifying their shapes so effectively that they ultimately called the very idea of the self into question" (Jameson, *Postmodernism*, 189).

In a single loop, Greenblatt maintains contact with one of his theoretical power sources—Foucault—while also giving expression to what Thomas calls the new historicism's "unacknowledged link to American progressivism" (Thomas in Veeser, 197).[16] The new historicism, according to Thomas, takes its place alongside other manifestations of neopragmatism in the United States, and thereby "reaffirms the liberal tradition of American progressivism and its sense of temporality" (197), despite its challenge to "narratives of progressive emergence." It thus also reaffirms that tradition's sense of individual agency—exactly the antithesis of Foucault's or Althusser's position with regard to the pervasiveness, at least in modern and now postmodern social formations, of deindividualized power—"Ideology," "discipline," "surveillance," "the tyranny of the Norm," and so forth. Rather than echoing Foucault's insistence upon the impending dissolution of that modern abstraction "man," the new historicism, luckily for liberal humanism, resuscitates that liberal humanist abstraction through "self-fashioning."

Against the anti-individualistic tendencies of both Marxism and poststructuralism, Greenblatt covertly reinscribes individual agency. In contrast, cultural studies maintains a more radical but nonetheless traditional emphasis on *collective* agency, which often takes the form of an appraisal of the potential for political resistance in various marginalized groups and cultural phenomena. Of course the search for resistance is a much-diminished version of the traditional Marxist goal of revolution. But as a derivative of British democratic socialism, cultural studies remains at least consonant with earlier forms of Marxism. For that very reason, as Robert Young suggests, cultural studies fits less comfortably with poststructuralism than does the new historicism (90). In any event, the cultural studies movement, partly because of its British origin, has been more directly radical-political than has new historicism. Some of the professional anxiety that Fish notes among new historicists and that he shares with them, on the other hand, has to do with the awareness that they *might* be political but are not. Or at least, they might write in more politically adversarial ways but do not. '

Fish's reaction to this anxiety is to deny that he shares it, while also denying that academic work of any sort can be political in any meaningfully public sense. According to Fish, if you are an academic, you can't be a politician or a truly public intellectual. The key figures in the early history of the cultural studies movement, however—Richard Hoggart, E. P. Thompson, Raymond Williams, and Stuart Hall—were all political activists and public intellectuals, more or less influential outside the academy as well as inside. And one of my favorite texts dealing with the public, political, often very powerful roles academic intellectuals have played is John Trumpbour's 1989 anthology, *How Harvard Rules: Reason in the Service of Empire*. Of course, the public-academic intellectuals who figure most largely in Trumbour's exposé are neither literary critics nor radicals. They are instead conservatives or liberal-conservatives such as Henry Kissinger, Robert McNamara, and Zbigniew Brzezinski. I wonder also what Fish thinks of the public, political, and often quite powerful roles more recent neoconservative academics such as William Bennett, Dinesh D'Souza, and Francis Fukuyama have been playing?

More succinctly and perhaps more clearly than in *Professional Correctness*, in his contribution to Veeser's *The New Historicism*, Fish expresses his view that nothing (except new individual studies of literature such as *Marvelous Possessions*) has happened because the new historicism isn't new and cannot be new. There, too, although acknowledging the apparent difference between their "materialist" critics—those more oriented, no doubt, to cultural studies—and the new historicists, Fish suggests that the difference between them is negligible: both groups want to do history and both want to be political in the same ways:

In short...New Historicists buy their freedom to do history (as opposed to meta-accounts of it) at the expense of their claim to be doing it—or anything else—differently. But of course that is a price the New Historicists will not be

91

willing to pay, for, like their materialist critics, they have a great deal invested in being different, and, again like their materialist critics, the difference they would claim is the difference of being truly sensitive to difference, that is, to the way in which orthodox historical narratives suppress the realities whose acknowledgment would unsettle and deauthorize them. Whatever their disagreements on other matters, both New Historicists and materialists are united in their conviction that current modes of historiography are (wittingly or unwittingly) extensions of oppressive social and political agendas. ("Commentary," 309)

Fish isn't claiming, of course, that forms and acts of oppression haven't occurred throughout history, nor that historians do not have an obligation to write histories about these forms and acts of oppression. Nor—I am guessing here—is he denying that historiography makes no public, historical, political difference whatsoever.

The textbook on American history that I read as a public high school student in the late 1950s contained one bland paragraph on slavery. This is not and could not be the case with history textbooks today, no doubt mainly because of the civil rights movement, but also because of the revisionary work of many academic historians, both black and white. Both history and historiography matter in obviously public, political ways. Though perhaps more distantly, so do literary criticism and one of its offshoots, the formation of the literary canon. Or canons. A reading of Paul Lauter's *Canons and Contexts* and at least a scan of the table of contents of his *Heath Anthology of American Literature*, or a reading of any of Sandra Gilbert and Susan Gubar's feminist studies and a scan of the table of contents of their *Norton Anthology of Women's Literature*, should dispel any notion that even strictly academic literary criticism makes no public, political difference.

Fish wants to dismiss the differences that both cultural studies and the new historicism make or promise to make by suggesting that making a difference is merely a matter of trying to be fashionable. Even though I believe that the new historicism makes less difference in several ways than does cultural studies, the trouble with Fish's argument is that he himself, through his neopragmatist cynicism, makes fashionable hay by claiming to make no difference. There is nothing new under the sun, according to Fish, including the new historicism, which is simply the old historicism dressed up with a few unnecessary and contradictory theoretical concepts. But, then, also according to Fish, the non-new historicism is there to be enjoyed for its own nonpolitical sake, as a matter of "professional success" within the academy. With such friends, perhaps the new historicism doesn't need enemies.

Beyond their neopragmatist readiness to opt for "professional success," the trouble with both Fish and the new historicists is that they offer models of historical change in which no real change is possible. Practice occurs, just as domination occurs (power, money, and agency are everywhere), and that's all we know in life, and all we need to know. As Thomas remarks: "For Fish change just happens. There is no struggle involved in it. But there are varieties of change. For instance, Fish's argument does not address the interests of those who suffer under existing conditions, which, to be sure, are always changing but do not seem to change their suffering" (*The New Historicism*, 101). Thomas goes on to note that the first American pragmatists—Peirce, James, Dewey, the Beards, and others—were believers in "progressivism" and in the political importance of their ideas in effecting change in the public arena (cf. Rorty). Fish's "professionally correct" cynicism and what he calls the "self-righteous" political anxiety and even guilt of new historicist critics such as Greenblatt and Louis Montrose are, no doubt, the historical reflex of a postmodern era in which the gap between what is sometimes viewed as the *merely* academic and the larger society and now global economy of capitalism is widening. The main difference between Greenblatt and Fish may finally be that the former continues to hope that his ideas and work will matter politically as well as academically, whereas the latter believes that it is his professional obligation to insist that his ideas, beyond the work that he does for his chosen "interpretive communities" of literary criticism and legal studies, make no difference whatsoever.[17]

Forget history and politics and even "the cultural text," Fish admonishes; let's go practice literary criticism, as we—the profession of English studies—have always done in the past and will continue to do just as long as somebody continues to pay the bills. But what guarantees that somebody—the public, namely—will continue to pay the bills for new-old readings of

"Lycidas"? Fish's desire to resucitate the old New Criticism is not reasonable argumentation so much as the proverbial academic ostrich sticking his head in the sand. Or as Rick Perlstein puts it in his review of *Professional Correctness*, Fish's contention that "the enemies of literary study are the New Historicism and cultural studies, and that more professionalism [i.e., a return to literary criticism as practiced by Cleanth Brooks and Stanley Fish] just might save the sinking ship" is politically benighted.

The real enemies of English and, indeed, higher education in general are numerous, powerful, and now both inside and outside the university. They include those who attack even Fish for "political correctness," and for the last three decades they have constituted a reactionary, anti-intellectual politics that threatens the very foundations of higher education. To assume that if we all just behave in "professionally correct" ways the bad politics will disappear has, if anything, even less purchase on the public realm and the real world than the seemingly merely academic (and, according to Fish, unprofessional) political agendas of the new historicism and cultural studies. For if Perlstein, Louis Menand, Cary Nelson, Gerald Graff, David Simpson, and many other analysts of the current academic scene are correct, there is most definitely a political context—and struggle—that even literary critics are embroiled in, whether or not they recognize it. Moreover, they had better learn to fight back if they want to continue to have a profession to practice. In this struggle, the new historicism, which has not seemed very new for quite some time now, is not likely to be one of the major combatants, in part because it has always been—*pace* Fish—professionally correct, neopragmatically doing what it does best, which is interpreting literary texts in more or less new ways. In contrast, cultural studies, with its interdisciplinary affiliations, bringing together academic professionals from many humanities and social science fields, its focus on contemporary cultural politics, and its more forthright ties to Marxism, radical feminism, and many versions of ethnic and postcolonial critique, looks increasingly like a united front—one site, at least, where the culture wars over the university and its future are being and will continue to be waged.

Postcolonialism and Its Discontents

6

How many goodly creatures are there here!
How beauteous mankind is! O brave new world,
That has such people in't.
—Shakespeare, *The Tempest*

With the advent of postcolonial studies, typically in English, comparative literature, and foreign language departments, much that once seemed marginal to the humanities and social sciences has begun to seem more significant if not yet central to higher education. But why should empire, its aftermath, and its traces in literatures and languages be of importance today, if indeed the colonial era is over, and we are now in a postcolonial era? In *Culture and Imperialism*, Edward Said writes:

> The world has changed since Conrad and Dickens in ways that have surprised, and often alarmed, metropolitan Europeans and Americans, who now confront large non-white immigrant populations in their midst, and face an impressive roster of newly empowered voices asking for their narratives to be heard.... To ignore or discount the overlapping of Westerners and Orientals,

> the interdependence of cultural terrains in which colonizer and colonized co-existed and battled each other... is to miss what is essential about the world in the past century. (xx)

No other factor has been so profoundly influential on all of the world's cultures than imperialism from the Renaissance forward. It does not make sense, then, to interpret the "post" in postcolonial as meaning that the colonial era has ended and that humanity has entered some nonimperialist New World Order.

It is *de rigueur* for postcolonial theorists to start their essays, books, and lectures by objecting to the word "postcolonial," because colonialism or its effects or both are still influential. The word is, perhaps, least objectionable as a periodizing term, referring to the decolonization of Europe's formal, political empires. Though empires and their downfalls—Rome, for example—are the stuff of classicism, the recent history leading to the alleged postcolonial condition starts with the independence of India and Pakistan in 1947–48 and continues through the emergence of independent nation-states in Africa, the Caribbean, Vietnam, and elsewhere. But even this relatively uncontroversial, period use of the term conflicts with claims that other modern cultures and societies are postcolonial: Ireland, Canada, South Africa, Australia, the United States.[1] And there is also the claim that, though formal political empires have been been mostly dismantled, the economic exploitation and "dependency" established through those empires have continued and perhaps even strengthened the stranglehold of "the West" on "the rest." Kwame Nkrumah, first president of newly independent Ghana, made this point in his 1965 book, *Neo-Colonialism: The Last Stage of Imperialism:*

> The essence of neo-colonialism is that the State which is subject to it is, in theory, independent and has all the outward trappings of international sovereignty. In reality its economic system and thus its political policy is directed from outside. (ix)

Nkrumah saw neocolonialism as the situation across Africa and, indeed, throughout "the less developed parts of the world" (x). He also saw it as "the worst form of imperialism," because for those able to profit from it, "it means power without responsibility," while "for those who suffer from it, it means exploitation without redress" (xi).

Once capitalism had sunk roots of exploitation in Africa, Nkrumah believed, it could dispense with formal political and military domination. It was not a question of "post" for him, but of a cancerous growth of impoverishment on the one hand (in Africa and the rest of the Third World) and increasing enrichment and power on the other (in Europe and North America). Those postcolonial theorists who now question the "post" take up the theme of economic dependency in terms of the increasing power of transnational capitalism and the globalization of the world's largest corporations (almost all of them based in the West or in Japan and Southeast Asia). The enormous and soaring national debts of Third World countries verify Nkrumah's basic argument: there is no "post" to economic imperialism (see, for example, Altvater et al.).

Postcolonialists sometimes also go on to consider the relationship between their "post" and the various other postisms that have sprung up since the 1960s: poststructuralist, postmodern, postindustrial, posthistorical and, more recently, posthuman. In her consideration of the "pitfalls of the postcolonial," Anne McClintock includes, along with the terms I have just listed, "post-cold war, post-Marxism, postapartheid, post-Soviet, post-Ford, postfeminism, postnational . . . [and] even postcontemporary" (10). In this chapter, I explore the discontents—productive ones, as I see them—of postcolonial theory in regard to several of these other post-terms, while also considering its relations with both multiculturalism and cultural studies.

Postcolonialism and Poststructuralism

As the echo of Lenin's *Imperialism: The Last Stage of Capitalism* in its title suggests, Nkrumah's *Neo-Colonialism: The Last Stage of Imperialism* takes a Marxist perspective on the persistence of Western domination through economic exploitation and dependency. "Last" means latest rather than final; for Nkrumah, it indicates a continuity rather than an impending break. Versions of Marxist analysis are evident also in many of the texts, manifestos, and declarations of independence written by those nationalist leaders and intellectuals who form what Said, for one, acknowledges as the first, original group of postcolonial (or, better, anticolonial) intellectuals. In *Culture and Imperialism*, Said mentions Amilcar Cabral, Aimé Césaire, Frantz Fanon, Mohandas Gandhi, C. L. R. James, Jawaharlal Nehru, Nkrumah, Walter Rodney, Leopold Senghor, and others—a representative rather than comprehensive list, since it does not include such major figures as Jomo Kenyatta and Mao Tse-Tung.

With the exception of Gandhi, all of these leaders and intellectuals were Marxists or socialists. A major discontent of postcolonial theory today is that, by and large, it is not Marxist but poststructuralist in perspective, and hence is necessarily critical of both the Marxism and the nationalism of the earlier anticolonialists. Writing as a Marxist, Aijaz Ahmad objects to "the surrender... to poststructuralism... on the part of that branch of literary theory which is most engaged with questions of colony and empire" (37). Ahmad continues:

> The newly dominant position of poststructuralist ideology is the fundamental enabling condition for a literary theory which debunks nationalism not on the familiar Marxist ground that nationalism in the present century has frequently suppressed questions of gender and class and has itself been frequently complicit with all kinds of obscurantisms and revanchist positions, but in the patently postmodern way of debunking all efforts to speak of origins, collectivities, determinate social projects. (Ahmad, 38)

The key difficulty is that poststructuralism substitutes a (theoretical) politics of *différance* for what is often seen rather nostalgically as an activist politics of solidarity and clear, unified identity. According to Ania Loomba:

> Recently, many critics of postcolonial theory have... blamed it for too much dependence upon post-structuralist or post-modern perspectives (which are often read as identical). They claim that the insistence on multiple histories and fragmentation within these perspectives has been detrimental to thinking about the global operation of capitalism. (13)

Both Ahmad and Loomba argue that the poststructuralist connection produces various "fragmenting," depoliticizing, and disabling effects, including both a stress on individual identities rather than on political and economic factors and a homogenization of models of power and subordination, hypostatized as the situations and psyches of *the* colonized and *the* colonizer. As Loomba puts it, "Postcolonial theory has been accused of precisely this: it shifts the focus from locations and institutions to individuals and their subjectivities. Postcoloniality becomes a vague condition of people anywhere and everywhere, and the specificities of locale do not matter" (17).

On the positive side of the ledger, the poststructuralist influence has led to the recognition of the complex "specificities" of individual identities, to the deconstruction of the binary oppositions that underwrite all versions of racism and most versions of both imperialist and nationalist ideologies, and to a philosophical stress on *différance* that is also now associated with "multiculturalism." Stuart Hall, who has spent much of his career both shaping the cultural studies movement in Britain and elsewhere and attempting to negotiate the apparent impasses between Marxism and poststructuralism, writes:

> The differences...between colonising and colonised cultures remain profound. But they have never operated in a purely binary way and they certainly do so no longer. Indeed, the shift from circumstances in which anti-colonial struggles seemed to assume a binary form of representation to the present when they can no longer be represented within a binary structure, I would describe as a move from one conception of difference to another..., from difference to *différance*, and this shift is precisely what the...transition to the "post-colonial" is marking. ("When was 'The Post-Colonial'?"247)

Différance comes from Jacques Derrida's important essay of that title, one that I spent several days reading and rereading and, I hope, understanding. Another discontent is that much poststructuralist theory is abstruse, technical, and difficult to fathom. It is not the sort of theory that would be of immediate help in the midst of a guerrilla war for the independence of one's nation or ethnic group. And, whatever its political intentions or valences, its intellectual difficulty makes poststructuralism highly academic and, in that sense, elitist. Even with its emphasis on breaking down binary, stereotypical patterns of misrepresentation and ideology, poststructuralism is not a theory that seems likely to have democratizing, liberating consequences of a practical sort. Insofar as postcolonial theory at least aims at the emancipation of the masses—of ordinary human beings everywhere in the world—*and yet* maintains the high level of abstraction and intellectual difficulty that it has learned from poststructuralism, then perforce, it would seem, it can never reach the masses. If one question it asks repeatedly is, "Can the subaltern speak?" a question that it sometimes asks of itself is, "Can postcolonial theory speak both for and to the subaltern?" To date, the answer seems to be negative.[2]

Marxism in various forms has reached masses and altered the shape of politics everywhere in the world, including the so-called Third World. Yet from a poststructuralist standpoint, as Robert Young contends in *White Mythologies*, "Marxism's universalizing narrative of the unfolding of a rational system of world history is simply a negative form of the history of European imperialism" (2). This is a criticism that Marxists such as Aijaz Ahmad find difficult to counter. For his part, Ahmad takes Said to task for "dismissing" Marx as a "Romantic Orientalist" who claimed that the only way forward for India was through the capitalist mode of production, imposed on it by British imperialism. Ahmad shows that Marx's thinking about India was much more complex than Said allows, and yet he concludes by criticizing Marx in roughly equivalent terms:

> By the time [Marx] came to write *Capital*, the aspiration to formulate premisses of a universal history remained, as it should have remained, but the realization grew that the only mode of production he could adequately theorize was that of capitalism.... It is from the theoretical standpoint of *Capital*...that one can now see the brilliance, but also the error, in many a formulation about India. (242)

In other words, despite his "brilliance," Marx finally did not escape from the Eurocentric perspective that his understanding of capitalism gave him.

Ahmad does not just blame Said for making much the same criticism of Marx from the poststructuralist position of "colonial discourse analysis." He blames him also for being an inconsistent poststructuralist, one who tries to combine elements of Foucault's theorization of discourse with elements of Marxism, especially Antonio Gramsci's conception of hegemony. In *Orientalism*, according to Ahmad, Said also mixes in large doses of the literary humanism he learned from Erich Auerbach and others. The result of this theoretical eclecticism—or, as Ahmad would have it, inconsistency—is both "radically anti-Foucauldian" and "one way of domesticating the revolutionary content of Gramsci's thought" (167, 169).

The problem of Said's theoretical "affiliations," to use one of his favorite words, is more generally a problem for postcolonial studies. Even Gramscian (or "Western") Marxism involves insisting on a universalizing and in some sense Eurocentric "metanarrative," based on a model of Enlightenment rationality and revolution, and also on a materialist epistemology. Both the historicism and the epistemology are called into question by poststructuralism. Foucauldian "discourse analysis," moreover, threatens to abandon the radical politics of Marxism altogether, in favor of mere textuality (back to literary criticism) and an ethics rather than politics of *différance*. Quite apart from whether either perspective is at all compatible with the liberal humanism that Ahmad thinks is Said's greatest sin, poststructuralist discourse analysis and Marxist historical materialism are ultimately incompatible. And yet it may be one of Said's virtues that he has been willing to poach ideas from Foucault and Gramsci, from Derrida and Raymond Williams and many others, without worrying too much about either logical or political consistency. It is at least fair to say, as Ahmad does, that "Said is our most vivacious narrator of the history of European humanism's complicity in the history of European colonialism" (163).

Postcolonialism and Postmodernism

What might be called the elitist effect of poststructuralism is compounded by the fact that postcolonial theory is dominated—or is said to be dominated—by three Western-educated academics teaching in elite American universities: Edward Said, Gayatri Spivak, and Homi Bhabha. Thus, in *Colonial Desire* (1995), Robert Young speaks of the "Holy Trinity" of the field, while Spivak and Bhabha themselves point to Said's *Orientalism* (1978) as the origin of postcolonial theory (Moore-Gilbert, 35). So, too, Bart Moore-Gilbert defines postcolonial theory as "work which is shaped primarily, or to a significant degree, by methodological affiliations to French 'high' theory—notably Jacques Derrida, Jacques Lacan and Michel Foucault," and goes on to focus on Said, Spivak, and Bhabha. Moore-Gilbert acknowledges, however, that it is "the 'intrusion' of French 'high' theory into postcolonial analysis that has perhaps generated the most heated of the many current debates" in the field (1). It is therefore reasonable to ask what the field amounted to before this "intrusion," and also if that intrusion is crucial rather than a parasitic distraction from the main tasks at hand, which are analyzing the historical and cultural effects of imperialism, nationalism, and racism in the modern and now postmodern world.

Insofar as it is centered in Western, mainly American English and comparative literature departments, postcolonial studies is not merely academic but literary in focus. While, along with feminism and African-American studies, postcolonialism is helping to diversify or pluralize "the canon" and the traditional liberal arts curriculum, its political purchase even within the university may not extend much beyond literature and language fields. At the same time, the influence of "the Holy Trinity" and that of a few of their friends and opponents such as Ahmad and Arif Dirlik has helped produce a postcolonial star system similar to that in some other academic fields—one of the effects of the corporatization of the university.

The point is not to criticize Said, Spivak, and Bhabha for becoming academic stars. Such stardom is now a standard feature of higher education. It is rather to stress the perhaps too-eager academic acceptance of their ideas and lessons, as opposed to the presumably more radical, hard-headed lessons of (among others) Ahmad and Dirlik. But stardom can also be construed as an effect of the postmodern condition: celebrity as simulation. Yet celebrity is one price that must be paid if academics are to become "public intellectuals." Russell Jacoby, who has attacked postcolonial studies as a jargon-ridden, illogical, and overcelebrated fraud ("Marginal Returns"), has also argued that genuinely public intellectuals have been swallowed up by the academy (*Last Intellectuals*). But Said, for one, is by almost any definition (except a very myopic one) a public intellectual. And the amount of media attention that Spivak and Bhabha have received has also helped to familiarize some portion of the public, at least, with postcolonial issues and controversies.

At the same time, the general star system in academia points to the postmodern spectacularization of some aspects of what goes on in universities—often the wrong aspects, or at any rate distortions of those aspects. If postmodern culture is preeminently one of "simulation" and "hyperreality," the university is now an important player in that culture. Old-style, left-wing public intellectuals of the kind Jacoby nostalgically recalls may have disappeared into the academy. But some new-style public intellectuals have emerged from the ivied cocoon into the limelight of "the society of the spectacle" (DeBord). And perhaps some of them are influencing postmodern culture and the world in general in positive ways.

Though it might be impossible to prove such a hypothesis, it also seems to be the case that, as Hall suggests, there has been a general transition from the Manichaean ideologies of the age of formal empires to a new, widespread emphasis on *différance*. If so, that transition can be at least partly attributed to the breakdown of the old empires. The liberation struggles of peoples and societies throughout the world in the twentieth century have soaked into Western, even imperialist and racist imaginings. The older intellectuals who fought against imperialism and racism and for the independence of their societies and cultures—Nkrumah, Jomo Kenyatta, Gandhi, Nehru, and many others—emerged, often in spectacular fashion, on the world stage as public intellectuals, leaders, and politicians. Although their acts and influences can only be studied and celebrated at a distance by today's academic postcolonialists, their work persists.

Nevertheless, the general, global "decolonization of the imagination" that has made up so much of the history of the world since 1945 has also included huge and often tragic uprootings and diasporas of millions of people, such as the migration and violence that accompanied the partition of India and Pakistan in 1948–49.[3] From Rey Chow's "multicultural" Hong Kong to Paul Gilroy's "Black Atlantic," the world has been and is, perhaps, even more today in motion, diasporic. Migrations from all parts of the world into the United States have also made this "superpower" among nations, one that has inherited the position of the main (neo)imperialist dominator from the older European centers of empire, increasingly multicultural and in that sense, at least, postcolonial. But whatever sorts of postcolonial freedoms are made possible by American democracy are contradicted or threatened by its corporate-military-imperial domination (see Kaplan and Pease, *Cultures of United States Imperialism*).

If one assumes (as I do) that nonessentialist *différance* is both ethically and politically preferable to essentializing versions of difference (racism, for instance), then today's postcolonial academics, whether they have the

103

status of public intellectuals or not, have the tasks of foregrounding the colonial, racist, and diasporic aspects of modern and postmodern history, at least for other faculty and for their students, and of promoting democratic, constructive versions of "multiculturalism" rather than phony, undemocratic ones. By phony multiculturalism, I mean the type that supports essentialist assumptions about race, culture, and identity while seeming to do otherwise. The forms of phony multiculturalism represent a danger within universities in versions of "nativism" or "centrism," which may or may not have the beneficial effect of moral uplift or "recognition" for the racial and cultural groups involved, but they are just as evident in the neoconservative backlash, which attacks both postcolonial and poststructuralist theory as subversive of "Western civilization," while seeking to reinvest that civilization with the hegemonic power and glory the neoconservatives believe it has always possessed.

Beyond the university, phony versions of multiculturalism are rampant in postmodern America, Europe, and the rest of the world. It is of major importance for theorists and intellectuals, whether postcolonial or not, to critique and condemn these versions wherever they appear. Numerous examples of what I mean can be found at your local amusement park and in the films and other products of the Disney Corporation. On one of the rides at Disney World in Orlando, Florida, the boat glides by several simulacra of African villages. The dummy Africans who loom out of the jungle have bones in their noses, war paint and scars on their faces, large spears in their hands, and are obviously every (white) American's worst Hollywood nightmare of cannibals. The recorded voice-over, in a soothing, down-home (white, perhaps Texan) accent, tells you to stay calm and maybe the savages won't attack. Around the bend, the boat suddenly leaves Africa and floats past a simulacrum of a Native American village. These are, says the voice-over, "peaceful" natives; here the "weary traveler" could expect hospitality, food, and shelter. "Why, this might even be Pocahantas's village."

At the Epcot Center, which has the appearance, at least, of a World's Fair, things get worse (that is, even more insidiously stereotypic). It's a multicultural sort of place, okay, but the international sites are all of a piece. In the Mexican building, one can go for a ride on the "Rio del Tiempo," which is supposed to represent Mexican history. The first miniature scene the boat passes represents an Aztec (or is it Mayan?) village, complete with pyramid, where the little indigenes are happily, peacefully planting and harvesting maize and perhaps some other crops (it doesn't matter: they are just supposed to be a happy, peaceful bunch of Indians). The next scenes are of equally happy, suddenly Mexican villages, complete with fiestas and Mariachi music. These villagers, too, are happy, peaceful farmers in a land without history. Well, there may be a bandido or two lurking among them—something about Pancho Villa, perhaps—but it's a bit hard to tell. Then the boat ride ends, and the happy time-travelers, having absorbed the Disney version of Mexican history, step into the interior of the building where they can shop for Mexican souvenirs and dine on tacos and salsa. The same relentless, cheerful, supposedly multicultural stereotyping is evident at all of the other Epcot sites: thus, "the spirit of Norway" consists of Vikings, trolls, codfish, skiing, and waterfalls (cf. Project on Disney, 42–44, 72–73).

"The postmodern condition," as Lyotard declares, means "incredulity toward metanarratives," which hardly makes the Epcot Center postmodern. On the contrary, racial, national, class, and gender stereotypes are all "metanarratives" of sorts. Both stereotypes and metanarratives simplify or ignore human complexities, diversities, specificities. Racism is a metanarrative that produces stereotypes according to these general rules: all human beings belong to one race or another; there are only a few pure, main races; mixed-race people don't count or are inferior to unmixed; and the races form a hierarchy from inferior to superior (currently coded as from precivilized to civilized, or underdeveloped to developed). Of course, there are also metanarratives of emancipation, all based on or stemming from versions of Enlightenment faith in reason: science, liberalism, Marxism, nationalism. The last term is a seeming anomaly in this list: in one direction, it is emancipatory for the members of the nation espousing it; in another, it is next of kin to racism, both exclusive and morally judgmental. But, then, racism has also often assumed the guise, at least, of science, and hence of Enlightenment rationality. As Christian Delacampagne explains:

> Can racism exist outside reason or without its support? No, because racism is
> nothing but *biologism*, that is, a face—extreme, exaggerated as much as you

like, but a face all the same—of modern scientific reason. Certainly, racism is only a caricature of rationalism; but just like any caricature, it cannot be understood without reference to its model. (87)

It would, perhaps, come as a shock to most of the visitors to Disney World to realize that it is a deeply imperialist, racist enterprise. But in economic terms, Disney is a transnational corporation with empire-building goals, and its racist-imperialist ideology—that is, its phony multiculturalism—is an exact match for its corporate scale and behavior. According to Richard Barnet and John Cavanagh:

> Disneyland is now a global empire; its Japanese incarnation outside Tokyo draws 300,000 visitors a week, and Euro Disneyland, a theme park on the outskirts of Paris occupying space one-fifth the size of the city itself, eventually hopes to draw more tourists than the Eiffel Tower, Sistine Chapel, British Museum, and the Swiss Alps combined. (25)

Slavoj Žižek contends that multiculturalism in all its variations is "the ideal form of ideology of . . . global capitalism" (94); he thus raises the question of whether there can be a "critical multiculturalism" that can effectively oppose "corporate multiculturalism" (see also Berlant and Warner). It might at least help if multiculturalists of the critical variety were to picket the Disney theme parks and distribute free copies of Ariel Dorfman and Armand Mattelart's classic of ideological demystification, *How to Read Donald Duck*. "Disney exorcizes history," they write (64), and also all questions of racial and social class exploitation. "Natives" both good and bad, both peaceful and savage, are reduced to children, a stereotypic process that also seeks to infantilize the Disney consumer of whatever age. The general pattern is one of fetishism, and the ultimate fetish is the almighty dollar.

Postcolonialism and Postindustrialism

To some extent, arguments about postmodernism parallel and overlap those about the emergence of so-called postindustrial society. The basic idea is that the most "advanced" economies in the United States, Japan, and western Europe have moved away from the "heavy"—and heavily centralized—manufacturing industries (steel, automobiles, and so forth) to a more "flexible" regime focused on information and service. The key text was Harvard sociologist Daniel Bell's 1973 *The Coming of Post-Industrial Society: A Venture in Social Forecasting*. Since Bell had already, in the midst of the Cold War and as the United States was getting embroiled in the Vietnam War, announced "the end of ideology," there was not much reason to assume that he was particularly good at "social forecasting." There is even less reason to believe so now, nearly three decades into the supposed era of postindustrialism.

The American and other highly "developed" economies have indeed been shifting away from heavy manufacturing in the directions of information and service. This transition has corresponded to the consolidation and globalization of the world's largest corporations, most of which now have capital assets worth more than the gross national products of many nation-states: "Ford's economy is larger than Saudi Arabia's and Norway's, Philip Morris's annual sales exceed New Zealand's gross domestic product," and so forth. "The combined assets of the top 300 firms now make up roughly a quarter of the productive assets of the world." At the same time, the gap between the wealthiest and the poorest societies is increasing; over half of the planet's six billion people are too impoverished even to participate in the global economy as consumers (Barnet and Cavanagh, 14–16). Meanwhile, through the computerization, robotization, and "outsourcing" of numerous industrial processes, the manufacturing of all sorts of commodities has been spread around the world. Heavy industry hasn't disappeared—steel and automobiles continue to be manufactured, of course—but the processes have been dispersed, and one consequence has been that nationally based labor movements and trade unions have been in retreat. In the United States, at the cost of plant closings and downsizings in many industries, the labor force has been "restructured." As the Clinton administration has boasted, both inflation and unemployment have been low during the economic boom of the last seven or eight years, and millions of new jobs have been created. But social class and income inequalities have increased, in part because many of the new jobs are part-time, low-wage jobs in the so-called service sector, which includes such activities as frying burgers at McDonald's.

For Daniel Bell, as Frank Webster notes in his critique of the postindustrial society thesis, economic and technological progress leads to the increasing automation of agriculture and industry, "thereby getting rid of the farmhand and later on the industrial working class while simultaneously ensuring increased wealth" and social stability (35). Abolishing farmhands and the proletariat is all to the good from Bell's neoconservative perspective, because what is eliminated is simultaneously "unpleasant manual labour" and "radical politics." For, Bell asks (in Webster's words), "how can the class struggle be waged when the proletariat is disappearing?" (35). And the disappearance of "radical politics" is also, of course, a major aspect of "the end of ideology."

But "unpleasant manual labour" has not been abolished; along with much manufacturing, it is only being "outsourced" to such Third World sites as the Philippines and the *maquiladora* area of northern Mexico. There industries formerly based in the United States go right on manufacturing commodities such as cars, shoes, and televisions while paying their new workers ten to twenty times less than they had been paying American workers. And for the time being, they can do so without being hampered by trade unionism, environmental regulations, and legally imposed health and safety standards. This transnational dispersion of manufacturing no doubt benefits the economies of Mexico, the Philippines, and other parts of the "developing world" in a general way. But the globalization of industrial capacity has not stopped the acceleration of the income gap between the wealthy, "developed" nations and the impoverished, "underdeveloped" ones. Nor has the increased prosperity of the developed nations reduced income inequality and poverty within their borders, but exactly the opposite.

For much of the world, all "postindustrialism" means is just a new, slicker version of what Nkrumah called "neo-colonialism." The one major improvement seems to be that the new economic and manufacturing regime does not need to be imposed and governed through the military and political apparatus of empire. In many newly independent nation-states, including ones such as Mexico and the Philippines that are ostensible democracies, both political power and a certain amount of economic power are wielded by what Frantz Fanon called the "national bourgeoisie." But wherever it has emerged, the indigenous bourgeoisie typically does not own the means of production; these today are largely owned by transnational corporations.

> Neither financiers nor industrial magnates are to be found within this national middle class. The national bourgeoisie of underdeveloped countries is not engaged in production, nor in invention, nor building, nor labor; it is completely canalized into activities of the intermediary type. Its innermost vocation seems to be to keep in the running and to be part of the racket. (Fanon, 149–150)

At the time Fanon was writing *Wretched of the Earth* (it was published in French in 1963), it was still common for the governments of recently decolonized states to demand or at least threaten the nationalization (that is, the socialization) of at least some of the means of production. By and large, however, to the national bourgeoisie, socialism meant "the transfer into native hands of those unfair advantages which are a legacy of the colonial period" (Fanon, 152).

For today's transnational corporations, the threat of socialist takeovers by the governments of Third World countries is minimal, because the corporations can always transfer their money and their manufacturing capacities elsewhere. For their executives and investors alike, the beauty of transnational corporations is that they are beholden to no single nation-state or governmental power anywhere. And in places where local or national businesses and industries were once developing or had a chance to develop, transnational corporations are able to buy them out or simply drive them out of business through hugely lopsided competition. While many parts of the "underdeveloped" world are gaining unprecedented sources of prosperity and new employment, they are also gaining new versions of exploitation and sources of inequality. Lima, Peru, for example, is today a more prosperous city than it was a decade ago. But almost all of the new businesses are American-, British-, or Canadian-owned, while some businesses started by Peruvians have gone under or sold out to foreign corporations. Thus, Inca Cola, which began as a homegrown business, is now owned by Coca-Cola.

Postcolonialism and Posthistory

One component in both Bell's "end of ideology" thesis and its near-relative, Francis Fukuyama's "end of history" thesis, is that now that the entire world (almost) has been decolonized and turned into independent nation-states, and now that communism is no longer a major rival to capitalism, even in the poorest regions the path is open to modernization (or economic development) and to democracy.[4] From now on, the world will become unified under the progressive banners of transnational capital and Western-style, democratic liberalism.

Needless to say, this rosy scenario of an "end of ideology" and an "end of history" is not an aspect of what usually goes under the rubric of postcolonial theory, with its dual claims that imperialism or at least its effects are still at work in the world and that, nevertheless, cultural and ethnic differences must be defended, studied, and valued. Further, any notion that history is turning into a benign posthistory is quite obviously belied by the many wars and threatened wars now occurring around the world. The ongoing aerial surveillance and bombing of Iraq by the United States; Israel's decades-long conflict with Palestinian nationalists and their supporters in the Middle East and North Africa; Russia's bloody conflict with Chechnya; the militarized division of Korea; China's occupation of Tibet and threatened take-over of Taiwan; the ongoing conflict between India and Pakistan; and interminable civil wars in many African and Central and South American countries do not suggest that a peaceful, prosperous New World Order has been or will soon be born.

A major question for postcolonial studies is the extent to which today's conflicts are outcomes or continuations of the violence of the imperialist conquest and carving up of the world from the Renaissance down to the present. On one level, as Fanon noted in *Wretched of the Earth*, the creation of independent nation-states out of former colonies was often the substitution of "the dictatorship of the national bourgeoisie" and of its "single party" for European domination: "The single party is the modern form of the dictatorship of the bourgeoisie, unmasked, unpainted, unscrupulous, and cynical" (165). The boundaries, seats of government, and often many of the institutions of the new nation-states were established during the imperialist era. As Fanon also notes, the partition of Africa by the European powers at the Berlin Conference in 1884–85 created artificial borders that became the borders of nation-states with little or no regard for traditional, indigenous territorial, cultural, and societal conceptions. These new nation-states are as a consequence inherently unstable, and they are also, as Nkrumah notes in *Neo-Colonialism*, hindrances to pan-African cooperation and economic progress.

A. Adu Boahen makes the same points when, in *African Perspectives on Colonialism*, he writes: "The partition of Africa by the imperial... powers led ultimately to the establishment of some forty-eight new states... in place of the existing innumerable lineage and clan groups, city-states, kingdoms, and empires without any fixed boundaries" (95). Boahen adds that "the creation of the states has proved to be more of a liability than an asset" (95). One outcome is that the larger states, at least, are "multi-ethnic," often with long-standing rivalries among groups, resulting in some instances in almost continuous civil war since independence. The recent, genocidal conflict between the Hutus and Tutsis in Rwanda is a case in point. Another outcome is that, merely by chance, some of the new states possess far greater economic resources than others—oil-rich Nigeria, for example, compared to land-locked Burkina Faso or tiny Gambia and Togo. Such economic disparaties also contribute to instability and the potential, at least, for war.

The "legacies" of European imperialism in Africa, according to Boahen, are not all negative. As in India and elsewhere, the imperial regimes imposed or developed "two new institutions—a new bureaucracy of civil servants and a new judicial system" (98). They also at least began to develop modern economic infrastructures, including "roads, railways, harbors, the telegraph and the telephone" (100). But these facilities were never adequate and were "very unevenly distributed in nearly all the colonies." They were, moreover, not designed to serve as the basis of industrial modernization within Africa, but rather to render more efficient the extraction of crops and natural resources. One result has been "neo-colonialism," as Nkrumah says, or economic exploitation and dependency minus formal political attachments to the West.

One further legacy of imperialism in Africa was the creation of national, standing armed forces. As in much of Latin America and elsewhere, the professional armies of the African nation-states have been "nothing but a chronic source of instability, confusion, and anarchy as a result of their often unnecessary and unjustifiable interventions in the political processes" of those states (Boahen, 99). In these and numerous other ways, all of Africa has been and will continue to be affected by imperialism. Further, if one defines modernity in strictly economic terms, and asks which of the recently decolonized nation-states in Africa or in other parts of the world are "developed" or "underdeveloped," the standard answer is and will continue to be that most of them are "underdeveloped"—that is, both impoverished and not yet, at least in economic terms, modern. From this perspective, there can be no question of countries such as Togo, Burkina Faso, or even Nigeria having passed beyond the stage of modernization into postmodernity. Indeed, even to pose the possibility in these terms suggests the ironic albeit unwitting cruelty of claims that the world in general has somehow progressed beyond the modern, much less that it is about to enter a nirvana-like "stationary state" called "posthistory."

Even within the prosperous, "postmodern," and "postindustrial" beneficiaries of imperialism and corporate globalization such as the United States and Britain, "the empire strikes back" and also writes back in many ways. In *The Souls of Black Folk*, W. E. B. Du Bois declared that "the problem of the twentieth century" would be "the color line." In both the United States and Britain, and in many other parts of the world, there is every sign that it will continue to be "*the* problem," or at least one of the main problems, of the twenty-first century. The only person who seems to think that racism is no longer a factor in American politics and culture is Dinesh D'Souza, whose *The End of Racism* is a posthistorical, end-of-ideology fantasy comparable to Fukuyama's. In contrast, Henry Louis Gates, Jr. gets it right:

> Ours is a...world profoundly fissured by nationality, ethnicity, race, class, and gender. And the only way to transcend those divisions—to forge, for once, a civic culture that respects both differences and commonalities—is through education that seeks to comprehend the diversity of human culture. (xv)

Racism and the virulent nationalisms that are rebalkanizing the Balkans and other parts of the world are and will continue to be shapers of history, of which there is no "end" or "post" in sight.

Postcolonialism and Multiculturalism

Gates's comment points to the issues and controversies that are often grouped under the rubric of "multiculturalism." This word is in turn some-times treated as a near-synonym for postcolonialism. In its usual mean-ings, it signifies a cultural diversity and pluralism that, in the context of any large nation-state today, is or should be self-evident. A multiethnic society of mostly willing immigrants, of descendants of slaves, and of approxi-mately one and a half million aboriginal inhabitants, the United States is intrinsically multicultural, and always has been. The concept of the "melt-ing pot" originally suggested that everyone could fit in—could become assimilated into mainstream culture as Americans rather than "hyphen-ated Americans." The trouble arises, at least for the critics of multicultural-ism such as Allan Bloom and Arthur Schlesinger Jr., when so-called minor-ity cultures insist on hyphenation—that is, when they emerge not merely to take their place alongside majority (white, European, middle- and upper-class) American culture, but also to insist on equal recognition and respect. Then they seem resistant to assimilation and even (according to their critics) to threaten to displace majority culture and take center stage.

In *The Disuniting of America*, Schlesinger asks: "What happens when people of different ethnic origins, speaking different languages and pro-fessing different religions, settle in the same geographical locality and live under the same political sovereignty?" His answer is, "Unless a common purpose binds them together, tribal antagonisms will drive them apart" (13). Why he takes such a Hobbesian view of human nature is unclear, especially since much of his analysis of the American multicultural experi-ence contradicts this view. Of course, America has always been multicul-tural, even while it has also been, as Schlesinger acknowledges, racist: "The curse of racism has been the great failure of the American experiment" (18–19). Schlesinger proceeds to treat present-day assertions of racial and cultural diversity and dignity as "threats" to the "common purpose" of the

United States, instead of as (at the very least) forms of resistance to white racism. He does so in part because he fails to define "common purpose" in his own liberal terms as freedom, justice, and democracy, and treats it instead as meaning a common culture. In other words, America's multicultures should all be thrown into the "melting pot" and reduced to a single culture.[5]

Schlesinger thus makes the neoconservative mistake of failing to distinguish between what Charles Taylor calls "procedural" versus "substantive" liberalism. Procedural liberalism prescribes only the legal framework within which individuals and groups such as ethnic, religious, and cultural minorities can choose their own goals and values. Substantive liberalism, in contrast, seeks to prescribe goals and values. While procedural liberalism allows for multicultural forms of *différance* and "recognition," nevertheless, Taylor indicates, it too can be "inhospitable to difference, because (a) it insists on uniform application of the rules defining . . . rights, without exception, and (b) it is suspicious of collective goals" (94). Even the best-intentioned forms of liberalism can be impositions upon patterns of individual and group difference. At the same time, procedural liberalism is the necessary form taken by every democracy. Indeed, both multiculturalists of the supposedly bad, essentialist sort and critics of such bad multiculturalism like Schlesinger commit the substantive error to the degree that they seek to impose either essentialist versions of culture and ethnicity or a version of a unified American heritage on everyone else.

Typical of the discourse on multiculturalism is the claim that there are good and bad variations of it, and that the bad are versions of "reverse discrimination"—that is, that they are separatist or "particularist" in a manner that repeats the exclusionary tactics of racism. Thus, Diane Ravitch, former U.S. assistant secretary of education, distinguishes between "pluralistic" and "particularistic" multiculturalisms: "Today, pluralistic multiculturalism must contend with a new, particularistic multiculturalism. The pluralists seek a richer common culture; the particularists insist that no common culture is possible or desirable" (276). Ravitch's main example of "particularistic" multiculturalism is the "Afrocentrism" of Molefi Kete Asante, which she interprets as insisting on displacing Eurocentrism altogether. Asante's response emphasizes that "pluralism" under unequal conditions is never really pluralistic; it is just a disguise for renewed practices of domination. Ravitch's "version of multiculturalism," he writes, "is not multicultur-alism at all, but rather a new form of Eurocentric hegemonism" (301). Asante continues:

> As part of the Eurocentric tradition, there seems to be silence on questions of hegemony, that is, the inability to admit the mutual conspiracy between race doctrine and educational doctrine in America. Professor Ravitch and others would maintain the facade of reasonableness even in the face of arguments demonstrating the irrationality of both white supremacist ideas on race and white hegemonic ideas in education. (302)

Asante further claims that he does not intend his version of Afrocentrism to take the place of Eurocentrism, or of the educational forms of white supremacism, but rather that it be considered on equal, nonhegemonic or nonhierarchical terms with white, majority culture. In other words, to Ravitch's claim to be arguing for a beneficent, pluralistic multiculturalism, Asante counters by insisting on exactly that: a pluralism that treats all cultures, whether "minority" or "majority," as equals. According to Asante, Ravitch "posits a *pluralistic* multiculturalism—a redundancy—then suggests a *particularistic* multiculturalism—an oxymoron—in order to beat a dead horse" (305).

Asante is clearly right about both the redundancy and the oxymoron involved in those phrases and concepts. The "dead horse" metaphor is also, in my estimation, accurate, because "particularistic multiculturalism" is one of the dead horses that Bloom, D'Souza, and other neoconsevative critics of higher education have beat into the ground ad nauseum. Perhaps such bad multiculturalism is a greater problem in the public schools than in colleges and universities. Nevertheless, as Nathan Glazer argues, "we are all multiculturalists now," in part precisely because of the failure to end racial discrimination, especially against African-Americans. For better or worse, Glazer contends, multiculturalism "has...won" (4). But even if "particularist," self-ghettoizing versions of Afrocentrism have emerged (and none of the other possible "centrisms" seem quite so threatening to Bloom and company, except perhaps womancentrism and gaycentrism, which exist only in the frigid imaginary of neoconservatism), they are bound to be self-defeating, for the very reason that makes multiculturalism

115

a fact of life for all of us. As Gates puts it: "whatever the outcome of the culture wars in the academy, the world we live in is multicultural already. Mixing and hybridity are the rule, not the exception" (xvi).

The contradictory, self-defeating quality of "particularist multiculturalism" is logically similar to white supremacism or to the more intolerant, race-based versions of nationalism—or for that matter, to the attempts of neoconservative defenders of "Western civilization" to bar the doors of the university against poststructuralist, postcolonial, multiculturalist, feminist, and gay-lesbian forms of debate and *différance*. Moreover, while it has been possible for its critics, however unfairly, to identify multiculturalism with particularism, or at least to try to divide and conquer by rejecting "particularist" and affirming "pluralistic" versions of multiculturalism, no one who has read anything written by Said, Spivak, Bhabha, or other postcolonialists can possibly doubt that their ideas are in accord with poststructuralism in its deconstructions of essentialist versions of racial, national, and cultural claims to purity, originality, and superiority. In today's diasporic world, everyone and everything is in motion or transit, and is necessarily hybrid. You never step into the same culture twice.

The multiculturalist and postcolonial insistence that the literary canon be revised to include the works and voices of authors of color is also and always an insistence that the canon, or for that matter the category of literature itself, not be merely taken for granted. And if "English literature" today is also Irish, American, Nigerian, Indian, and Australian, the English language itself is a marvel of hybridity and borrowings from many other languages. I suspect few professors of English today worry about maintaining the purity of the dominant, European literary heritage—the canon, in short—but occasionally someone will wander into the main office of my department and ask a secretary, in lieu of the less accessible chair, about the purity of the language (grammatical if not political correctness). I sometimes find it difficult to convince undergraduates that the language we share isn't a strict linguistic and even legal code, whose half-mystical laws were inscribed by God on tablets of stone at the time of creation (that God's native tongue seems to have been ancient Hebrew hardly matters). I like to offer these disbelieving believers examples of the hybrid, kinetic nature of the language they speak and struggle to write, such as a few pages of Gloria Anzaldúa's *Borderlands/La Frontera: The New Mestiza*, in which she uses

English, Spanish, and Nahuatl, all spoken on "the U.S.-Mexican border [which] *es una herida abierta* where the Third World grates against the first and bleeds" (3). Also useful is Salman Rushdie's essay on *Hobson-Jobson*, the late nineteenth-century dictionary of such Anglo-Indian terms as "pajamas," "bungalow," "mango," "thug," "guru," and "pundit," among many, many others. Even more eye-opening may be a sample of Australian aboriginal literature, such as Banjo Worrumarra's "Pigeon Story," which starts:

> Now—
> PIGEON—
> Pigeon START OFF—
> him bin—
> I talk to you—
> with the Pidgin English, Pidgin—
> white man tongue, Pidgin. . . .

It can be humbling for students to realize that, though Banjo Worrumarra can speak and write both English and "Pidgin English," neither they nor I nor the vast majority of Americans or even of white Australians know his aboriginal language.

There are three main positions in the debates about multiculturalism, each with its weaknesses or dangers but also its strengths. Particularism entails versions of ethno- or cultural-centrism that reproduce the logic of racism in a positive mode (so-called reverse racism). But it is often through particularism that underrepresented races and cultures are able to make significant gains in recognition and representation.[6] Multiculturalist pluralism, in contrast, is always dependent on procedural liberalism whose chief weakness is its inability to take sides, to render judgment, or to hierarchize ideas and cultural artifacts. Yet its necessary, significant strength lies in its fairness, or in its leveling, egalitarian effects. Finally, those who reject multiculturalism in favor of some version of cultural universalism (one culture—usually Western, European civilization—for all) are also engaging, wittingly or not, in a version of racist logic. Yet some cultural values must be universal—respect and justice, for example—and there must also be some means of distinguishing between the universally valid and constructive and whatever does not measure up to that standard.[7] Ideally, as Charles Taylor suggests, a positive multiculturalism would synthesize

117

the constructive aspects of all three positions, while avoiding the weaknesses—perhaps an impossible task, and yet one that must be constantly attempted, advocated, and renewed.

Postcolonialism and Cultural Studies

In the flurry of publications about Raymond Williams that followed his death in 1987, a number of commentators noted that, despite his socialist politics and his progressive views about higher education, he was rather stubbornly a "Little Englander." Throughout his career, Williams had little to say about imperialism, British or otherwise, and also about race and racism within Britain or elsewhere. This limitation in Williams's work has led some to question whether there is or can be any adequate rapprochement—let alone identity—between cultural studies and postcolonial studies. Thus, in *Views Beyond the Border Country: Raymond Williams and Cultural Politics*, the editors, though in general celebrating Williams's career including his seminal influence on cultural studies, write that his "ideas about culture...reinscribe the narratives of Western colonialism and imperialism" (Dworkin and Roman, 13). According to this line of argument, though "steadfastly opposed [to] imperialism," Williams was nevertheless a British intellectual writing from the metropolitan center; he did not and perhaps could not understand, let alone assume, the perspective of a non-British, nonwhite, imperialized subject, nor even parlay his Welsh working-class background into a position structurally parallel to that of an Irish intellectual.

In one direction, this argument is so obvious that it hardly needs repeating: Williams was a white, male, British, and Cambridge-trained intellectual, with all the limitations as well as power of access that those facts suggest. In another, however, it points to a surprising absence in his work of any extended engagement with the immense role that British and more generally European imperialism and racism have played in shaping the modern and now postmodern world. In most of his work on British culture—*Culture and Society, The Long Revolution, Keywords, The English Novel, Communications*—Williams expressed little awareness of how imperialism has affected and, indeed, empowered that culture. It was partly to make up for this deficiency in Williams's work that Said wrote *Culture and Imperialism*, which can be read as a sequel or supplement to *Culture and Society*.

Williams, of course, does not represent cultural studies in general. In *The Black Atlantic*, Paul Gilroy notes the influence of the British "culture and society" tradition that Williams traced and that formed "the infrastructure on which much of English cultural studies came to be founded." Gilroy goes on to say, "This origin is part of the explanation of how some of the contemporary manifestations of this tradition lapse into what can only be called a morbid celebration of England and Englishness" (10). Gilroy criticizes both the British New Left and the earlier "British Communist Party's historians' group" for reproducing the "nationalism and ... ethnocentrism" of the culture and society tradition "by denying imaginary, invented Englishness any external referents whatsoever. England ceaselessly gives birth to itself, seemingly from Britannia's head" (14).[8]

Gilroy, who studied at the Birmingham Centre for Contemporary Cultural Studies, does not go so far as to suggest that the concept of culture as such is Western and ethnocentric. But that suggestion, at least, is made by some of the contributors to *Views Beyond the Border Country*, including its editors. What these criticisms and suggestions underscore is that cultural studies and postcolonial studies are in some sense incompatible intellectual and academic developments. To assess any of the claims and counterclaims about this alleged incompatability, there is perhaps no better starting place than a consideration of what Williams *did* have to say, no matter how limited or slight in relation to the totality of his work, about race, empire, and the aftermath of empire.

It is also the case that several of the participants in the formation and work of the first institutional incarnation of cultural studies at Birmingham have placed race, ethnicity, and empire high on their own agendas. The obvious example is Stuart Hall, whose account of the origins of cultural studies includes the observation that "a key role in the formation" of the British New Left "was played by various (then student) colonial intellectuals." Including Hall, these intellectuals "came from outside Britain, and ... were connected to, but never part of the dominant institutions of the British left" (11). Gilroy, one of Hall's students at Birmingham, served as a coeditor of an anthology of "working papers" produced at the Centre, *The Empire Strikes Back*, and he also authored *There Ain't No Black in the Union Jack* (1987) before going on to write *The Black Atlantic*. All three books are major contributions both to postcolonial studies and to "black British cultural studies."

Apart from Hall and Gilroy, the other "colonial intellectuals" in most accounts of early cultural studies are neglected figures. Equally neglected, however, are Victor Kiernan and Eric Hobsbawm, both of whom have had much to say about modern empires, imperialisms, and racisms. I am not suggesting that either Kiernan or Hobsbawm has ever had much influence among the practitioners of cultural studies, but that is part of what I mean by their being neglected. Both were active in the Marxist Historians' Group, and both have produced major studies of imperialism that partly contradict Gilroy's claim about the Anglocentrism of the British Left. I have in mind works such as Kiernan's *The Lords of Humankind, European Empires from Conquest to Collapse*, and *America: The New Imperialism*, and Hobsbawm's *Industry and Empire* and *The Age of Empire, 1875-1914*.

Despite Kiernan and Hobsbawm, and despite the fact that Hall and other colonial intellectuals were influential in the formation of the British New Left and, hence, of cultural studies, charges of "Englishness" and "ethnocentricism," especially as applied to the three intellectuals who are usually seen as the pioneers of the movement—Williams, Richard Hoggart, and E. P. Thompson—are difficult to refute. Williams's most extensive consideration of imperialism in relation to British culture comes in *The Country and the City*. But in her contribution to *Views Beyond the Border Country*, Gauri Viswanathan contends that "Williams's reading of Britain in relation to global power suffers from the reintroduction of both the language and the concepts of economic and ideological determinism in the absence of a relational and conj[un]ctural analysis of imperialism" (224). In regard to British and more generally Western culture, Williams thinks in terms of a certain reciprocity: the material or economic base or mode of production limits and shapes culture in various ways, but culture interacts with the base, shaping it in turn. In regard to non-Western cultures, however, the reciprocity drops away: imperialism shapes these cultures in Williams's articulations, but is not shaped by them in turn. In short,

120

according to Viswanathan, in "his analyses of British culture Williams radically questions that same analytical framework of economic determinism by which he simultaneously explains British imperialism" (225).

Perhaps it would be fairer to say that Williams never offered an analysis of any non-Western culture. He did not even offer extended analyses of the cultures of Britain's "internal colonies"—that is, the cultures of "the Celtic fringe," including Ireland, Scotland, and Wales. (One can, perhaps, consider Williams's fiction as, in part, studies of what it meant to him to be Welsh.) "The English novel" for Williams was still the *English* novel, and not just because it was written in English, but because, at its best, it dealt with working-class and rural aspects of experience that seemed to Williams fundamentally—if perhaps not essentially and immutably—English. Even if one accepts Viswanathan's critique, however, there is the further question as to whether the limitations she and other postcolonial analysts find in Williams's work are true more generally of the cultural studies movement Williams influenced so profoundly. Is cultural studies restricted by a conception of culture that is somehow inevitably Western, metropolitan, and imperialist?

One of the difficulties this question immediately runs into is that, as it has developed well beyond the range of concerns that Williams addressed, and also as it has developed in the thirteen years since his death, cultural studies has no particular unity, and certainly no focus on "Englishness," that could possibly make it incompatible with postcolonial perspectives. Cultural studies is most definitely multicultural, eclectic, and hybrid. A second point I have already mentioned: the involvement of a number of prominent postcolonial intellectuals, including Hall and Gilroy, in cultural studies. And a third is that, throughout its history, and even in such early works as Williams's *Culture and Society* and E. P. Thompson's *The Making of the English Working Class*, cultural studies practitioners have attacked essentialist notions of culture and identity and insisted upon their social, historical construction. That they have often done so from a Marxist perspective, insisting on the economic influences, at least, upon the cultural or ideological superstructure, in no way detracts from this point: you do not have to be a poststructuralist to insist that culture is, well, culturally constructed.

The critique of cultural studies by certain adherents to postcolonialism, moreover, seems reversible: the same charges can be leveled at postcolonialism. There is, first, the charge that the latter field or set of issues has
emerged only in and through mainstream literary scholarship, and more
especially within and through, as Loomba notes, "English literary studies"
(96). And again, the main theoretical discourses that compete for hegemony in postcolonial studies, Marxism and poststructuralism, are of
European origin.

One upshot is the apparently contradictory spectacle of a theoretical
discourse that, while it promises to represent non-Western, ex-colonized
perspectives, can be seen as doing just the reverse. Said's *Orientalism* and
also his *Culture and Imperialism* are primarily analyses of Western discourse about Eastern societies and cultures. Said is quite explicit, moreover, about his indebtedness especially to Foucault, Gramsci,
and—yes—Raymond Williams. So, too, even when asking if the "subaltern"
can "speak," Spivak writes in English to a largely Western readership and
acknowledges her debts to both Marx and Derrida. And when Bhabha is
writing about "hybridity," he too is doing so in English, and also indicates
that for "sly civility" or any other "hybrid" relationship to occur between
colonizer and colonized, the mediating language is likely to be English or at
any rate European.

According to Ahmad, "what is remarkable is that with the exception of
Said's own voice, the only voices we encounter in [*Orientalism*] are precisely those of the very Western canonicity which, Said complains, has
always silenced the Orient" (172). Ahmad is no doubt also right that Said is
deeply indebted to the "High Humanism" of Eric Auerbach, Leo Spitzer,
and others. But it would perhaps be fairer to argue that Said's postcolonialism is on some level indistinguishable from cultural studies, or anyway
that it has developed through the work and influence of Raymond
Williams. This is all the more ironic, given the high praise that Ahmad
accords Williams (46–49). Ahmad sees Williams as developing in an
increasingly leftward, Marxist direction, and declares:

> The work of his last decade went from strength to strength... though the
> breadth of its engagements was hardly to be contained in a given book. In the
> process, Williams helped to sustain a level of critical discourse not easily dis-

lodged by the kind of new fashions and new orthodoxies that came to dominate literary studies—in sections of the British Left itself but, even more, in the
United States. (49)

At the end of this passage, Ahmad expresses his Marxist hostility to the various versions of poststructuralist theory, including Foucauldianism, that
have challenged Marxist historical materialism in a variety of ways.

Acknowledging neither the influence of poststructuralism on
Williams's thinking nor the full influence of Williams on Said's thinking,
Ahmad reaches what seems to me the mistaken conclusion that
Orientalism and the later essays that went into the making of *Culture and
Imperialism* are either Foucauldian in a doctrinaire way or marred by a
"theoretical eclecticism [which] runs increasingly out of control: sweeping,
patently poststructuralist denunciations of Marxism can be delivered in
the name of Gramsci, using the terminology explicitly drawn from
Althusser, and listing the names of communist poets like Aimé Césaire,
Pablo Neruda and Mahmoud Darwish to illustrate the sites of resistance"
(200). No doubt it would be unfair to Ahmad to infer from this statement
that for any noncommunist even to name "communist poets" is either a
logical inconsistency or sacrilege. More to the point is the issue of theoretical "eclecticism," which Ahmad repeatedly dismisses, in Fredric Jameson,
Gayatri Spivak, Ranajit Guha, and others as well as in Said, as a version of
"postmodern pastiche" (202 and elsewhere). But Williams himself, and
more generally the cultural studies movement that he helped to generate,
committed the (theoretical) sin of theoretical "eclecticism" many times
over. Citing Said's insistence that texts must be studied in their "affiliations"
with the social, economic, and political, Hall points out that eclecticism
rather than theoretical consistency (or dogma) has been one of the
strengths of cultural studies, part of what has allowed it to hold "theoretical
and political questions in an ever irresolvable but permanent" and productive "tension" (Hall, "Cultural Studies," 271–272).

That Williams never engaged in direct theoretical debate with
Foucault, Derrida, or even Louis Althusser may be a virtue, but is more
likely another limitation of his work (compare Said's critical engagements
with especially Foucault and Derrida in *The World, the Text, and the Critic*,
or Jürgen Habermas's with these and many other theorists in *The*

123

Philosophical Discourse of Modernity and elsewhere). But Williams's "culturalist" reformulations of the Marxist base-superstructure paradigm and of certain Marxist conceptions of ideology as mere "false consciousness" moved him, and cultural studies after him, in the direction of the poststructuralist emphasis on "discourse." This emphasis in turn allows both Williams and Said to focus on issues of representation and misrepresentation in the linguistic, cultural, and political meanings of these terms (see, for example, Said's "Representing the Colonized"). And poststructuralism has also supplied Said and many other cultural critics and theorists with tools for theorizing other forms of both inequality and *différance* in relation to race, class, and gender.

In conclusion, one of the reasons—perhaps the main reason—that postcolonialism, cultural studies, and multiculturalism have all become major issues and forms of research and teaching in higher education is democratization, though an alternative term for this process might be hybridization. The key problem isn't the emergent militancy of these new academic discourses, as their neoconservative critics insist. It is instead that of a worn-out universalism: the failing attempt to repress or control the increasingly fragmentary and particularist, and yet also increasingly homogenizing, political, economic, and cultural effects of transnational capitalism. Not all of the political charges and countercharges involved in postcolonial studies, cultural studies, and multiculturalism are or ever will be clear, but the ethical and political imperative these all entail is clear: to try to be inclusive, democratic, and multicultural rather than exclusive, authoritarian, and monocultural.

Between Liberalism and Marxism

7

The Populism of Cultural Studies

Discuss unto me; art thou officer?
Or art thou base, common, and popular?
—Shakespeare, *Henry V*

"Between" is misleading, but it stems from my having written the first version of this chapter for a 1998 conference on "The Broken Middle: Liberalism and Cultural Studies." The organizers at Yale's Whitney Humanities Center apparently hoped that the speakers would bridge or repair that "broken middle." Perhaps they wanted us to show how liberalism and Marxism were being or could be combined in cultural studies, or else how cultural studies, despite its origins in the Marxism of the British New Left, had also been a product of "the liberal imagination."[1] That phrase is Lionel Trilling's; the organizers seemed also to expect talks that would invoke Trilling, however improbably, as one of the godfathers of cultural studies. Although I and several of the other speakers alluded to Trilling, my argument went in a contrary direction. Though cultural studies was never merely the academic offshoot of the British New Left, much less the product of any orthodox Marxism, neither did it develop within an ideologically safe space "between" liberalism and Marxism. Obviously, too, impressive though his cultural criticism was, Trilling did not help found *The New Left Review* and never taught at the Birmingham Centre for Contemporary Cultural Studies.

The conference organizers were hospitable and unobtrusive. But two or three of the participants insisted on conflating cultural studies with their imagined versions of multiculturalism. According to them, multicultural-ism (and therefore, cultural studies) warps in the direction of single-cultur-alism and racial exclusiveness of one sort or another.[2] The chief culprit was David Bromwich, whose main claim to authority about either multicultur-alism or cultural studies is his 1992 book, *Politics by Other Means: Higher Education and Group Thinking*. Bromwich there accuses—from his pre-sumably liberal perspective—both the nonacademic Right and the acade-mic Left of being herd animals incapable of independent thought. In rela-tion to both cultural studies and the theory disease, he seems especially worried about "an iconoclasm that supposes a new social system can be created by acts of textual solidarity" (167). Since I do not know any "icono-clasts" who suppose that utopia equals "textual solidarity," Bromwich, who happens to teach at Yale, makes me think that strange notions pass there about what goes on in the wider world, including the academic world. In any case, in his conference paper, Bromwich offered a version of this untenable syllogism: cultural studies equals multiculturalism equals, at its worst, Afrocentrism (though he noted, fairly enough, that that "centrism" is no different in its "group thinking" from Eurocentrism).

As another participant asked, "What has any essentializing, ethnocen-tric version of anything got to do with cultural studies?" After all, one of the central tenets of cultural studies has been the social constructedness of identities—race, class, nationality, gender, religion, and so on. If one sub-stitutes "ideology" for "social constructedness," the basic meaning remains, though the Marxist orientation of cultural studies comes into view. Whatever else liberalism may be, it is capacious or baggy enough to entertain the idea that identities are social constructed. But an under-standing of that social construction as ideological runs contrary to liberal humanism and individualism. This is partly because, in most of its usages, including those derived by cultural studies from Gramsci and Althusser, ideology involves social class. But the eviscerization of social class in much recent cultural studies work is the chief way that it departs from Marxism and moves, if not toward liberalism, toward populism.

The history of cultural studies was at first written as a progress from Arnoldian and Leavisite liberal humanism toward Marxism. Raymond Williams's departure from the British Communist Party and then, after *Culture and Society*, his move into a qualified Marxism that shares much with some forms of liberalism complicates the story.[3] Since the 1970s, that story has more often been written as a falling away from Marxism, in the directions both of democratic socialism and of what Jim McGuigan, in his book of that title, calls "cultural populism."[4] According to McGuigan, at first "cultural studies named the enemy confidently from theoretical positions informed . . . by Marxism and then . . . by feminism ([and] to a lesser extent, [by] black politics). The grounds of such critical thought were increasingly called into question in the 1980s" (113). And Angela McRobbie writes, "A critique of Marxism inside cultural studies [was] inevitable" (6). Among other issues, McRobbie cites postmodern "incredulity" toward the emancipatory "metanarratives" of the Enlightenment, including both liberalism and Marxism.[5] Feminism and ethnic, postcolonial studies have focused on types of cultural struggle—against sexism, against racism—that bring the Marxist emphasis on social class as "the principal motor of history" into question. "Identity politics" means many things, including the postmodern meltdown of the old metanarratives of emancipation, but in relation to social class, as Katha Pollitt notes in a recent article in *The Nation*, "race and gender are crucial means through which class is structured. They are not side issues" (9; see also Butler).

Whether one understands these developments as improvements upon a seminal but primitive Marxism, or as a weakening, loss of focus, or violation of radical solidarity, cultural studies has never been a movement that might just as well be called Marxist studies. According to Stuart Hall, "There never was a prior moment when cultural studies and marxism represented a perfect theoretical fit" (279). Yet a key feature of cultural studies, at least in Britain, has been its insistence on the centrality, if not always primacy, of social class, in relation to identity as well as to other categories. Moreover, any acknowledgment of the importance of class implies that economic factors, and therefore some version of the Marxist base/superstructure paradigm, are fundamental to understanding both identity and culture. At the same time, perhaps one weakness of cultural studies has been its failure to explore the full implications of Max Weber's distinction between class and status. For both Weber and Marx, a class is defined in terms of its relation to the economic mode of production and ownership of property. But status involves other, often more intricate political and cultural factors, including gender, race, ethnicity, education, religion, and so forth, that are often in tension or even contradiction with the main economic factors that define class. The Marxist tradition tends to treat status in terms of ideology, and yet status for individuals often involves forms of self-interest, authority, power, and even profit that have little or nothing to do with false consciousness.

While cultural studies derives from a radical tradition that looks back to William Cobbett and Robert Owen as well as to Marx and Engels, it also derives from Leavis and Arnold, who at least understood that culture and class are related, though both wanted to understand that relationship from the top down—that is, in terms of an idealism that Marx's materialism stood on its head. Arnold defines culture's antithesis, "anarchy," largely as class conflict, or the ways the Barbarians, the Philistines, and the Populace pursue their separate interests at the expense of the common good. Culture is the *deus ex machina*, Arnold hopes, that will transcend sectarian and class conflict and "Hellenize" Britain, leading it into the paths of "sweetness and light." While Arnold advocated more Hellenism to cure class conflict, Marx asserted that culture is always based upon economic forces and class interests. This thesis Arnold had to deny in order to represent culture—high culture, at least—as transcending class and economics. But high culture has never had the class-harmonizing function Arnold hoped it would. As *The Communist Manifesto* puts it, the "class culture" on which the bourgeoisie prides itself "is, for the enormous majority, a mere training to act as a machine" (487). This brutal reality remains brutally real today, despite both liberal and neoconservative claims to the contrary, despite the apparent absence of an aristocracy at least in the United States, and despite the alleged leveling of cultural value hierarchies in the postmodern condition.

In his biography of Arnold, Trilling notes that Arnold expected "the State" to serve both as "a perfectly fair umpire" in resolving class conflict and as the means for diffusing high culture through education. But there has never been such an umpire, says Trilling, though there may be more or less imperfect approximations of one. Himself located somewhere between Arnold and Marx, Trilling adds: "Arnold, facing a time of strong class feeling, wished to avoid [the] notion of a State based upon class power.... Class struggle, even to the outcome of a neat balance of power in the State, was what he feared." But Arnold, Trilling declares, "was building with a fallacy" (231).

Throughout his career, Trilling acknowledged the importance of economic factors in shaping culture.[6] A liberal intellectual who accepted many of Marx's ideas, he was, perhaps, as much an American forerunner of cultural studies as even an avowed Marxist like Edmund Wilson. On the other hand, when McGuigan charges cultural studies with retreating from Marxism into cultural populism, he means that it downplays or ignores economic factors including social class. Noting "the terror of economic reductionism" expressed by the founders of cultural studies, McGuigan points to the many occasions when they said, in effect, "The Marxist base/superstructure paradigm is a necessary starting place for thinking about culture and ideology, but it is also too crude. The relations between cultures and economic modes of production are multi-leveled and reciprocal rather than mechanically deterministic."

For Williams, who makes these points in "Base and Superstructure in Marxist Cultural Theory" and also in *Marxism and Literature*, neither a crude economic determinism nor a complete abandonment of base/superstructure analysis made sense. To lose sight of the economic altogether, or even to treat it as another aspect of a given social formation, on a par with politics or religion, meant losing sight of class conflict as the central dynamic of history. Yet Williams also insisted that culture is an active, productive process or set of processes that can't be neatly separated from economic factors. In a sequel to his "Base and Superstructure" essay, Williams examines "communication" as a "means of production" (50–63). Given the proximity of the terms, one can substitute "culture" for "communication" and reach the same result. Williams writes that "communication and its material means are intrinsic to all...forms of labour and social organization, thus constituting indispensable elements...of the productive forces" (50). Though rejecting McLuhan's "technological determinism"

129

(52), Williams argues that "a theoretical emphasis on the means of communication as means of production . . . should . . . encourage new approaches to the history of the means of communication themselves" (53).

The emphasis on communication—more specifically, mass communication—has led cultural studies to become, as much as anything else, the study of the forms and processes of mass or so-called popular culture in modern and postmodern societies. But critics of this emphasis contend that what happens in much cultural studies is merely a carnivalesque inversion of the high/low cultural value hierarchy, or a valorization of mass cultural products such as soap operas and the pleasures their consumers derive from them—audience reception studies, in short, often with little or nothing said about how these products are produced or who owns the means of production. The issue of *The Nation* containing Katha Pollitt's article is the fourth in a series on "The National Entertainment State," and is headlined, "Who Controls TV?" One learns more about that question from *The Nation* than from a number of recent cultural studies books on television.

The neglect of economic factors, including social class, is McGuigan's main complaint in *Cultural Populism*. This is also Francis Mulhern's lament in his recent essay, "The Politics of Cultural Studies," another example of seeing its history as a falling away from Marxism. Mulhern writes that, reacting against the elitist *Kulturkritik* of both Leavisism and the Frankfurt School, cultural studies has insisted, "one-sidedly, on the active and critical element in popular cultural usages," and has "overlook[ed] the overwhelming historical realities of inequality and subordination that condition" those "usages" (45). Mulhern continues:

> A minority in cultural studies has stood out against these tendencies, but without much success. "Populism" is one charge laid against the majority inclination, and with good reason. But populism, in all its varieties, sees itself as oppositional. (46)

This sort of pop culture populism is, however, not nearly so oppositional as it thinks, except perhaps in relation to academic issues. "Given that most . . . popular culture today," Mulhern writes, "takes the form of commodified recreation or aestheticized subsistence activity . . . organized as a market in 'lifestyles,' the spontaneous bent of cultural studies is actually *conformist*—at its worst, the theoretical self-consciousness of satellite television and shopping malls" (46).[7]

According to this populist and popular brand of cultural studies, the consumer is never wrong, because her "tactics" of interpretation and pleasure hunting can always be viewed as "resistant" to the "grand strategies" of mass culture. Stuart Hall's notion of "articulation," moreover, is less than helpful; it merely allows its users to escape from the burden of causal explanation and appears to mean little more than the new historicist metaphors of "negotiation" and "circulation."[8] Nor is there much reason to distinguish between pop culture populism and those brands of liberalism and neoconservatism quick to identify the public good with the marketplace. From such a populist position, there isn't even any basis for criticizing the aesthetic aspects of commodities: if they are popular, they must be good somehow or for something.[9] Rejecting cultural elitism, the shopping mall populism of a lot of cultural studies effervesces into a class-innocent pluralism indistinct from liberalism's general laundering of political and economic alternatives. Such a position is analytically no more helpful than Adorno's condemnation of all mass culture as kitsch.

Since the Birmingham Centre's early accounts of youth subcultures, a lot of the vitality of cultural studies has stemmed from its focus on the political uses to which consumers put aspects of mass culture. But while analyzing the signs especially of working-class "resistance" in reggae and punk rock, as Dick Hebdige does in *Subculture*, is both reasonable and, if anything, obvious, discovering "resistance" among the consumers of the Disney channel or of Calvin Klein jeans is, to put it mildly, a stretch (cf. Frith). On a flight to London recently, I sat next to a lawyer from Cleveland who told me that, though successful, he's bored by his job. So when he gets home to the suburbs on a nice summer evening, he puts on his Sony Walkman, mounts his riding mower, and guillotines the grass whether it needs it or not. The Walkman, he confided, doesn't work, but it prevents interruptions.

The lawyer's story confirmed a hypothesis of mine about the riding mower subculture of middle America. I have neighbors who spend more time roaring around on their Clipper Supremes than watching television. Though the degrees of "resistance" may differ, the lawyer's account, I said

131

to myself, shows that the riding mower subculture is not all that different from gangsta rap in "resisting" power and ideology. The broken Walkman is just further evidence that, as Baudrillard contends, "the masses" equal the postmodern "implosion of meaning." Among some enthusiasts, there's even status competition over who can mow the smallest lawn with the largest, loudest, most expensive machine. This shows the subculture's rejection of economic rationality, in favor of a postmodern economy of wasteful expenditure, not unlike Kwakiutl *potlatch*.

But I'll let someone else write the definitive *New Leaves of Grass* analysis of the riding mower subculture of middling America. In Don DeLillo's *White Noise*, Murray Siskind, who hopes to found a department of Elvis studies at the College on the Hill, tells Jack Gladney that he doesn't understand some of their other colleagues "in popular culture":

> "I understand the music, I understand the movies, I even see how comic books can tell us things. But there are full professors in this place who read nothing but cereal boxes."

To which puzzlement Jack responds: "It's the only avant-garde we've got" (10). But though bringing mass culture topics into the curriculum may once have been avant-garde or radical, it is hardly so today, except perhaps within specific disciplinary contexts.[10] Thus, it may still be a bit carnivalesque to deal with film or television in some English departments, and yet most universities now have film and mass communications units. Business and journalism courses, moreover, routinely teach how to advertise, if not how to critique advertising as capitalist ideology.

When we set up our cultural studies program at Indiana, there was immediate interest in it from people in several disciplines—film, journalism, folklore—who were already working on mass cultural forms and processes. For my young colleagues in telecommunications who wanted to break away from the vocational, positivist emphases of their unit, the new program was a chance to join forces especially with people in film studies who were also doing sophisticated theoretical and critical work. But if there was controversy within the telecom department, there was none in the university at large. The deans loved what they saw as our *au courant* proposal for the program, which of course we did not call "Marxist studies." But Marxist studies wasn't what the young Turks from telecom wanted, or for that matter the rest of us. What we wanted was a program where the theoretical issues circulating within the larger cultural studies movement could be debated, refined, used. So our program is necessarily eclectic although not pluralist: feminist, gay, poststructuralist, Marxist, post-Marxist—you name it, we've probably got it. Meanwhile, its main focus is contemporary mass culture.

But even when our theoretical emphasis is, say, psychoanalytic, we think of ourselves as "cultural materialists," which means in part that we continue to recognize the economic factors that limit and shape the mass-produced, mass-mediated commodities that constitute most contemporary culture. Our eclecticism is neither pluralistic nor liberal, if by that term is meant tolerantly nonjudgmental and all-inclusive. Nor is it liberal, if what is meant is the humanist but elitist stess on the Western literary canon as the basis of a liberal education. On the contrary, our program is both contentious and politically progressive in aim. I think that we all agree with Edward Said's definition of the work of "oppositional intellectuals"—our work—as the production of "noncoercive knowledge...in the interests of human freedom" (*World*, 29).

So while it's true that the history of cultural studies can be told as a falling away from Marxism, and while it's also true that cultural populism is too cosily at home with capitalist consumerism, I do not think that the general development is away from Marxism into or back to liberalism. For one thing, celebratory analyses of mass cultural products often find in them sources of sexual pleasure and resistance to what Foucault calls "the tyranny of the Norm," and therefore of at least potential liberation for individuals if not for society at large, that can't be neatly reduced to any of the three main political terms I've used here: Marxism, liberalism, populism. For another, the key factors in shifting cultural studies away from Marxism—poststructuralism, feminism, and ethnic, postcolonial studies—have also prevented it from simply reverting to liberal humanism.

Yet the populism of much cultural studies runs several risks, including a lack of focus. It offers no basis for political activism because it doesn't directly support the sort of public agenda that Marxist, feminist, gay-lesbian, ethnic, and postcolonial studies support. Further, cultural populism too often surrenders even the weak weapons of aesthetic criticism. Whereas artistic and literary analysis, as with Williams, Leavis, Trilling, and Arnold, has often doubled as social criticism, cultural populism slides into a facile sociologism that, I imagine, most sociologists don't find interesting. And yet cultural populism is perhaps a small price to pay for a theoretical inclusiveness that remains focused on the chief modes of domination— gender, race, class, and "the tyranny of the Norm." This focus makes much cultural studies work quite distinct both from literary criticism and scholarship and from vacuous celebrations of mass cultural commodities, including cereal boxes and riding mowers. It also makes it different from the canonical and canonizing liberal humanism that the neoconservative critics of higher education now love to fetishize.

In the graduate-level Introduction to Cultural Studies that I teach and for which I wrote *Crusoe's Footprints*, we explore the social construction of value hierarchies. We start with nineteenth-century British examples, partly because Victorian culture has been my main area of research and partly because modern and postmodern forms of mystification, involving what Ellen Meiksins Wood calls "the retreat from class," had not yet taken hold. Thackeray on "snobs," high versus low church, the divisions of early railway travel into three classes, the discourse about literary genres—all Victorian culture was organized in social class terms. Thus, with literary genres, the high end of the scale—epic and tragedy —is identified as aristocratic. The mainstream novel is of course bourgeois, and seen as such by its major producers—Thackeray, Dickens, Trollope. The low end—melodramas, broadsides, penny dreadfuls—is invariably identified as "lower" or working class. While this hierarchization of genres in class terms more or less reflects actual production and consumption practices, it also personifies both genres and specific texts. Poems, novels, and plays are figured as members of the higher, middle, or "lower" classes. In his critique of Arnold's literary "touchstones," Northrop Frye might have been critiquing Victorian culture in general:

> Arnold's "high seriousness" evidently is closely connected with the view that epic and tragedy, because they deal with ruling-class figures and require the

high style of decorum, are the aristocrats of literary forms. All his Class One touchstones are from, or judged by the standards of, epic and tragedy. Hence his demotion of Chaucer and Burns to Class Two seems to be affected by a feeling that comedy and satire should be kept in their proper places, like the moral standards and the social classes which they symbolize. (*Anatomy*, 21–22)

Among the secondary texts that I assign, Peter Stallybrass and Allon White's *The Politics and Poetics of Transgression* offers many vivid examples of the ways eighteenth- and nineteenth-century cultural value hierarchies, customs, and behaviors were organized in relation to social class. Among my favorites are "the learned pig" and "the ditch of truth." Both are carnivalesque, "symbolic inversions" of normal and normalizing hierarchies, on the immense grid of mind-over-matter assumptions, metaphors, and concepts. The learned pig, of course, stands on its head the human-over-animal hierarchy. "The ditch of truth," from Victor Hugo's *Les Misérables*, is an apt metaphor for all of those modern epistemologies—scientific positivism, fictional realism and naturalism, Marxist historical and economic materialism, Darwinism, Nietzschean genealogy, and Freudianism—that plumb the depths to explain surface phenomena. Hugo's romantic, muckraking masterpiece about poverty, social class, and revolution is itself based on such a materialist epistemology. Hugo calls the Parisian sewer system the ultimate "conscience of the town where all things converge and clash":

> There is darkness here, but no secrets. . . . Every foulness of civilization . . . sinks into the ditch of truth wherein ends the huge social down-slide, to be swallowed, but to spread. No false appearances, no white-washing, is possible; filth strips off its shirt in utter starkness, all illusions and mirages scattered, nothing left except what is, showing the ugly face of what ends. (Qtd. in Stallybrass and White, 141)

If all modern, supposedly scientific or materialistic epistemologies are versions of "the ditch of truth" or of plumbing the depths, then how can postmodern assertions that there are only surfaces and simulacra be understood as analyses or explanations?

To say that cultural value hierarchies, customs, and behaviors are organized in social class terms leaves open the question of whether they, like the hierarchy of social classes itself, are determined by economic factors

135

(the "economic mode of production" in Marxist terms; the "division of labor" in the language of the classical, capitalist economists), or whether those terms are instead simply powerful metaphors, useful in identifying and understanding other value hierarchies besides social class. There is the related question of whether other very basic, familiar hierarchies and the metaphors derived from them may be equally or perhaps even more fundamental (that is, more formative of other hierarchies) than social class. While class struggle was the general motor of history for Marx and Engels, and therefore the most fundamental category structuring ideology (and, hence, structuring all of culture), the unequal power relations derived from gender difference are at least as fundamental. According to feminist historians such as Gerda Lerner, class inequality has its remote origin in gender inequality. And since gender difference derives from the body, perhaps it is more fundamental than class. The body has always and in all cultures served as a main source of symbols and metaphors for expressing other evaluative, hierarchical relations (Douglas). Menenius Agrippa's speech to the plebs in the opening scene of *Coriolanus* about "the body's members" rebelling "against the belly" is a case in point. To this patronizing harangue, the First Citizen replies that "the cormorant belly... is the sink o' the body," betraying

> The kingly crowned head, the vigilant eye,
> The counselor heart, the arm our soldier,
> Our steed the leg, the tongue our trumpeter.

This exchange leads to Menenius's identification of the belly with the Roman Senate and the First Citizen with "the great toe" of the body politic. And the genitals? Where do they belong in the hierarchy of body parts? Stallybrass and White posit four main categories to which the value hierarchies they analyze belong: "psychic forms, the human body, geographical space, and the social order" (3). Since the most graphic, simple, and immediate of these is the body, as in *Coriolanus*, the body may seem more basic than the other categories. This prioritization also makes sense in psychoanalytic terms; it includes gender difference and gives due (perhaps excessive?) regard to the genitals.

Stallybrass and White sketch a Bakhtinian rhetoric of value hierarchies that my students find immediately useful. Because I assign Nietzsche's "What Is Noble?" chapter from *Beyond Good and Evil* as one of the first texts we read, I use it to illustrate this rhetoric. Its main elements are, first, the nonironic assertion of hierarchy (high is high, and low is low). Thus, at the start of "What Is Noble?" Nietzsche declares: "Every enhancement of the type 'man' has so far been the work of an aristocratic society... [one] that believes in the long ladder of an order of rank and difference in value between man and man, and that needs slavery in some sense or other" (201). The most obvious sort of challenge to such straightforward assertion is symbolic inversion, as with "the learned pig" and "the ditch of truth," rhetorically turning "the world upside down." When "the crowd" gains the upper hand and "slave morality" sweeps all before it, Nietzsche argues, then "in the world of historical values, counterfeit *rules*" (218). In short, throughout the social and symbolic order the lower usurps the place of the higher, which is what the plebs are threatening to do in *Coriolanus*. Besides straightforward assertion and symbolic inversion, there are also various forms of symbolic hybridization such as democratic leveling, understood not as the low taking the place of the high but as the collapse of hierarchies into some amorphous, perhaps "broken" middle or muddle. Nietzsche has a literal sort of miscegenation between low and high in mind when he writes that the cause of "the slowly arising democratic order of things" is "the intermarriage of masters and slaves" (209). There is also a fourth rhetorical possibility, less easy to illustrate, involving the complete rejection of high/low formulations of value. Nietzsche is only reasserting "noble" values when he writes that the "noble type of man experiences *itself* as determining values... it is *value-creating*" (205), but presumably the truly "noble" man can make up his own values and impose them on others. Feminist attempts to imagine and create a gender-free language provide a better illustration of the difficulties involved in altogether avoiding or eliminating evaluative, hierarchical language.

Most cultural forms and phenomena fall somewhere between the extremes of high and low, noble and base. Nietzsche's great worry is that everything is downrushing not to the abject lower depths, but into the mediocrity of "the crowd" or "the masses," composed not of militant

137

working-class types but of bourgeois and petty-bourgeois types, mere "shopkeepers." Much nineteenth-century British culture has more to do with varieties of middlingness than with the extremes of high and low. Thus, Champagne Charlie, Ally Sloper, and other swells, toffs, shoppers, barmaids, snobs, prostitutes, chorus girls, and cads populate Peter Bailey's recent study, *Popular Culture and Peformance in the Victorian City*. At the same time, the urban types—or, better, *roles* (cads, etc.)—that Bailey privileges were of little importance to social history's first major incarnation, Marxist labor history. As told by E. P. Thompson and others, the making of working-class solidarity and radicalism from the French Revolution through the Chartist decade of the "hungry 40s" gets derailed by the story of its unmaking in the second half of the century. As Bailey contends, this standard, decline-and-fall narrative is simplistic for several reasons. In what Bailey identifies as "the most influential account of this dilution of class consciousness" (130), Gareth Stedman Jones sees mass militancy transmogrifying into popular "escapism," or the commodified attractions of the music hall, the sports arena, and the seaside holiday. So did capitalism bribe or "distract" working-class radicalism into the twin cages of "respectability" and apolitical vulgarity? Or did it help to provide new forms of culture, entertainment, value, status, and even identity that put class conflict on the back burner, so to speak? Certainly Champagne Charlie both understood and popularized a sort of social mobility and in-mixing that had little to do with the rigors of work and trade-union organizing:

> From Coffee and from Supper Rooms,
> From Poplar to Pall Mall,
> The girls, on seeing me, exclaim,
> "Oh, what a Champagne Swell!"

The Victorian city offered a rapidly expanding scene for leisure pursuits, for mass or popular culture, and many of these pursuits, as Bailey makes clear, emphasized role playing: strolling and shopping, music hall, theater, and Ally Sloper's con games and womanizing. From the Great Exhibition of 1851 on, the symptoms of an emergent "consumer society" proliferated: mass daily journalism, the first department stores, the first advertising agencies, mass tourism, and the advent of marginalist eco-nomics. (This revision of orthodox, capitalist economics, exemplified in Britain by W. S. Jevons's 1871 *Theory of Political Economy*, scrapped the old labor theory of value, as in both Adam Smith and Marx, in favor of a con-sumption theory; utility defined as consumer desire became the sole mea-sure of value.) And consumerism meant that more and more individuals of all classes began to be able to buy what they wanted, everything from food to Cook's tours. At the very least, one of the effects of prosperity and the proliferation of consumer goods was to help loosen the ties that unified working-class solidarity.

As Bailey notes, the older social-labor history accounts of the Victorian era make much of working-class "respectability." After the 1840s, as Victorians themselves often pointed out, trade unionism became respectable, inclined to work within the political and legal system rather than against it. Workingmen presumably also began imitating their betters (despite Arnold's characterization in *Culture and Anarchy* of the "popu-lace" as drinkers, brawlers, and smashers). However, in his "role analysis" of "working-class respectability," Bailey contends that any self-respecting worker, with enough cultural "knowingness," could slip into and out of a variety of roles, some respectable, some not so respectable. This is a per-fectly commonsensical observation, yet one that social historians have not always observed. The earlier tendency, seconding Marx and Engels, was to identify a factory worker as just that and no more: an exploited, underpaid, alienated, but hopefully increasingly angry prole who would one day turn into a revolutionary of the right sort. Even the very first factory workers, however, were factory workers only part of the time. The "performance" aspect of social history that Bailey emphasizes involves the fact that all of us play many roles every day. Prosperity enhances people's ability to do so, whatever their original class or status, and sometimes also to change status and even class. Insofar as class identity is determined mainly by work or occupation, it is qualified by or comes into conflict with the various roles that people adopt when they are not at work, when they are at play. From midcentury on, consumerism in Europe's and America's urban spaces meant, in part, new opportunities to play an ever-growing number of non- or after-work roles.

Many people today express their identities as much or more through consumption and their leisure activities as through their work. Bailey has taken some clues in this regard from cultural studies (but even very recent versions of cultural studies persist in trying to find moments of supposedly political "resistance" in, for example, women's consumption of soap operas). For many Victorians, what Marx called "the idiocy of rural life" had been left behind for the "glamour," "knowingness," and relative nomadism of urban life. Urban role playing amounted to a sort of social liberation involving an at least transient social mobility (a shop clerk didn't have to inherit £10,000 a year to become a swell or a toff during his off-hours). "Glamour" and "knowingness," moreover, are both important categories in Bailey's account of the advent of modern consumer society. Related to these is what Bailey calls "parasexuality," by which he means the increasing, tolerated, or "licit" commercialized employment and display of attractive young women—barmaids and chorus girls, for example. His studies of both of these perhaps minor but nevertheless characteristic occupations for women are highly interesting additions to Martha Vicinus's account of both vocations and avocations open to "independent women" in mid- and late-Victorian Britain. And "parasexuality" is a suggestive category in helping to understand how the erotic machinery of much mass culture works.

Bailey's social history of the emergence of commercialized leisure and consumer society shows that "knowing" actors and actresses of all classes on the urban stage were increasingly able to play and enjoy the roles they wanted to play—both during their leisure time and as occupations in the "leisure industries." A shop clerk or an omnibus driver could become a swell, a theatergoer, or even a music hall performer. A chorus girl could become a prostitute or a shopper or a watcher of other chorus girls or even the wife of an aristocrat. In modern urban history, work routines, occupations, and social classes all begin to lose some of their rigidity. Leisure expands, popular culture expands, the mass media come on stage. Desire and pleasure become categories to reckon with for historians, sociologists, and economists. But even though status, role playing, and various other categories related to individual identity complicate the picture, social class stratification does not disappear.

Champagne Charlie's urbane knowingness, which includes knowledge of how to mock and transgress social class boundaries, styles, and values, suggests in part how concepts of the "high" and "noble" have undergone various cultural metamorphoses into the forms of modern and now post-modern "sophistication." This last term is both privileged and defended in several recent analyses of literary and cultural theory. Indeed, within social science and humanities disciplines, to be a theorist has, for the last two or three decades, been generally treated—whether fairly, logically, or other-wise—as a higher, more sophisticated calling (or status) than to be a mere plodding empiricist. In large part, it has been the usurpation of these disci-plines by high (especially poststructuralist) theory, with its correlative claims to cultural capital, that has so aroused the *ressentiment* of the acad-emic bourgeoisie (so to speak).[11] In any event, two recent studies that posit both sophistication and theory as important, interrelated categories are Joseph Litvak's *Strange Gourmets* and Vincent Pecora's *Households of the Soul.*

According to Theodor Adorno, "in the managed world of the culture industry" or mass media, neither "aesthetic naïveté" nor the "noble sim-plicity" of classical art can exist (*Aesthetic Theory*, 336). What takes their place is, on one side, the cynicism of advertising, and, on the other, the per-haps equally cynical sophistication of critical intellectuals like Adorno. The ability of capitalism not just to tolerate but rather to mass produce and market—that is, exploit—both mass and high culture, both ideology and its relentless critique, was for Adorno the major problem of cultural modernity. Citing Adorno at the start of his highly sophisticated study of the many ways simpler, more primitive, "nobler" forms of economic exchange have been invoked by critics of capitalist modernity, Pecora writes: "if every superfluous adjunct of capitalism—from the work of art...to the fins on the 1959 Cadillac...is already a protest against instru-mental reason, if...the commodity fetish represents by its very nature 'something not entirely absorbed'...by...commerce, then capitalism is in every transaction a subversion of itself" (ix). Sophisticated communities of taste, whether noble, gay, fashionable, or otherwise, can simultaneously recall versions of the "noble household" or "archaic *oikos*" *and* serve as leading, perhaps avant-garde, models for the fashions set in motion by capitalist consumerism. This fact, well understood by Thorstein Veblen, is central to the aesthetic and cultural theories of Adorno, Roland Barthes, and Pierre Bourdieu, among others. Cultural studies practitioners, echoing

Foucault, keep repeating that power breeds resistance, promotes only to discipline carnival, and conjures up the abnormal to verify its normality.

Also citing Adorno at the start of his highly sophisticated defense of sophistication, Joseph Litvak writes: "In the vast restaurant of [contemporary] culture, there is no room for either naturalness or naïveté" (12). But there *is* room for sophistication, albeit of the necessarily cynical variety Peter Sloterdijk identifies as "enlightened false consciousness." Litvak and Pecora both analyze how culture and cultural value hierarchies have developed over the last two centuries, often in resistance but always in relation to capitalism, industrialization, and bourgeois conformity, including sexual conformity. Critical of "the pluralistic consensus, the happy law of *chacun à son goût*, now operative in cultural studies" (149), Litvak, from the standpoint of queer theory, offers close readings of *Pride and Prejudice*, *Northanger Abbey*, *Vanity Fair*, *Remembrance of Things Past*, and the cultural theories of Adorno and Barthes in order to defend intellectual and sexual sophistication against both the insidious homophobia of the mass media (Adorno's "culture industry," although, as Litvak shows, Adorno himself sometimes expressed homophobia) and the "terroristic regime of good taste" (25) that thinks it can infallibly tell high culture from the rest.

Litvak emphasizes that homosexuality has often been identified both with intellectuality (academic and otherwise) and with the tastes, at once fashionable and suspect to the less sophisticated, that take pleasure in the new, the camp, the queer. Echoing Nietzsche, he argues for "a gay alchemy, a gay science that we might also call a hom(e)opathy" (94). Taking his title from Proust, "l'étrange gourmet" or "man of strange appetite" (94), Litvak is well aware that "the naive sophistication that Proust practices" (112) can be easily confounded with the sorts of cultural, intellectual, and social class snobbism that, for example, Thackeray both mocked and practiced. Analyzing the homophobia implicit in Thackeray's "bitchy art" (60), as Eve Sedgwick calls it, Litvak shows how the puppet master of *Vanity Fair* wants to have his cake and eat it too by attacking while enacting social climbing. In the imposing, preposterous "fat dandy," Jos Sedley, "Thackeray enthusiastically plays up the scandal of that oxymoronic figure, the obtuse style queen" (56). With sophisticated irony, Thackeray mocks false sophistication; and with equally sophisticated irony, Litvak deconstructs the falseness (contradictions) of that mockery. That "Thackeray's snob already doubles...as a protohomosexual" (56) seems debatable, however, given Jos's obsession with Becky, who poisons him at the end of the novel to cash in on his life insurance. And one also wonders if the heterosexual marriage plots that are a staple of canonical novels like Austen's are necessarily, inherently homophobic? But Litvak is certainly right to see in Thackeray's passive-aggressive social class *and* sexual resentment a homophobia that both disavows and desires sophistication. Further, the classed figures of the dandy, the snob, and "the charming young man" are, as Litvak contends, central to the history of the novel and more generally to Victorian culture and its standard incarnation, the gentleman. A sizable portion of the history of Victorian fiction concerns how the less-than-gentlemanly figures of the snob and the dandy are mocked and demonized, perhaps as scapegoats for the proto-homosexuality that the gentleman heroically displaces from himself (47).

While Litvak focuses upon what gives individual pleasure, both intellectual and sensual, and also upon particular novels, Pecora focuses upon the many ways the Aristotelian conception of the "noble household" resurfaces in modern sociological, anthropological, and literary theory from Hegel to Baudrillard. Taking his title from Nietzsche's critique of nostalgia for a "'remote, primordial, and inclusive household of the soul' that is, quite literally, an imaginary, philosophical version of the noble *oikos*" in Aristotle (80), Pecora offers an insightful analysis both of much Victorian and modernist fiction, especially in relation to imperialism, and of a wide range of theories of modernity. In novels as various as H. Rider Haggard's *King Solomon's Mines* and Joseph Conrad's *Lord Jim*, "One can be a true master abroad in ways hardly possible at home, a sentiment that remains a powerful ideological component of imperial conquest well into the twentieth century" (175).

Pecora identifies versions of "the noble household" in much of the "romantic ethnography" of the last two centuries, from Rousseau to Lévi-Strauss and beyond. His most challenging claims are that the Aristotlean *oikos* shows up everywhere in modern thought and, more specifically, that the linguistic turn exemplified by poststructuralism, far from abandoning or deconstructing the nostalgic search for "the noble household," continues that search: "Aristotle's *oikos*/marketplace dichotomy would be profoundly reinterpreted by a . . . French tradition of critical social and anthropological thought—running from Durkheim to Mauss to Bataille—that would abandon Marx's labor theory of value and Aristotelian concern for proper use as well as his critique of capitalism's mystified production of surplus value in the market economy. Instead, the Durkheimian tradition put forward a value theory based on the reciprocity of exchange itself in modern society," modeled upon gift exchange in precivilized societies (211–212). Pecora shows how, for Durkheim, Mauss, Bataille, Lévi-Strauss, and also for Lacan, Derrida, and Baudrillard (among others), "the gift" provides a "nobler" version of economics than either capitalist or Marxist utilitarianism. According to Pecora, substituting "the signifier" for "the gift" leads to Derrida's theory of *différance* and also to the many versions of "alterity" in current cultural theory, including postcolonial studies (see Derrida, *Given Time*). However, claiming that all values originate in exchange, while pointing back to primitive versions of "the noble household" involved in "gift exchange" like the *Kula* ring of the Trobrianders, leads Pecora also to Baudrillard as "the reductio ad absurdum of the romantic tradition in social theory." In Baudrillard, "the capitalist marketplace itself begins to simulate," if not "nobility," then a sort of primitive circularity in exchange that looks more like *potlatch* waste or expenditure—those riding mowers, again!— than like utilitarian functionalism or instrumental reason (278).

Litvak's and Pecora's studies of sophistication and value can be situated within Jukka Gronow's clear, concise history of ideas related to modern consumerism and "the mechanism of fashion" (47), a version of Adorno's "culture industry." "Good taste" and sophistication of all sorts, as Bourdieu argues in *Distinction*, are forms of "cultural capital" that circulate in relation to money, market values, and social class. But the "antinomy of taste" in Kantian aesthetics—the fact that "taste" is both private and somehow public, intensely subjective and yet also demonstrably objective— makes it possible to read *Strange Gourmets*, and to some extent also *Households of the Soul*, as falling somewhere between Humean subjectivism, according to which everything is a matter of individual preference, and Bourdieu's objectivism, according to which any individual's classifications by taste are always expressions or functions of social class. As Gronow paraphrases Bourdieu, "Tastes are class tastes" (28). Yet, as Champagne Charlie shows, social class boundaries are permeable in many ways, including Thackeray's "snobbism" and Bakhtin's "carnival." And sexuality, including Bailey's "parasexuality," has been perhaps the most potent violator of class boundaries throughout history.

Litvak recognizes that "the class politics of sophistication are inseparable from its sexual politics" (3), while also recognizing that sophistication often consumes with gusto the bodily, the vulgar, the opposite of whatever is supposedly high cultural. But his interest in the ways intellectual sophistication (including "theory sophistication") and homosexuality have been identified, both negatively and positively, leads him to neglect forms of especially working-class pleasure, both cultural and sexual, that are ordinarily seen as naive or unsophisticated. So, too, while the nobility of Pecora's "noble household" carries an aristocratic valence that corresponds to nineteenth-century and modern conceptions of high culture, once Pecora begins to find a similar nobility in non-Western, so-called primitive societies and in primitive forms of gift exchange that are more egalitarian than hierarchical, the boundaries of social class under capitalism begin to blur. True, this is perhaps less Pecora's doing than that of the many "romantic" social theorists, including Marx, whom he surveys. But one nevertheless wonders about forms of nonutilitarian exchange, generosity, ritual, and community that lie below the horizons both of the traditional aristocracy and of the bourgeoisie.

In contrast to Bailey, Litvak, and Pecora, cultural studies populists who downplay or ignore social class in their studies of the popular consumption of mass-produced commodities wittingly or unwittingly align themselves with those postmodernists who assert that reality has vanished into the maelstrom of mass-mediated simulations. Social class also blurs or vanishes, as in Baudrillard's *In the Shadow of the Silent Majorities*, with its claim that "the masses"—no class distinctions in that term!—equal the "refusal of meaning." Both mass-mediated "simulations" and Baudrillard's theory about them are examples, moreover, of that mirrorlike "superficiality" that Jameson identifies as "the first and most evident" symptom of the postmodern condition:

> The emergence of a new kind of flatness or depthlessness, a new kind of super-
> ficiality in the most literal sense, [is] perhaps the supreme formal feature of all
> the postmodernisms. (*Postmodernism*, 9)[12]

This "new kind of superficiality" is related to definitions of the postmodern as involving the collapse of the modernist high versus mass culture dichotomy. As Andreas Huyssen puts it, "the great divide" between modernist high culture and commodified mass culture no longer exists; especially with the eclipse of the possibility of an emancipatory democratic, mass culture under socialism, "high art" has been "preempted by the rise of mass mediated culture and its supporting industries and institutions" (15). According to this view, there is no longer any alternative to the capitalist massification and commodification of all culture—thus there emerges, supposedly, a new sort of classless or at least dehierarchized society.

The postmodern or late capitalist "triumph" of "mass mediated culture" does not mean, however, the leveling or disappearance of social class hierarchies, either in relation to the actual social positions people occupy or in relation to the symbolic forms of culture. Bailey's "knowingness," Litvak's "sophistication," and Pecora's "noble household" persist. Bourdieu's *Distinction* is a powerful demonstration of how high-low value hierarchies of all sorts, correlated to social class, permeate all aspects of culture and society in post–World War II France. There and elsewhere, the hierarchies of literary and artistic genres, for instance, are vertical "deep structures" that carry over even to television—*Masterpiece Theatre* versus *The Simpsons*—and to music—classical versus country-and-western or rap. As deep structures, class-related value hierarchies bisect and organize all of the surfaces that postmodernist theory privileges. The rhizomatic, often deliberate superficiality of much postmodern culture including its theorization ordinarily entails not the disappearance of high/low hierarchies but their carnivalesque inversions and in-mixings—the Boston Pops, Roy Lichtenstein's cartoon paintings, the *New Yorker* (which Clement Greenberg once described as "quality kitsch").

A recent article in the *New York Times Magazine*, that other barometer of liberal, middlebrow good taste, is entitled "Luxe Populi," and subtitled "Luxury for All." Written by Holly Brubach, the magazine's "style editor," its thesis is that the "luxury trade"—which happens, like a lot of cultural theory, to be mainly French, and which consists of perfumes, evening gowns, pricy wines, and so forth—used to cater to an elite called the "old rich." But the luxury trade, it seems, is now democratizing, reaching out to the great middle-class majority—or anyway, reaching out to that lucky upper echelon of the great middle class with enough money and sophistication to emulate their betters. This new bunch of luxury lovers Brubach calls an "aristocracy of taste." But even if one grants that the luxury trade is getting a bit more democratic, as it descends the social class ladder it does so with consummate good taste and caution, and of course does not kick over that ladder in any inelegant haste to plunge into the depths of vulgarity. Certainly it does not plunge into the abyss of the meaning-imploding masses who shop at Wal-Mart. Also, even if only metaphorically, it appears that there *is* an "aristocracy" or two in the otherwise leveling haze and scandal of postmodern American superficiality.

With "Luxe Populi" and the *New York Times Magazine* at the upper middle, at least, of the totem pole of postmodern culture, it is essential to recall what lies at its base. One way to do so is to note the dozens of recent, albeit no doubt tasteless, sociological studies of poverty, welfare, and racial discrimination such as Ken Auletta's *The Underclass*. Sometimes called "the residuum" and identified as refuse ("the ditch of truth" again) in nineteenth-century discourse, today's underclass is usually defined as so impoverished that it lies *beneath* the working class (and all other classes) in the pecking order of postmodern America (and Europe, and elsewhere). Despite persistent rumors of the vanishing of both the underclass and the industrial proletariat, there are numerous accounts of their persistence even in supposedly "postindustrial" America. According to some of these accounts, if the proletariat is disappearing (shrinking, at least), that is because of downsizing; it is in danger of sinking into the jobless underclass. Further, a recent article in *American Demographics* titled "The New Working Class" points out that "in a supposedly classless society, nearly half of Americans consistently identify themselves as working class" (Heath, 51; see also Jackman and Jackman).

Recent low unemployment and general economic productivity may be providing a modicum of new prosperity for many workers and even for those "beneath" them, but all commentators note that inequality between the wealthiest and the poorest is on the rise. An article on this topic in *The Christian Science Monitor* points out that "income inequality is worse in the US than in other industrial nations" (Francis, 16). In 1997 in the United States, "the top 1 percent of households received 7.3 percent of the national after-tax income"; in just two years, that figure is now closer to 12.9 percent—higher than at any time in history. And the growing inequality is apparent on a global scale as well, with so-called Third World countries falling further and further behind the West. "The gap in per capita income between the industrial and developing worlds tripled over the past three decades—from $5,700 in 1960 to $15,400 in 1993. . . . The incomes of about 1.5 billion people in some 100 countries were lower in the 1990s than in earlier decades" (Brown, 116). All this is familiar bad news, but it is also news that, at least in the United States, gets ignored or overlooked in a variety of ways, perhaps most obviously through the pervasiveness of the assumption that "progress is our most important product" and that progress, at least in the long run, will trickle down to everyone.

In any event, studies of the urban underclass show all too clearly that America's social pyramid has a bottom as well as a top, and suggest that social class continues to structure all aspects of postmodern culture. In relation to our work, education, I agree with George Lipsitz that "the erasure of class differences" even in the context of higher education needs to be countered by an active teaching about class. In colleges and universities today, there are many more courses about race and gender than about social class. I also agree with John Guillory that "the proper context for analyzing [both] the school" and literary canon formation is social class (viii). In *The Politics of Social Class in Secondary School*, Ellen Brantlinger demonstrates that class inequalities influence all aspects of what happens in high schools, including students' attitudes toward education and toward each other. And Jonathan Kozol's *Savage Inequalities* is a powerful indictment of the massive failure of American public education to live up to its democratic ideals, dooming millions of children to poverty and the so-called underclass. It is not possible to read such studies and still agree with the Arnoldian, liberal (and now also neoconservative) belief that "the true apostles of equality" are "the men of culture."

For these and many other reasons, theorizing and mapping the relationships between culture and social class will remain basic to whatever it is that we continue to call cultural studies. "Our students will come to their own conclusions when they read texts about social class," writes Lipsitz. "But whatever they conclude, they will be better prepared for the future if they know that for many people at many different times there has been a class struggle even more important than the one between the teachers and the students" (20).

Informania U

8

Initially the screen shows a hazy blob that in fact contains all of the words of all of Shakespeare's plays. It's a 3D space that you can fly through, so that you can grab the computer's control knobs and zoom in to find a play. . . . Moving within a play and among plays is done by traveling in this space rather than by pulling books off a shelf.
—Neil Gershenfeld, *When Things Start to Think*

How all occasions do inform against me.
—Shakespeare@*Hamlet*.lit

In *The University in Ruins*, Bill Readings argues that the old *raison d'être* of higher education—nation-based cultures and national identity making—is on the wane. Through the metamorphosis of the university into a transnational corporation, the various disciplines of knowledge are losing any sense of connection to a central mission or ideal such as culture or the liberal arts. Readings takes several of his cues from Jean-François Lyotard, who wrote his now-famous *Postmodern Condition* (1979) as a "report on knowledge" and higher education for the government of Quebec. Lyotard there opines that the university is "nearing what may be its end" (xxv), in part through the fragmentation of the various disciplines into mutually incomprehensible "language games," and in part through the computerization and commodification of "information." Much the same message is evident in the contributions to the 1997 Open University volume, *The Postmodern University? Contested Versions of Higher Education in Society*, edited by Anthony Smith and Frank Webster. In his contribution, sociologist Zygmunt Bauman writes: "The postmodern condition has split one big game of modern times into many little and poorly co-ordinated games, playing havoc with the rules of all the games, and shortened sharply the lifespan of any set of rules" (21). Like Lyotard, Bauman sees both computerization and corporatization as contributing to this outcome. Concerning the second factor, Bauman declares:

> While remodeling themselves ever more vigorously after the pattern of corporate capital, universities are all too eager, and if not eager then obliged, to cede the right to set the norms, and perhaps most seminally the ethical norms, to [higher education's] newly embraced prototype and spiritual inspiration [the marketplace]. This means stating its own principles ever more gingerly and meekly, and feeling awkward and apologetic whenever those principles clash with the rules sacrosanct to business. (20)

For his part, Readings prefers to call today's university "posthistorical" rather than "postmodern," both because he disapproves of the more celebratory versions of postmodernist advocacy (or theory) and because he claims that the historical mission of the university, the archiving and dissemination of "national" cultures and literatures, is being voided. Here again he echoes Lyotard, who also claims that no one any longer expects universities to produce citizens charged with emancipatory "ideals," but only experts and professionals trained in certain pragmatic "skills" *Postmodern,* 48). I shall consider the question of "posthistory" more fully in the next chapter. Here it seems to me evident that, despite terminology, Readings offers basically the same arguments that can be found in Lyotard and in *The Postmodern University.* My point isn't to diminish his originality and insightfulness, but rather to stress that *The University in Ruins* belongs to the fast-growing subgenre of critiques of higher education that depict it as succumbing to the forces of postmodernization, and especially to transnational capitalism and its mushrooming sector of communications and information industries. As Readings puts it, in the "posthistorical university," not just culture but "knowledge" as such "tends to disappear, to be replaced as a goal by facility in the processing of information: something should be known, yet it becomes less and less urgent that we know what it is that should be known" (86).

Readings does not find easy solutions to what he sees as the ruination of the posthistorical university. On the contrary, he accepts its corporatization and its decoupling from issues of national history, culture, and identity as inevitable, indeed as a *fait accompli*. We academics must learn to "dwell in the ruins" and make the best of a bad situation. Certainly Readings does not see a solution in any emergent academic formation. Cultural studies, for one, has arisen just as the centrality of nation-based cultures is waning, but when institutionalized as a new sort of interdisciplinary discipline, it is only an empty framework without substance:

> There is a direct ratio between the intensity of apocalyptic claims for the institutional potential of Cultural Studies and their absence of explanatory power. What allows Cultural Studies to occupy the entire field of the humanities without resistance is their very *academization of culture*, their taking culture as the object of the University's desire for knowledge, rather than as the object that the University produces. Culture ceases to mean anything as such; it is dereferentialized. (99; his emphasis)

Like "excellence," "culture" becomes another general equivalent that, because it is so general, ceases to have any intrinsic meaning. Through cultural studies, the university goes in search of culture just as culture has ceased to mean anything. But culture has always carried meanings other than just the goal of liberal arts education. And Readings's suggestion that those who advocate and practice cultural studies encounter no resistance is debatable, to say the least, given the resistance to it from academic traditionalists as well as from neopragmatists such as Stanley Fish. Nevertheless, it may be that culture is too general a term to do more than bring scholars together from a variety of disciplines in a common enterprise of investigating and debating more specific issues. Perhaps the most common feature shared by those engaged in cultural studies is an emphasis on social critique, and sometimes this emphasis, with or without any of Marx's other ideas, at least approaches a "radical critique of everything existing" (Marx and Engels, 12). Perhaps, too, critique is what Readings means when he offers his own general equivalent—"Thought"—for the enterprise that he hopes will begin to occupy the ruins of the posthistorical university. It isn't Thought-as-critique that is gaining centrality in higher education, however, but the quite different, uncritical category of *information*.

According to Readings, what will allow (thoughtful) professors and students to dwell effectively among the university's ruins is "Thought." By this capitalized term, he clearly means something different from the types of academic, disciplinary rationality that helped produce the ruins in the first place.

> The referent of teaching, that to which it points, is the name of Thought. Let me stress that this is not a quasi-religious dedication. I say "name" and I capitalize "Thought" not in order to indicate a mystical transcendence but in order to avoid the confusion of the referent with any one signification. The name of Thought precisely is a name in that it *has no intrinsic meaning.* (159)

But this is just what Readings has earlier said is the problem with "culture": it comes to mean everything, and therefore it has "no intrinsic meaning." Readings does not do enough, it seems to me, to show how Thought is or could be different from the standard forms of academic rationality. In any event, Readings brings Kant back into the picture: philosophy, the discipline devoted to Thought, needs to be reinstalled at the empty center of the ruined university. But not, of course, philosophy as it is presently constituted in philosophy departments, with their various -isms and answers, including logocentrism. For Readings, Thought instead signals the ongoing questioning or creative "dissensus" that he understands as an ethical obligation for both teachers and students. One can ask, however, whether Thought has ever not been, at least ideally (in Thought) at the center of the university and of teaching.

There are, of course, different types of Thought. One current and, indeed, fashionable type goes under the rubric of "critical thinking." As I noted earlier, most of my colleagues in English claim that their main goal is to foster critical thinking among students, and the same is true of teachers in many other disciplines.[1] But one teacher's critical thinking is not necessarily another's. Perhaps in part because of this new "conflict of the faculties," there are now numerous experts, textbooks, and instructional programs aimed at teaching both teachers and students how to become critical thinkers. I suspect that most versions of critical thinking now offered are not what Readings means by Thought. Many of them seem rather to inculcate forms of instrumental rationality and technical problem solving without any overarching philosophical, ethical, cultural, or political aim or design. Certainly the "critical" aspect of such thinking does not add up to the "radical critique of everything existing." One textbook titled simply *Thinking* asks, "What is thinking?" This is probably a good question to raise in a textbook on thinking, but here is the (non)answer:

> Right now you are thinking. Think about it. What *exactly* are you doing now? What is happening in your head as you think?... Simply put, how does your brain work?

The authors of *Thinking* don't leave these questions suspended Ariel-like in thin air, but immediately reassure their student readers: "Do not feel bad if you do not know the answer[s] because neither do the experts" (Kirby and Goodpaster, 5).[2]

What would it mean, however, to install Thought in Readings's sense at the center of the posthistorical university? It would mean, for one thing, to leave open-ended, in the form of questions or questioning, that which is too often presented as closed, as "fact," "information," or "knowledge" prepackaged by the experts (the professors). There is a sound pedagogical principle involved in this idea: both students and professors learn more through inquiry and discovery than through what Paulo Freire has called "the banking" version of instruction. Nevertheless, I suspect that most professors believe that what the university, whether "in ruins" or not, should continue to produce and deliver is knowledge—that is, the final results of the critical thinking done by professors in our various disciplines.

Neither "thought" nor "knowledge," however, works any better (or worse) as a general equivalent for the entire academic enterprise than "culture," and for the same reason: they are too general to have more than abstract significance as goals. Readings's argument is self-defeating, because the logic of the general equivalent that he invokes empties all possible general equivalents of specificity and intrinsic value. Of course, as much as he argues that Thought *should* occupy the ruins, he is also arguing, because of the transformative power of globalizing capital, that what has really taken over the center of the educational enterprise is *the* general equivalent, money.

However, there is another candidate for general equivalent, one that Readings stresses along with money: information. The argument that cultural studies is becoming hegemonic in higher education pales before the emergence of two interconnected interdisciplinary enterprises, "cognitive science" and "informatics." At my university over the last couple of decades, a high-powered group of computer scientists, psychologists, philosophers, linguists, and mathematicians have united around work on artificial intelligence. They initially formed an interdisciplinary program in Cognitive Science. From this starting point, they have proceeded to forge our newly approved "School of Informatics." Part of their rationale for the creation of the School is that similar programs, departments, and schools already exist or are developing in universities around the world. According to the website of our new School of Informatics,[3] similar programs, departments, institutes, or schools have been established at Penn State, Michigan, Syracuse, Oregon, Stanford, Berkeley, George Mason, Illinois, and other places in the United States, as well as at Edinburgh, Queens (Ontario), Oslo, Delft, Athens, Manchester, Nagoya, Kansai, and other universities abroad. On the "Overview" page, one learns that "'informatics' is a term of European origin having to do with the collection, classification, storage, retrieval and dissemination of recorded knowledge treated as a pure and applied science. Indiana University defines informatics as the art, science and human dimensions of technology. It is information technology applied to human problems."[4]

Besides the global proliferation of informatics as a new academic field, a further rationale for the creation of our school is spelled out in a statement on its website by our vice president for academic affairs, Kenneth Gros Louis: "National studies show that hundreds of thousands of jobs in information technology went unfilled last year [1998]. In addition, a study by the U.S. Department of Labor reports that employers are increasingly looking for computer specialists who are not only technically skilled, but also knowledgeable about the employer's industry. By its very design, the School of Informatics addresses these trends." Nothing could be more practical and, it seems, sensible. But even with its scientific origins and intentions, the School of Informatics, on one unsympathetic interpretation, will be just another vocational school, without much if any connection to what higher education used to stress: culture, the liberal arts and sciences. According to Readings, what is occurring is "the replacement of a highly suspect organicist notion of culture by... *information*, exactly the mechanical or technological specter of mere lifeless facts against which the idea of culture was supposed to protect" (87). Then, too, even if information rather than money is the new general equivalent at the heart of the "ruined university," what makes it so powerful is in large part its easy quantification and transformation into money: jobs for students; grants for researchers; and the high-tech industries pouring millions of dollars into higher education to provide the information technology to make informatics a reality. The *Indiana Daily Student* for 24 February 2000 headlined the news that "Sun Microsystems... will bring one of the largest supercomputers in the world to the [IU] Kelly School of Business." The university's administrators praise Sun's leadership and foresight, and Sun's CEO, Scott McNealy, praises IU's leadership and foresight. According to IU President Myles Brand, "Sun commits itself to an ongoing, highly integrated relationship with IU that will have enormous payoffs for students, researchers and others." Clearly, with its potential for "enormous payoffs," information is the new pot of gold at the end of the academic rainbow.

Both the deal with Sun Microsystems and the new School of Informatics exemplify the general and accelerating trend of higher education toward computerized corporatization. The proponents of the new school, while stressing its cutting-edge status, also insist that in most respects it will be (better) business as usual. In at least four ways, they claim, the new school will simply improve upon what the university has always done or tried to do: (1) it will produce and deliver information—especially information about information; (2) it will do what other forward-looking and prestigious universities are doing or planning to do; (3) it will train students in a systematic way for jobs and careers that exist in the real world; and (4) it will create a space or place for faculty from different disciplines to share issues and expertise, and thereby help to create a shared set of academic values, beliefs, and goals—perhaps even, eventually, a core curriculum.

The notion of a core curriculum is an implicit possibility rather than an explicit goal for the creators of the new school. In my experience, the bigger the university, the more difficult the establishment of a core curriculum becomes (quite apart from whether such a curriculum is a good idea). Nevertheless, for the advocates of the new school, "information" is what binds all academic enterprises together. Further, those who have signed on as its charter members, many of them participants in the older cognitive science program, constitute a promising and already productive collaboration across several disciplines. And there is the encouraging news that all disciplines will or could have some stake in the new school. This prospect has led my department, English, to begin recruiting at least one professor with expertise in "electronic literacy," and other departments are also scrambling to jump on the informatics bandwagon.

On one level, all of this is heartening. I like the idea that my university is trying to stay in the forefront of current academic and intellectual developments. I like, too, the interdisciplinary collaboration that is one hallmark and source of our new School of Informatics. I respect, moreover, those faculty who see real benefits, both practical and theoretical, for their own research and teaching stemming from their participation in the school. These people aren't nutty professors, or at any rate they aren't any nuttier than the rest of us; they know what they are doing and why they are doing it. And no one, it seems to me, can quarrel with the goal of creating courses and educational opportunities that will steer students toward successful careers.

But there is a burden of inevitability, not to say finality, about the school that has troubled it from the start. One of the arguments in its favor has been that "if we don't do it, somebody else will, or is already doing it." But this argument has seemed, even to some of those who offer it, a case of the tail wagging the dog. There has been a strong sense that the pressure to create the school has come from outside the university, and especially from the so-called high-tech industries that are, it appears, clamoring for informatics graduates to fill the jobs that are already waiting for them. And there has been the related concern that the school is technology driven. It isn't just the (virtual?) jobs that are already begging for infograds that seems troubling, nor even the increasing interactions between corporations like Sun and the university, but also the proliferation of new machinery that is rapidly and quite visibly filling up the spaces among the ruins—spaces that Readings hoped would come to be occupied by Thought.

The thought that machines are invading the spaces once reserved for Thought is, I suspect, unsettling also to some informatics professors. Even if in "postmodern" or "ruined" form the university persists, computerization is ringing "the knell of the age of the Professor," writes Lyotard, because "a professor is no more competent than memory banks in transmitting established knowledge" (*Postmodern*, 53). Anxiety about the possible extinction of the professoriate is stirred by news of related technological developments such as so-called distance learning; a second, "academic Internet" based at the Indianapolis campus of my university; all sorts of Web-based courses and course-design programs; and above all the development of entire "virtual universities"—Phoenix University, the Western Governors' University, the California and Canadian Virtual Universities, and so on. The other main source of this worry, the prevalence of part-time instructors and consequent erosion of tenure-track positions, is of course also related to the corporatization of higher education.[5]

The fear of extinction could be somewhat allayed if it were not that most of the techno-objects crowding into university libraries, offices, dormitories, and even dining halls are "thinking machines." These machines, it seems, do what professors do, and at least threaten to do it better.[6] Advocates of "virtual" or "distance" education make no bones about what they see as the meltdown of the traditional university, classroom, and even professor. In his best-selling *The Age of Spiritual Machines*, Ray Kurzweil predicts that by 2029 "human learning" will be "primarily accomplished using virtual teachers and . . . neural implants," while most learning and even the creation of "significant new knowledge" will be done "by machine with little or no human intervention" (221). Just what all of us humans (including professors) will do with our presumably vastly increased spare time is a bit unclear, but we will still need to learn a few things, like how to access digitalized information, in case we ever need to.

Writing about the present instead of the future, Michael Gell and Peter Cochrane assert: "Effective learning can be realized by providing a student with a computer, loading the educational software, and walking away" (252). Gell and Cochrane believe, in fact, that the "virtual" classroom can be far more "effective" (or at any rate, efficient) than the traditional one. Professors, after all (especially absentminded ones), are a lot less efficient than computers. Gell and Cochrane also contend that universities as we have known them have constituted inefficient "monopolies" on education, which can and should give way to new, more efficient, and more consumer-oriented "knowledge businesses," including new combinations of the old universities and the telecommunications industries. That "knowledge businesses" are creating a new cultural arena Gell and Cochrane call "edu-tainment" seems not to faze them—they express little or no anxiety about the "McDonaldization" or "Disneyfication" of education—but there are now hundreds of so-called corporate universities, include the Disney Institute (which offers "infotainment") and McDonald's "Hamburger U."

In contrast to Gell and Cochrane's advocacy of the "virtualization" of higher education, the evidence from "the great pioneer of distance learning," the Open University in Britain, does not suggest that computers can do it better than professors, but rather that "a computer terminal is an unsatisfactory alternative" to face-to-face education (Smith and Webster, 13). Computers and other technological aids can supplement what human teachers do, but not altogether supplant them. Or so it appears, at least for the time being. Even Gell and Cochrane still have in mind "virtual" or tele-vised instructors, guiding students through course materials. Right now what computers do well is complex computations and the storage, manip-ulation, and communication of various kinds of relatively static informa-tion. But chess-playing computers can beat world chess champions, and they will get better. By 2020, according to Kurzweil, computers will reach the power and flexibility of the human brain and zoom right past us (3). There are, moreover, a wide array of "intelligent" possibilities depicted in physicist Neil Gershenfeld's *When Things Start to Think*, such as "smart" paper and even shoes. So the thought of a computer occupying a philoso-phy classroom and instructing students, perhaps both human and machinic (that is, cyborgian), in how to engage in the activity that Readings names Thought is hardly far-fetched.

In his 1997 book with the distinctly dystopian title *Slaves of the Machine*, Gregory Rawlins, a professor of computer science at Indiana, writes:

> Computers are now doubling in complexity every eighteen months. Twenty years from now it probably won't make much sense to call these devices "machines." Even if it isn't purposeful or self-aware, it's hard to call something a machine if its behavior is so complex, reactive, and apparently purposeful that it behaves more like a cat than a toaster. (17)

Or more like a professor. Teaching and reading machines are old stories. So, too, in a sense, are computers. But just on the the horizon, Rawlins notes, are "intelligent machines" that will be self-evolving, capable of adapting to a wide range of environments—that is, capable of growing increasingly complex and powerful on their own (see also Kurzweil). And who or what will teach the machines?

As Gell and Cochrane suggest, however, much more elementary and readily available technology already exists that, if the university mandated or encouraged its use, could take over the job of classroom teaching from either Gregory Rawlins or me. I could have my classes videotaped, and then have future students replay the simulacra of myself in subsequent semesters in perpetuity (provided the videotapes were occasionally copied). I do not know that there are any rules that would prevent my sim-ulacra from doing my teaching for me. On the contrary, at York University in Toronto, nontenured faculty are being required to videotape their courses and also put them online.[7] But with or without administrative approval (or coercion), if I did present videotapes of my lectures in my absence, there might be complaints from students—though it is interest-ing to speculate what they would complain about (cf. Kurzweil, 96–97)—and I might cease getting raises. Perhaps the administration, how-ever, would simply seize the videotapes as its "intellectual property" and send me packing.

In its rush to take commercial advantage of video and online courses produced by nontenured faculty, the high-handed York University administration provoked a strike which, as David Noble points out in "Digital Diploma Mills," resulted in a contract that provides faculty with at least some protection and rights against a future that will increasingly place both their jobs and the face-to-face classroom in jeopardy. Like the downsizing in manufacturing industries, the downsizing of tenure-track faculty positions is now occurring partly through the automation and commercialization of instruction. In these circumstances, students may start sending their own simulacra to class, or just stay home and boot up the online courses they need to graduate from some new virtual program or university. And when will the first diploma, in lieu of a human student, be awarded to a computer?

Besides the increasingly liminal, simulacral role of faculty in higher education, there are at least two issues concerning the creation of our School of Informatics that warrant further Thought. The first concerns the nature of "information" and the consequences of installing it categorically at the center of higher education. And the second concerns the nature and consequences of the proliferating machinery on which we professor-purveyors of various sorts of information, and our students, are increasingly dependent.

The creation and delivery of information is what universities have always been about, of course, and in this general sense, information is synonymous with knowledge. But in more specific ways, the two terms are not synonymous, or not exactly synonymous. If in one direction knowledge equals information, in another it equals Thought in Readings's meaning of that term. This triad does not form a reassuring syllogism, whereby information equals knowledge, knowledge equals Thought, and therefore information equals Thought. On the contrary, information equals, on most accounts, undigested data waiting for Thought to interpret or say what it means.[8] According to Theodore Roszak in *The Cult of Information*: "In its new technical sense, *information* has come to denote whatever can be coded for transmission through a channel that connects a source with a receiver, regardless of semantic content" (13; cf. Webster, 21–29). Information even equals, in a sense, "holes in paper," as Gernot Wersig indicates:

Electronic data processing people always tended to promise more than they could deliver. So, even at a time when their machines were not able to process more than holes in paper, they started to call it information processing, which led to the establishment of the discipline which was later called informatics (especially in Europe). (221)

Translate "holes in paper" into the binary code of digital machines, and the result is the same.

In his thoughtful analysis of the Internet, philosopher Gordon Graham writes that there is a naivete "sometimes evident in enthusiasts for the Internet, especially educationalists.... This lies in their assumption that in the Internet we have a vast storehouse of information" (89). While the Internet is indeed "a vast storehouse" or archive of ever-increasing information, it also stores and delivers vast quantities of misinformation, disinformation, and trivial information. The naive assumption that it contains *only* information is, Graham continues, "sustained by the technical use of the term 'information'":

> In the expression "digital information" the word "information" is used in its barest sense and means no more than a set of electronic impulses which can be made to produce text and images on a screen. Information in this technical sense *has no epistemological implications*. (89; my emphasis)

You don't need to verify information and thus prove its truth; all you need to do is receive it from your computer, your TV, or some other source. Knowledge, on the other hand, does have "epistemological implications," involving the twin ideas of truth and verification.

Besides knowledge, there are several other terms that have had major roles in traditional discourse about education and that "information" now threatens to displace or erase: Thought, understanding, culture, the liberal arts, wisdom. In *The Idea of the University: A Reexamination*, Jaroslav Pelikan writes:

> It is difficult [to discuss] knowledge, whether as an end in itself or as a means to some other end, without introducing the distinction between knowledge and information. Thus a dictionary of synonyms... explains that whereas *information* often "suggests no more than a collection of data or facts either discrete or

integrated into a body of knowledge," the term *knowledge* "applies not only to a body of facts gathered by study, investigation, observation, or experience but also to a body of ideas acquired by inference from such facts or accepted on good grounds as truth." (34–35)

Pelikan goes on to say that "information tells us the What and knowledge the How," and adds: "that leaves, of course, the Why, which, ever since the Hebrew Bible and the Greek thinkers, has been the province of wisdom" (35). Pelikan, reconsidering John Henry Newman's *Idea of the University*, has written a learned, thoughtful, and perhaps also wise book. But it is also a curiously ill-informed book. Published in 1992, Pelikan's study of "the idea" of the university has nothing to say about virtual instruction, the increasing role of computers in all aspects of what goes on in the university, or the rise of "information" as the new, central focus of the academic enterprise. Pelikan's book, just eight years after it was published, strikes me as poignantly dated.

Setting aside the question of just how computers might be able to help with "wisdom," we should recall that from the Enlightenment onward the main goal of university education has been widely held to be the production of the cultivated (albeit not necessarily wise) individual. Readings argues that this goal was originally tied to notions of citizenship and national identity, but that these have eroded through the globalization of capital. John Guillory argues that specifically literary, humanistic culture as educational goal has eroded because of the rise of the "technical-managerial class." The two arguments mirror each other, because the new class has emerged in tandem with transnational capital. Both developments, moreover, are causes and effects of the development of the high-tech computer industries, so it stands to reason that information is replacing culture in "the ruined university." But does it also stand to reason that the substitution of information for culture is causing the ruination of the university? Perhaps not; and yet I suspect that the university is today a more ruinous place than it used to be, in part because the new category at the heart of its enterprise is more vacuous—both epistemologically and ethically—than the older, more traditional categories I have mentioned.[9]

As to the second issue, certain kinds of machinery have always been necessary for conducting research and sometimes teaching, especially in the sciences. However, the current dependence of faculty and students in all disciplines on computers is unprecedented. Never before has a single type of machine, the personal computer hooked up to the university's systems and the Internet, been so necessary for carrying on every sort of academic work. Hypertext, class webpages, Internet assignments, electronic bibliographies, and distance learning are rapidly becoming standard rather than experimental. At the same time, a glitch in the system—a virus, a power outage—can cause problems across an entire campus and, indeed, throughout academia. The general response to these problems is, So what? We want our universities, our offices, our students, and ourselves to be wired, whatever the minor headaches or even the larger consequences.

My electronic double (*mon semblable, mon frère*) has moved into my office and is present, often turned on, when I am talking to students or colleagues. It isn't eavesdropping yet, so far as I know. But already it puts vast amounts of information at my fingertips, and much more is on the way. This is the good news. Is part of the bad news cybersurveillance? Can I trust my electronic shadow (is it really "user friendly")? In their article on e-mail in *Academic Keywords*, Nelson and Watt give several examples of college and university administrations that make a regular practice of surveilling faculty use of e-mail and other university-supported programs. Some schools have quite strict rules about "personal" versus "professional" uses. It does not lower the level of my paranoia when I consider that many of my e-mails combine personal with professional messages. I realize my university will not penalize me for congratulating a doctoral student who has just defended her dissertation on also getting married, but that's exactly the sort of blurring between personal and professional that happens all the time. And even if the boundary between personal and professional can't be effectively policed, the suspicion that some administrator or his satraps (perhaps a computer with far more brainpower and access to information than I'll ever have) may be scanning all the messages that are sent and received over university-owned computers is, to say the least, disconcerting.

There is also the annoyance—at least, that's how I view it—of increasingly frequent "upgrades." Everyone who uses computers, whether for work or leisure, experiences upgrading. "Computers are now doubling in complexity every eighteen months," Gregory Rawlins declared in 1997. The speeding up of innovation in the high-tech industries is the main theme of

James Gleick's *Faster: The Acceleration of Just about Everything* (1999). Even before the advent of the Internet, computer power, following "Moore's Law," began doubling every eighteen months and at an accelerating rate (Gleick, 77; Kurzweil, 306). So, too, Paul Virilio's version of "crash theory" stresses "speed" building toward its absolute limit and history's vanishing point. Meanwhile, I, for one, do not have time to wax nostalgic about the machine or program I was using just a couple of months ago, before it was replaced by a newer, better version. Upgrading, we are told by the university's technopros (who proliferate with the machinery), is a normal aspect of technological and perhaps—*perhaps*—social progress.[10] But it is not now and has never been the case that the two sorts of progress are identical, nor even that social progress necessarily results from technological progress. In much current discourse about technology and its effects, the term "neo-Luddism" crops up, sometimes with the claim that the author or speaker will hew a sensible path between "the neo-Luddites" and "the technophiles" (Graham, 6–20; Robins and Webster, 1–9; Shenk). Despite his dystopian title, Rawlins seems to be of this sensible sort: he is, after all, a computer scientist.

In *Slaves of the Machines*, however, Rawlins also notes that new and better technology is bombarding its supposed human masters at an accelerating rate: "already, computers make computers" (37); this reproductive capacity is allied to an increasingly adaptive capacity that will lead to machines that "eventually become," like children, "indecipherable, then uncontrollable" (124). At this point in Rawlins's account, I found myself thinking of some of the wonderful-monstrous machines that inhabit science fiction, from Karl Čapek's robots in *R.U.R.* through the array of bizarre, unpredictable machines in Stanislaw Lem's fiction.[11] In *The Futurological Congress*, Lem's narrator, Ijon Tichy, says: "Who'd ever have guessed, in my day, that digital machines, reaching a certain level of intelligence, would become unreliable, deceitful, that with wisdom they would also acquire cunning?" Tichy has just "ingested" a book, in the form of a pill, called *The History of Intellectronics*, from which he learns about "Chapulier's Rule" or "the law of least resistance."

> If the machine is not too bright and incapable of reflection, it does whatever you tell it to do. But a smart machine will first consider which is more worth its

while: to perform the given task or, instead, to figure some way out of it. Whichever is easier. And why indeed should it behave otherwise, being truly intelligent? For true intelligence demands choice, internal freedom. And therefore we have the malingerants, fudgerators and drudge-dodgers, not to mention the special phenomenon of simulimbecility or mimicretinism. A mimicretin is a computer that plays stupid in order, once and for all, to be left in peace. (83–84)

Lem's list of misbehaving machines extends through "confuters" and "robotches," "dynamoks" and "cyberserkers," "electrolechers" and "solicitrons," and on to "The Great Mendacitor," which was "for nine years in charge of the Saturn meliorization project," but "did absolutely nothing on that planet, sending out piles of fake progress reports, invoices, requisition forms..." (85). This sounds suspiciously like certain university bureaucrats, though I realize Lem is talking about futuristic thinking machines.

Even if the machines we now have are (by and large) wonderfully reliable, in *Data Smog: Surviving the Information Glut*, David Shenk points to yet another problem. Shenk claims that his book "is neither techno-utopian nor neo-Luddite. It is *technorealist*—appreciating the benefits while recognizing and responding to [technology's] drawbacks" (16). The key "drawback" Shenk is concerned about is named twice in his title: "data smog" and "the information glut":

> At a certain level of input, the law of diminishing returns takes effect; the glut of information no longer adds to our quality of life, but instead begins to cultivate stress, confusion, and even ignorance. Information overload threatens our ability to educate ourselves, and leaves us more vulnerable as consumers and less cohesive as a society. (15)

These are by now familiar charges. Entropy, after all, has been an important concept in information theory ever since Claude Shannon's seminal 1948 article, "A Mathematical Theory of Communication." And as one formulation involving entropy would have it, more is less: too much information becomes disorganized, chaotic, reverting to randomness. Shenk may be a "technorealist," but his claim that "information glut" can lead to "ignorance" and undermine "our ability to educate ourselves" seems counterintuitive, if not exactly "neo-Luddite." Isn't information the opposite of ignorance? Just here, however, the distinction between knowledge and information may be helpful; Shenk stresses the related distinction between information and understanding. His point is that the storage and generation of information that computers allow exceed the grasp of any individual. The more one tries to take it all in, the more knowledge in the sense of understanding or comprehension diminishes.

Perhaps all machines have unintended side effects, including those that, like "information glut," are baneful rather than beneficial. One does not have to be a neo-Luddite to understand that new technologies often behave in quite unpredictable ways. "Unforeseen consequences," writes Neil Postman in *Technopoly*, "stand in the way of all those who think they see clearly the direction in which a new technology will take us" (15; see also Tenner). Thus, to cite one very familiar recent example, as the new millennium approached, billions of dollars was spent worldwide to correct the Y2K bug in computer systems. Nevertheless, down to the last minute, the experts could not be sure that massive power outages—just one of the possible "unintended consequences"—would not occur. Far more ominous was the possibility that failures in the systems controlling nuclear weaponry and nuclear energy facilities, especially in Russia and the Ukraine, might trigger disasters on the scale of Chernobyl or worse. But January 1, 2000, dawned; the apocalypse stayed aloof; history did not end; and the Y2K spectre faded away.

The experts and the news media waxed euphoric because, while something bad might have happened, nothing bad did happen. And so Y2K will go down in the annals of technohistory as a hugely expensive glitch that did no damage (apart from the huge expense), because the experts corrected it before it did damage. Meanwhile, the high-tech electronic industries have fueled an unprecedented level of prosperity (for many) and of stock market euphoria, at least in the United States, that are producing a number of "unforeseen consequences," among them an apparent corroboration of Francis Fukuyama's market-driven "posthistory" argument. In 2000 even more than in 1999 (and despite the economic difficulties of the "Asian tigers") free market capitalism, underwritten by global trading into the trillions of dollars in currencies, stocks, debts, and even (non)products that do not now and may never exist, seems to be the future. Despite other, much more serious signs that industrialization and the worldwide population explosion are causing irreparable damage to the environment (deple-tion of the ozone layer and global warming are the most publicized of these signs, but by no means the only ones), American and west European pros-perity continues almost unabated as of January 1, 2001.

Here it may be worth invoking that exemplary English professor Marshall McLuhan, both because he can be seen as a forerunner if not one of the founders of cultural studies, and because he has recently returned to the limelight, not as the prophet of the utopian possibilities of the mass media, but as an important predecessor of postmodern "crash theory." McLuhan argued that new technologies can have massive, unpredictable effects on individual minds and entire cultures and societies.[12] The "trauma of liter-acy" opens tribal, "closed societies" and gives birth to civilization. Papyrus facilitates the power and bureaucratic cohesion of the Roman Empire. The printing press causes modern nationalisms and nation-states to emerge from the coccoon of the Middle Ages. The telegraph and the railroad string together the far-flung European empires of the nineteenth century. And the electronic media are reversing the effects of print culture, wiring the entire world into a "retribalized" "global village."

While these now familiar ideas and their corollaries have often been interpreted as technological utopianism, they can be interpreted in dystopian ways related to "crash theory" (aka "trash theory"), a highly apocalyptic variety of postmodernism which, however, is not necessarily neo-Luddite, partly because it sees the future in terms of a McLuhanesque techno-determinism. "The wake of human progress can disappear again into the night of sacral or auditory man," or worse, as McLuhan put it, but there is nothing to be done about it. For one thing, it was by no means clear to McLuhan that James Joyce's "collideorscope" or any other new gadget, real or imagined, can save mankind from the traps and catastrophes that precisely are new gadgets, traps, and technologies (*Gutenberg*, 75). At least three crash theorists, Jean Baudrillard, Arthur Kroker, and Paul Virilio, have at various times and to varying degrees acknowledged McLuhan's influ-ence, and all three also see new technologies as catastrophes.

In *Data Trash*, Kroker (with Michael Weinstein) writes: "McLuhan's 'global village' with its promise of technology as a religious 'epiphany' has passed" (52).[13] This judgment seems doubtful, because Kroker's own brand of apocalyptic postmodernism begs to be read as a continuation of McLuhanism by other means. Kroker's first book dealt with McLuhan, Harold Innis, and George Grant as the main players in "Canada's principal contribution to North American thought," which is "a highly original, comprehensive, and eloquent discourse on technology" (7) that Kroker extends. In his recent manifesto about the "virtual" trashing of the human, Kroker declares: "Cross McLuhan's nervous system outerized by the media, with Nietzsche's 'last man'... and you get crash theory" (*Data Trash* 143), which is more or less Kroker's theory. Much the same can be said of Baudrillard's ideas about "simulation," "hyperreality," and the "implosion" of the mass media and the masses into "posthistory," which again add up to a version of crash theory (and Baudrillard also acknowledges his indebtedness to McLuhan).[14] In partial contrast to Kroker and Baudrillard, Paul Virilio, while also owing something to McLuhan, offers a technically more detailed version of crash theory, including an analysis of a wide range of postmodern and, perhaps, soon-to-be posthistorical technoscientific developments and their military origins and effects. Virilio sees war as inseparable from the accelerating technologies that war produces; war is, therefore, the future—humanity's or posthumanity's self-destruction, the ultimate "accident" waiting to happen.

For all three crash theorists, and also for McLuhan, the machines that people invent to save labor or time, to create new machines or products, to store and communicate information, and to defend or destroy each other turn out to have huge "unintended consequences," which in cancerous ways soon become main effects.[15] Any machine, of course, can crash: cars do it; airplanes do it; nuclear reactors do it; so do spaceships, computers, stock markets, entire societies, and even empires. According to Virilio: "[The accident] is the intellectual scapegoat of the technological.... To invent the train is to invent derailment; to invent the ship is to invent the shipwreck.... Today the question of the accident arises with new technologies" (*Reader*, 20). For Virilio, an accident is the unintended, usually destructive event that, like its shadow, always and necessarily accompanies an intended event. And the largest of the accidents that technological innovation is hastening mankind toward, "the accident to end all accidents," is the end of the world or at least of reality as humanity has known it, and therefore also "the end of the road for history" (*Open Sky*, 70, 125–126).

Kroker does not exactly predict the absolute end of reality or history, only the end of the "human," cannibalized by the "flesheating" technovirtualization of reality: "Crash theory is . . . post-humanist (not anti-humanist—what is there to be against if the 'human' is dead and now a subject of endless resurrection effects?)" (*Data Trash*, 143). So, too, Baudrillard, in *The Illusion of the End* and elsewhere, declares that "the end" of everything or of history is an "illusion." This is, however, because of the transmogrification of reality into "hyperreality," in which everything is an "illusion" or "simulation." Rejecting "the technological optimism of Marshall McLuhan," Baudrillard nevertheless adopts McLuhan's metaphor of "implosion" to describe how the mass media have swamped reality in the "hyperreality" of "simulations," a process for which "there is no alternative . . . no logical resolution. Only a logical *exacerbation* and a catastrophic resolution," whatever that last phrase means ("Masses" 206, 218; his emphasis).

Baudrillard, Virilio, and Kroker all interpret McLuhan's media theories as optimistic and at least surreptitiously religious (salvation through electricity—see Carey). In doing so, all three downplay or overlook McLuhan's many pessimistic pronouncements, and hence downplay the extent to which he anticipated their versions of crash theory.[16] They also tend to downplay or mask through irony the celebratory (but not optimistic) and at least quasi-religious moments in their own ideas. A secular version of apocalyptic thinking, utopian-dystopian discourse is always double-edged: no matter how bleak or monstrous the futures depicted by science fiction writers, for example, those futures may nevertheless seem exciting and even desirable in contrast to the drab, all-too-normal present. And such fictional versions of "hencity" (Lem, 88) also function as revelations: at last (supposedly), the truth about history and the future stands unveiled, and this too—the apocalyptic act of unveiling—is exciting, positive even in its negativity. So it is with the dismal technofutures or nonfutures predicted by crash theory: the imagination of the smash-up of social reality is more exciting than unspeculative, pedestrian accounts of that reality. This is another reason why Baudrillard, Kroker, and even Virilio aren't neo-Luddites: they are too enthusiastic about the futures they predict and about their own predictive rhetoric.

Crash theory is a form of dystopian thinking that says that technology backfires, and that its accumulating *and* accelerating accidents are either rapidly approaching or have already banged up against the ultimate catastrophe, the end of history or of reality or of the human. The basic premise of crash theory—that machines including communications media have taken over and are now the main causal mechanisms of social and historical change—is McLuhan's premise as well. "The medium is the message" states this idea quite clearly. The premise is at least partly dystopian, moreover, because it represents the human condition as one of profound alienation—one in which, as in George Lucas's first movie, *THX-1138*, humans have indeed become "slaves of the machine."

McLuhan's other most famous claim, that the mass media are "imploding" mankind into a "global village," today seems both prescient and obvious, but again not clearly utopian. Of course, communications technologies have always had the effect of uniting people (even in disagreement) by overcoming the distances between them. As McLuhan points out, this was as true of canoes and smoke signals in Native America as it is of airplanes and telephones in modern America. Over the last twenty years, moreover, discourse about the globalization of capital has accelerated. But is that discourse optimistic or pessimistic? For a transnational capitalist, the answer is positive; for a Marxist or even post-Marxist, the answer is just as clearly negative. Which side, positive or negative, did McLuhan take about the coming "global village"? This is not so clear. At the start of *Understanding Media*, McLuhan writes:

> After three thousand years of specialist explosion and of increasing specialism and alienation in the technological extensions of our bodies, our world has become compressional by dramatic reversal. As electrically contracted, the globe is no more than a village. Electric speed in bringing all social and political functions together in a sudden implosion has heightened human awareness of responsibility to an intense degree. It is this implosive factor that alters the position of the Negro, the teen-ager, and some other groups. They can no longer be *contained*, in the political sense of limited association. They are now *involved* in our lives, as we in theirs, thanks to the electric media. (5)

While this passage sounds optimistic, a "village" isn't necessarily utopia, and "explosion" and "implosion" do not suggest that anyone is in control of the process. McLuhan's terminology suggests instead that the process is both violent and out of control, and perhaps more destructive than constructive.

In *Understanding Media*, there is little that seems utopian and much that seems terrifying about the media's "outering" of mankind's senses through the wiring of the worldbrain or "noosphere." Besides at least worrying about "enslavement" to machinery (even the Indian is the "servomechanism" of his canoe [*Media*, 46]), McLuhan says that any technological "exstension" of the human body is simultaneously a "self-amputation" (45), and goes on to declare that "the new media technologies by which we extend and amplify ourselves constitute huge collective surgery carried out on the social body with complete disregard for antiseptics" (64). One result is contagion, a universal epidemic, and "no society has ever known enough about its actions to have developed immunity to its new extensions or technologies" (64). Prior to this passage in which humanity performs massive surgery on itself without adequate protection, McLuhan also states:

> With the arrival of electric technology, man extended, or set outside himself, a live model of the central nervous system itself . . . a development that suggests a desperate and suicidal autoamputation, as if the central nervous system could no longer depend on the physical organs to be protective buffers against the slings and arrows of outrageous mechanism. (*Media*, 48)

For Hamlet, "the slings and arrows" came from "fortune"; for us, they come from what we ourselves have produced but failed to control, "outrageous mechanism."

If McLuhan's claims about the physical harm done both to the individual body and to the body politic by the electronic "outering" of the "central nervous system" seem less dystopian (and less like a horror movie) than those made by Kroker about the "fate" of "human flesh" in the "electronic abbatoir" (*Data Trash*, 134–135), that is partly because of the former's ambivalence—his shuffling between positive and negative views of technology sometimes within the same paragraph or even sentence. But Kroker also expresses ambivalence, though his may be partly or wholly ironic. The "data trashers" of the Internet, or their machines, or both, according to Kroker, are nothing less than bloodthirsty "vivisectionists, vampiring organic flesh, and draining its fluids into cold streams of telemetry" (134). However, although a virtual electronic cannibalism is the order of the day in postmodern irreality or virreality, it's not all bad. "We are data trash. And it's good," Kroker announces in McLuhanesque, headline fashion. He continues:

> Data trash crawls out of the burned-out wreckage of the body splattered on the information superhighway, and begins the hard task of putting the pieces of the (electronic) body back together again. Not a machine, not nostalgia for vinyl, and most certainly not a happy digital camper, data trash is the critical (e-mail) mind of the twenty-first century. Data trash *loves living* at the violent edge.... *When surf's up on the Net, data trash puts on its electronic body and goes for a spin on the cyber-grid.* (158; my emphasis)

As often with McLuhan, Baudrillard, and Virilio, so with Kroker: it isn't easy or even possible to distinguish between irony and sober assertion. Whether or how any of their works can be read as politically useful social criticism sways in the electronic-eschatological imbalance. Kroker's virtual-apocalyptic rhetoric leaves the fate of the postmodern reader twisting in the windtunnel between being cannibalized by digital virtualization and joining the zombie-cannibal elite of "data trash" (well-educated, neo–white trash, apparently), who enjoy going for spins on their cybercycles through posthistory's flame wars.

One of the unintended consequences of recent technological innovation is crash theory itself. Virilio, Baudrillard, and Kroker are all theorists of "the postmodern condition," while McLuhan is now a liminal figure, posted somewhere between the modern and its post-condition. Of course, "post" today, no matter what it prefixes, sounds an apocalyptic, end-of-millennium note. McLuhan's work in the 1960s and '70s must be read in the context of ideas about "the coming of postindustrial society," to quote Daniel Bell's 1973 title: the movement away from the "Fordist" regime of heavy industry to that of "flexible accumulation," based on electronics and information technologies, and with many jobs located within the "service" rather than the industrial sector of capitalist economies (see also Harvey). These developments in turn underlie the shift to economic globalization and transnational corporations, with the correlative weakening or, in some cases, collapse of modern nation-states (Guéhenno, Miyoshi).

As apocalyptic theorists of postmodernism, Baudrillard, Kroker, and Virilio evoke and sometimes employ other post- terms, including postindustrial, postnational, and posthuman. All of these terms, moreover, crop up in recent debates about posthistory, as in Baudrillard's *The Illusion of the End* and, from a very different perspective, Francis Fukuyama's *The End of History and the Last Man.* I will consider their versions of posthistory more fully in the next chapter. In contrast, it seems to me much more difficult to reject the more thoughtful (and less apocalyptic) claims about the twin birth of postindustrial and postmodern society. Together with these "posts," and in some sense as one of their unintended consequences, I would include "posthuman," if not in Kroker's highly apocalyptic sense, then certainly in Katherine Hayles's more measured definition in *How We Became Posthuman: Virtual Bodies in Cybernetics, Literature, and Informatics.*[17]

Through her careful analysis of the history of cybernetics and computer technologies since World War II, Hayles demonstrates that "the death of the subject" and the arrival of the "posthuman" are not mere theoretical speculations on the part of nutty poststructuralists and postmodern crash theorists, but are instead in large measure the unintended consequences of scientific work on information, artificial intelligence, and electronics. From the time of the Macy Conferences on Cybernetics in the mid-1940s forward, and despite Norbert Wiener's and others' attempts to cling to vestiges of "the liberal humanist subject," a key outcome has been "a new way of looking at human beings. Henceforth, humans were to be seen primarily as information-processing entities who are *essentially* similar to intelligent machines" (Hayles, 7).

The short version of Hayles's argument is that, because of the power and influence of the cybernetics model, which converts—or tries to convert—everything into flows and patterns of information, the liberal humanist subject has turned into the posthuman cyborg. For Hayles, a key difficulty entailed by this transformation is "dematerialization" or "disembodiment." In cybernetics and cyberspace, information is treated as floating free from its material "instantiations," including both the human body and the machine:

> Whether the enabling assumptions for this conception of information occur in information theory, cybernetics, or popular science books...their appeal is clear. Information viewed as pattern and not tied to a particular instantiation is...free to travel across time and space. Hackers are not the only ones who believe that information wants to be free. The great dream and promise of information is that it can be free from the material constraints that govern the mortal world. Marvin Minsky precisely expressed this dream when...he suggested it would soon be possible to extract human memories from the brain and import them, intact and unchanged, to computer disks. The clear implication is that if we can become the information we have constructed, we can achieve effective immortality. (13)

What are the costs of the cybernetic vision of disembodied information? Even if she does not buy into the more apocalyptic ideas of crash theorists such as Kroker and Virilio, Hayles attributes a profound and pervasive cultural alienation to the radical separation of information from material bodies, specificity, and rootedness. Both the alienation and the danger are strikingly evident in Minsky's claim. The "erasure" of the human body (or, in another now familiar formulation, its refashioning as cyborg through what Haraway calls "the informatics of domination") entails the erasure of older versions of human nature, including "the liberal humanist subject." Hayles doesn't think that waging a rearguard struggle to retain these older versions of identity can stop the conversion of humanity into posthumanity. At the same time, "if we want to contest what these technologies [of information and virtual reality] signify, we need histories that show the erasures that went into the creation of virtuality, as well as visions arguing for the importance of embodiment." Hayles continues:

> Once we understand the complex interplays that went into creating the condition of virtuality, we can demystify our progress toward virtuality and see it as the result of historically specific negotiations rather than of the irresistible force of technological determinism....We can acquire resources with which to

rethink the assumptions underlying virtuality, and we can recover a sense of the virtual that fully recognizes the importance of the embodied processes constituting the lifeworld of human beings. (20)

Perhaps. But my guess is that the work of most of my colleagues in our new School of Informatics will go in a contrary direction—Minsky's direction—and will lead to the creation of ever-better machines and "information flows," ever-increasing profits for the high tech industries and perhaps (though this is hardly crystal clear) for the university, but also the increasing subordination of both human bodies and human beings, as well as their educations, to those machines and flows. We are indeed becoming (and have been since the takeoff of the first industrial revolution in the late eighteenth century) "slaves of the machine."

Apocalypse 2001
or, What Happens
after Posthistory?

9

What seest thou else
In the dark backward and abysm of time?
—Shakespeare, *The Tempest*

While they may worry about the annoyance of upgrading and about
entropy and information overload, I doubt that most of my colleagues in
informatics are interested in Marshall McLuhan, much less in crash theory
or even in arguments about "posthistory" and "posthumanity." Yet I hope
that they will read *The University in Ruins* and *How We Became Posthuman.*
Katherine Hayles offers a history of cybernetics and its byproduct, "posthumanity," insisting as she does so that history matters: if "we" expect to do
anything about "disembodiment" and technoscientific alienation, we must
operate within and through historical understanding. Bill Readings, too,
operates much of the time as a historian, although he seems more inclined
than Hayles to accept than to contest the thought that history, along with
the university, today lies in "ruins."

Readings often applies the adjective "posthistorical" to the university.
He does so in part because he wants to avoid celebratory notions about
having progressed beyond modernity, and in part because he believes the

university is no longer concerned in any significant way with history. But his use of "posthistorical" means that his argument invites comparison with the highly celebratory "end of history" thesis offered by Francis Fukuyama and his seconders: transnational capital has triumphed over its rivals; there is nothing to be done now except to allow the free play of market forces to usher in a utopian era of prosperity and general if not absolute equality for all. Yet nowhere does Readings express Fukuyama's faith in the benign workings of the marketplace, and "posthistory" for him is obviously dystopian. Because I believe, with Hayles, both that history's clock isn't about to run down and that historical understanding has a crucial role to play in criticizing and perhaps changing the world (including the university), I will end *Who Killed Shakespeare?* with a critique of current theories about "posthistory."

From Fukuyama's neoconservative perspective, though minor social change will continue, history in the old-fashioned sense of major political, ideological, and military conflict has ended with the triumph of liberal democracy and capitalism over its rivals, fascism-Nazism and communism. From the postmodernist perspectives of Jean-François Lyotard and Jean Baudrillard, what has ended is perhaps not history as such, but historiography, or the ability to explain social change: the "metanarratives" that used to underwrite traditional historical accounts have lost credibility or lapsed into mass-mediated "simulation." Matched against these endings of history are the critical perspectives of a variety of theorists and critics, including both Hayles and Readings, for whom the struggles of history and the necessity of developing rational accounts of those struggles have clearly not ended in a "postmodern sublime" or phony transcendence through mass-mediated "hyperreality," much less in some imagined final triumph of capitalism. In *Posthistoire: Has History Come to an End?*, moreover, Lutz Niethammer demonstrates that the ideas about "posthistory" of Baudrillard, Lyotard, and Fukuyama are not new, but themselves have a lengthy history extending back at least to Hegel. Like repeated prophecies of Armageddon or the Second Coming, the longer the history of the idea of posthistory, the more suspect that idea becomes.

Pointing out that the word *posthistoire* was originally a German rather than French neologism, Niethammer traces a major aspect of the history of posthistory in a lineage of mainly German intellectuals, stretching back to Hegel, who have proclaimed or predicted the end of history not through some grand, destructive apocalypse such as nuclear annihilation or ecological breakdown, but through the triumph of bourgeois liberalism and economic progress.[1] According to Hegel, the emergence of the democratic nation-state coupled with capitalism was the culmination of World History. But was this necessarily a positive development? For the intellectuals whom Niethammer surveys, the answers are variously negative. From the perspective of *posthistoire* theory, technological, bureaucratic rationalization (that is, modernization) entails the reification and massification of all values, meanings, and cultural forms. Capitalism commodifies everything, reduces all values to the monetary. Industrialism does not liberate through the factory system, but instead converts society into a gigantic factory (or, after Foucault, prison-house—the universalized "panopticon" of the "carceral society"). And democratization coupled with mechanical reproduction levels all cultural hierarchies and distinctions of authority (Ortega y Gasset's "revolt of the masses").

As Niethammer indicates (31–32), in Max Weber's famous "iron cage" passage that concludes *The Protestant Ethic and the Spirit of Capitalism*, modernity and the forces that drive it—capitalism, democratization, industrialization—defeat themselves through their very success. Weber does not quite identify progress with decadence, as does Nietzsche, but progress is nevertheless its own undoing, leading to a rationalized, disenchanted social order governed by experts and bureaucrats, the soulless "last men." "The posthistory diagnosis sees the social formation as marked to its core by an objective, power-structured process of standardization, which no longer promises any qualitative movement but is moving towards petrification" (Niethammer, 148). According to this gloomy diagnosis, among whose originators must be counted Edmund Burke and Joseph de Maistre as well as Hegel, bourgeois economics and democracy lead inexorably to the reign of mediocrity or worse. In "posthistory," a "standardized humanity" will "treat otherness as pure deviation and place it in the hands of doctors or the police—a one-dimensional normality in the face of which specificity would disappear" (8). Niethammer's phrase "one-dimensional normality" echoes Herbert Marcuse's *One-Dimensional Man* (1964) but also Foucault's "tyranny of the Norm" in *Discipline and*

Punish (1977). Though many of the diagnosticians of *posthistoire* have been, like de Maistre, reactionaries whose politics were more or less consonant with fascism and Nazism, Niethammer stresses that roughly the same thesis of an "end of history" in the leveling entropy of mass culture and society can be found among the Frankfurt School Marxists (Marcuse, Adorno, Benjamin) as well as among postmodernists (Lyotard, Baudrillard).

The "posthistory diagnosis," Niethammer argues, is less an objective assessment of the social and cultural developments making for modernity (or modernity as mass society) than it is the shared "negative utopia" of intellectuals across the political spectrum reacting to their own "marginalization" (148). Despair at either their impotence to resist or their complicity with the march of modernity that has produced, among other horrors, two world wars, Stalinism, and the Holocaust, has led many intellectuals to follow what Ernst Jünger called the *Waldgang* or "forest way"—that is, to wash their hands of history, to imagine themselves as somehow escaping or transcending it (68–69). For many intellectuals, Niethammer believes, the "posthistory diagnosis" has been "a specific form of projective self-exoneration" (143). He especially measures "how strongly the hopelessness of the posthistorical perspective is bound up with the presumption, tragedy and decline of educated middle-class individualism in the political practice of the wartime years" (85) for such thinkers as Jünger, Heidegger, Carl Schmitt, Hendrik de Man, Bertrand de Jouvenel, and Arnold Gehlen. These intellectuals, all more or less sympathetic to Nazism, developed theories of "the end of history" based upon a despairing view of the cultural entropy identified with modern mass society. But a version on the left of Jünger's *Waldgang* is Adorno's "Grand Hotel Abyss" (Jay, 18); though Niethammer does not say so, *posthistoire* theory reaches one of its philosophical culminations in Adorno's *Negative Dialectics* (1966), with its bleak claims that "the unity of world history which animates the philosopher to trace it as the path of the world spirit is the unity of terror rolling over mankind" (341) and that "all post-Auschwitz culture, including its urgent critique, is garbage" (367).

Agreeing with Niethammer, Perry Anderson in *A Zone of Engagement* also notes that "the idea of a closure of history has a more complicated pedigree than is often assumed" (285). But neither he nor Niethammer explore how that idea has been central to liberal political and economic theory. Both present Antoine-Augustin Cournot as, along with Hegel, one of the founders of *posthistoire* theory, and Cournot was also "one of the ancestors of neo-classical economics" especially in regard to price theory (Anderson, 294). However, from Adam Smith forward, liberal economics has modeled end-of-history scenarios. In his *Principles of Political Economy*, for instance, John Stuart Mill speculates anxiously about the culmination of social and economic progress in what he calls, echoing Smith, "the stationary state." Mill writes: "The doctrine that, to however distant a time incessant struggling may put off our doom, the progress of society must 'end in shallows and in miseries,' far from being, as many people still believe, a wicked invention of Mr. Malthus, was either expressly or tacitly affirmed by his most distinguished predecessors" (2:753). In *The Wealth of Nations*, Smith himself had distinguished "progressive" societies from "stationary" and "declining" ones: "The progressive state is in reality the cheerful and the hearty state to all the different orders of [any] society. The stationary is dull; the declining melancholy" (81).

For Smith, China was a key example of a society which, "though it may perhaps stand still, does not seem to go backwards" (73). Because Smith identified history with progress (that is, with perpetual economic expansion), much as Hegel identified it with the forward movement of the World Spirit, a society like China which had once been "progressive" but had subsequently become "stationary" for centuries was in a sense posthistorical—a premonition of what Lester Thurow, with the 1970s downturn of the American economy in mind, called a "zero-sum society." Between Smith and Thurow, liberal economics has been haunted by the specter of what would come after progress and therefore after meaningful history. Smith didn't envisage such an ending for Britain or any of the other "progressive" nation-states of western Europe and North America, but Malthus's theory of the inevitable limits that population imposes on economic growth, coupled with the ideas of the falling rate of profits and diminishing returns in agriculture elaborated by David Ricardo and others, pointed inexorably to a social condition after progress that approximates the dystopic visions of the *posthistoire* theorists.[2]

Though Mill was not alone among liberal economists in speculating about an inevitable end to progress—that is, history —in a stationary state, he was unusual in regarding that prospect as anything other than dismal.

183

Of course, the ends-of-capitalism predicted by the utopian socialists and by Marx were also versions of stationary states arising, in a sense, after history. Mill was close to agreeing with them when he wrote that the stationary state might be, "on the whole, a very considerable improvement on our present condition":

> I confess I am not charmed with the ideal of life held out by those who think that the normal state of human beings is that of struggling to get on; that the trampling, crushing, elbowing, and treading on each other's heels, which form the existing type of social life, are the most desirable lot of human kind, or anything but the disagreeable symptoms of one of the phases of industrial progess. (2:754)

The "struggle for riches," Mill opined, had succeeded "the struggle of war," and this was better than that human talents and energies "should rust and stagnate" (2:754). Nevertheless, the ideal social condition would be that in which, "while no one is poor, no one desires to be richer, nor has any reason to fear being thrust back, by the efforts of others to push themselves forward" (2:754). Besides, "a stationary condition of capital and population" did not necessarily mean a "stationary state of human improvement" (2:756); Mill imagines a condition beyond war and beyond the "struggle for riches" in which all individuals would be free to pursue their own mental, moral, and cultural "improvement" without impediment (2:756).

This genealogy of a liberal branch of posthistorical speculation is significant in part because much of the current debate has been aroused not by Niethammer's *posthistoire* intellectuals, nor even by the stimulus of the related endgame themes of postindustrialism and postmodernism, but by renewed liberal and neoconservative articulations of what Smith and Mill called "the stationary state." Here Thurow takes his place. More recently (1989), Francis Fukuyama, a student of Allan Bloom's, published a much-debated essay in *The National Interest* called "The End of History." Three years later, Fukuyama expanded the essay and responded to some of its critics in *The End of History and the Last Man.* Though contending that the recent apparent victories of liberal democracy and "free market" capitalism over their major rivals, especially fascism-Nazism and communism,

184

represent "the end of history" in the sense of major, global ideological, political, and military conflict, Fukuyama does not draw on Mill and classical economics. Instead, he indicates his indebtedness to several of the *posthistoire* theorists whom Niethammer analyzes—Weber and Nietzsche among them, but above all Hegel and one of Hegel's most influential twentieth-century interpreters, Alexandre Kojève.

Both in his 1989 essay and in the later book, Fukuyama operates as a sort of reformed Hegelian, the reforms consisting mostly, as Fukuyama's critics have frequently pointed out, of ignoring or rejecting many of the difficulties in Hegel and much of the pessimism in *posthistoire* theory after Hegel. Thus, in *Specters of Marx*, Jacques Derrida calls Fukuyama's book "the grammar school exercise of a young, industrious, but come-lately reader of Kojève," characterized by a "sophisticated naiveté" and a neoconservative "evangelism" (56–62). Fukuyama, according to Derrida, offers no improvement over "the classics of the end" that formed the staple of Derrida's own philosophical education in the 1950s: "the canon of the modern apocalypse (end of History, end of Man, end of Philosophy, Hegel, Marx, Nietzsche, Heidegger, with their Kojevian codicil and the codicils of Kojève himself)" (15). For Derrida, if Fukuyama has succeeded in proving anything, it isn't that history has ended with the collapse of Marxism and the triumph of liberalism-capitalism, but that the "problematics" engaged by "the Marxist tradition," as opposed to those "Marxist dogmatics linked to the apparatuses" of a now toppled "orthodoxy," remain more urgently relevant than ever (64).

Alex Callinicos also contends, in his response to Fukuyama, that the collapse of the socialist regimes in eastern Europe and the Soviet Union has no bearing on the relevance of Marx's critique both of capitalism and of Hegelianism (19). And Niethammer treats Fukuyama as an intellectual lightweight, much of whose interpretation of Hegel relies on Kojève, a major *posthistoire* speculator (Kojève's charismatic lectures on Hegel in Paris in the 1930s influenced many French intellectuals including Georges Bataille, André Breton, Jacques Lacan, and Maurice Merleau-Ponty).[3] Fukuyama deletes much of the terror and violence that both Kojéve and Hegel associated with the end of history (for Hegel, that ending had its specific violent beginnings in Robespierre, the Reign of Terror, and Napoleon). Fukuyama also overlooks Kojève's Stalinism, at least at the time of his 1930s lectures (Callinicos, 27). Fukuyama's *The End of History and the Last Man*, Niethammer says, thus gives "the impression of a kind of bandwagon operetta, in which the latest world model—the combination of consumer capitalism and liberal democracy—peacefully travels the globe and vanquishes the evil empire" (91, n. 12).

Against the pessimistic, even nihilistic tradition of *posthistoire* that Niethammer maps, Fukuyama offers an optimistic, cheery apocalypse: the "good news has come" (Fukuyama, xiii). This "evangelism," as Derrida calls it, consists precisely of the triumph of those forces—capitalism, democratization, industrialization—that Weber, Jünger, Adorno, Heidegger, and most other *posthistoire* thinkers have read as causing the end of (meaningful) struggle, the collapse of ethical and social distinction, the demise of high culture and the arts, and the massified "petrification" of the unique, the different, the nonconforming. On one level, Fukuyama seems to be doing little more than Mill in translating gloomy speculations about the coming stationary state into optimistic terms. But Fukuyama is aware of some of the reasons for pessimism in the *posthistoire* tradition. Throughout his book, he relies upon Hegel's master-slave narrative, the version of *ur*-history from *The Phenomenology of the Spirit* that Kojève also focused upon in his *Lectures*, and more especially upon the thesis that the desire for "recognition" motivates social, cultural, and political behavior just as powerfully as does the economic desire to fulfill basic physical needs. The model of "universal" human nature that Fukuyama borrows from Hegel/Kojève is thus, as Callinicos (31) and Derrida (62) note, a dualistic one. History cannot be explained solely in economic terms, as in orthodox Marxism; it also has its seemingly irrational side, which, Fukuyama contends, boils down to the craving for "recognition" by both individuals and societies.

This thesis, which separates economics (based on supposedly rational self-interest) from politics (based on supposedly irrational striving for recognition), allows Fukuyama to explain war, nationalism, and indeed, at least by implication, most of what goes on under the rubric of culture in noneconomic terms. The same tactic allowed Joseph Schumpeter to explain modern imperialism and war as the results not of capitalism, but of the atavistic survival of aristocratic militarism and vainglory, an argument that Fukuyama uncritically recycles (260–265). As good free marketeers from Richard Cobden through Schumpeter down to Milton Friedman have maintained, let capitalism alone—practice free trade—and economics will eradicate war, imperialism, and other vestiges of the feudal and barbaric past including poverty. Fukuyama overlooks Hegel's warnings about capitalistic enterprise unregulated by the state—warnings that clearly foreshadow Marx and Marxism. But, then, Fukuyama also seems unable to learn anything from earlier optimistic prophets of the final victory of liberal capitalism over its enemies (including its own internal contradictions). "On the very eve of World War I," he declares, "Norman Angell published... *The Great Illusion*, in which he argued that free trade had rendered territorial aggrandizement obsolete, and that war had become economically irrational" (4–5). That Fukuyama is repeating precisely the same optimistic argument about the global political benefits of capitalism does not faze him; it's just that Angell's prediction was premature.

But, even in the absence of aristocracies, the seemingly irrational craving for recognition that, according to Fukuyama, underlies cultural and political activity will continue to pose a major problem for posthistorical societies. Once liberal democracy has been universally installed, and once free market capitalism has worked its happy miracle of banishing poverty, will everyone be happy in the posthistorical society of equals? Fukuyama thinks that the answer *may* be yes, but only if "we" are able to figure out new, pacific ways to satisfy the apparently innate craving for recognition.

> Hegel... understood that the need to feel pride in one's humanness would not necessarily be satisfied by the "peace and prosperity" of the end of history. Men [*sic*] would face the constant danger of degenerating from citizens to mere *bourgeois*, and feeling contempt for themselves in the process. The ultimate crucible of citizenship therefore was and would remain the willingness to die for one's country: the state would have to require military service and continue to fight wars. (329)

But it's possible to imagine a number of nonviolent outlets to avoid the "boredom" (330) and self-contempt of the coming universal bourgeoisification of the world: sports, distinction in the arts, and above all (and here, no doubt, can be heard the voice of Fukuyama's RAND Corporation affiliation) success in business ("It is in the very design of democratic capitalist countries like the United States that the most talented and ambitious

187

natures should tend to go into business, rather than into politics, the military, universities, or the church" [316]). In other words, the new universal bourgeoisie (and of course, in the United States "we" know that "we" are always already middle class, unless "we" happen to be black, Hispanic, Native American, unemployed, homeless, incarcerated, or single mothers on welfare) will be able to overcome what Nietzsche for one saw as our slavish qualities by striving to be more bourgeois than ever. In the brave New World Order of eternal peace, plenty, and boredom, "we" will all struggle together to be the best members of the bourgeoisie that "we" can be, and the very best of us will successfully struggle to become CEOs of Fortune 500 companies.

Fukuyama believes, moreover, that most of the world is headed toward the same embourgeoisement as the goal of "universal history" (for his defense of Kant's and Hegel's notions of "universal history," see 55–70). This thesis that the entire world (or the historical portion of it, at any rate?) is headed toward the same, universal happy ending in liberal-capitalist peace and harmony then leads to the remarkable penultimate paragraph of his book:

> Rather than a thousand shoots blossoming into as many different flowering plants, mankind will come to seem like a long wagon train strung out along a road. Some wagons will be pulling into town sharply and crisply, while others will be bivouacked back in the desert, or else stuck in ruts in the final pass over the mountains.

So much for the unevenness of global capitalist development, Bonanza-style, but Fukuyama's westernizing fantasy continues:

> *Several wagons, attacked by Indians, will have been set aflame and abandoned along the way.* There will be a few wagoneers who, stunned by the battle, will have lost their sense of direction . . . while one or two wagons will get tired of the journey and decide to set up permanent camps at particular points back along the road. (338; my emphasis)

But most of the wagon train will make it over "the final mountain range," despite obstacles and "Indians," to the Happy Valley that Fukuyama names "the end of history." In offering this Boy Scout analogy for "universal history" and its upbeat ending, Fukuyama does not say who, especially in a post-Nazi, postcommunist world when swords are supposedly turning into ploughshares, his belligerent "Indians" symbolize, much less ask himself why his posthistorical vision takes the form of a John Wayne western. Because he worries a lot about Iraq, Iran, and Islamic fundamentalists, perhaps the wild Indians symbolize those apparent antagonists to the universalization (i.e., globalizing standardization) of westernizing capitalism? But what can Fukuyama possibly be thinking about actual, non-Hollywood Native Americans, as opposed to the last of the Mohicans? Are *they* part of the wagon train headed to Happy Valley, or not?

One unpleasant aspect of Hegel's version of "universal history" that Fukuyama minimizes is the great philosopher's clear and repeated insistence that World History did not include everybody: it was only "universal" for those peoples and nation-states in its vanguard; the vast majority of past and present societies had fallen or would fall by the wayside. Many societies and cultures—whole continents, in fact—were not part of the World Spirit's master plan. Thus, the entire continent of Africa lay beyond history's pale:

> Africa proper, as far as History goes back, has remained . . . shut up; it is the Gold-land compressed within itself—the land of childhood, which lying beyond the day of self-conscious history, is enveloped in the dark mantle of Night. (Hegel, 91)

History is "universal," Hegel believes, for *us Europeans*, but not for Africans, in relation to whom "we must quite give up the principle which naturally accompanies all *our* ideas—the category of Universality" (93). Large sections of Asia are also "unhistorical," though in China, Hegel declares, "History begins" (112). But just as Adam Smith had contended, Hegel's China has long since ceased being historical: with India and Persia, it has fallen into the "immovable" condition of oriental despotism, while the World Spirit has rolled westward, taking its wagonloads of rationality and progress—that is, history—with it. Today "China and India lie, as it were, still outside the World's History" (116), waiting for European conquest and imperialism to put them back on the high road of Reason. Perhaps the wild "Indians" who attack the wagons in Fukuyama's fantasy of history's end will never be reasonable from "our" perspective—in which case, no more than for Hegel will history, even the history of liberal capitalism, ever be "universal."

For both the eager student (Fukuyama) and the master-philosopher (Hegel), moreover, the unchanging notion of what a genuine (historical) wagon looks like is a nation-state on the European model. But how can history become pacifically "universal" without getting beyond this short-sighted, unevenly disintegrating, and—if modern history teaches any lessons—dangerous model? Fukuyama ignores the very different genre of endgame stories that speculate about the decline and eventual demise of nation-states, as in Jean-Marie Guéhenno's *The End of the Nation-State*.[4] The collapse of the communist regimes in eastern Europe and the Soviet Union, which Fukuyama understands as the triumph of democracy and capitalism, is an obvious symptom. The rise of the European Union is another, which, contra Fukuyama, cannot be understood merely as the development of a loose federalism among the free-standing nation-states of the modern era. Transnational capitalism is, moreover, a major factor in the weakening of all nation-state structures: "it is now the mobile private corporations, and not the geographically rooted nation-states," writes Masao Miyoshi, "that drive the world economy" ("Sites," 63; see also Miyoshi, "A Borderless World?"). According to Richard Barnet and John Cavenagh, "as national economies become increasingly intertwined, nations are breaking up in many different ways, and no alternative community is yet on the horizon" (22). Together with globalizing communications technologies, transnational capital is producing a "networked world" in which "the only universality that remains [is] that of money" (Guéhenno, 108). Overpopulation accompanied by the mass migrations of peoples, no longer ordinarily by wagon train, are further eroding national boundaries and legitimacies, as are separatist nationalisms within many nation-states: Chechen, Quebecois, Kurdish, Kashmiri, Tamil, Palestinian, Irish, Basque—even white supremacist and states' rights advocates within the United States. These processes, both globalizing and localizing, are weakening national governments and arousing new demands for international or postnational structures of law and order.

"The nation is no longer the natural framework of security, and we are beginning to dream again, so far unsuccessfully, of a world government"

(Guéhenno, 14; see also Miyoshi, "Sites" 72). But the thought of what comes after the nation-state—of what *should* come after the nation-state—does not enter Fukuyama's imagination anymore than it did Hegel's. Fukuyama devotes barely six pages out of four hundred to the United Nations, and then only to identify it with "the manifest failure of the League of Nations to provide collective security" which "has led to the general discrediting of Kantian internationalism and of international law in general" (281). True, Fukuyama believes that Kant was right (just as he believes that Hegel was right). But the New World Order will be based on the collaboration of "democratic" nation-states all practicing "free market" capitalism. And these free-wheeling prairie schooners of the future will be all the more secure in their wagonhood because of their universal practice of supposedly democratic capitalism. (Presumably the surviving "Indians" will be happy on their reservations and maybe even allowed a bit of symbolic status, like the Navaho Nation.) But Fukuyama does not begin to imagine a postnational world order, anymore than he avoids the wagon train versus Indians fantasy: his ideas consist mainly of a watered-down Hegelianism filtered through Allan Bloom, Kojève, Reaganomics, and Hollywood.

Fukuyama's "end of history" thesis is a variation of the "end of ideology" thesis offered by Daniel Bell and others as early as the 1950s (Bell, 1960). Clearly, too, declarations of the emergence of "postindustrial society" (Bell again in 1973, among others) and of the transformation of modernity into postmodernity are closely related themes (see Harvey, 121–200). All of these post- themes converge in Jean Baudrillard's recent exercise in "posthistorical" prophetic journalism, *The Illusion of the End*. As usual, Baudrillard behaves as if he has gotten to the end first, surveyed it, and returned to report to the rest of us that it is an illusion: it isn't going to happen because it can't happen, or anyway if it can it has already happened, so that the sense of its being about to happen is an illusion.

History, Baudrillard opines, "vanished" (which may or may not mean ended) some time ago, perhaps in the 1980s. Therefore, those who, like Fukuyama, announce its future demise are behind the times. "The Great Incinerators of history" have already done their work, and all that arises from the "ashes" now is the simulacral "Phoenix of post-modernity" (27). And yet there has been no "final solution," because much of the past "is today recyclable"—the past is repeating itself at least in the Disneyfied simulations of hyperreality, and therefore "*History will not come to an end*" (27; his emphasis). So Baudrillard has it both ways at once—history ended, vanished, or maybe reversed itself (10) awhile ago, and yet history "will not come to an end"—even as he seeks to trump, in his exorbitant way, both the gloomy and the celebrant prophets of *posthistoire*.

According to Baudrillard, there are more ways that history has ended than are dreamt of in the philosophies of Fukuyama and the *posthistoire* pessimists. Those ways include:

(1) "the acceleration of modernity," especially through the mass media, to the point of "'escape velocity,' with the result that we have flown free of the referential sphere of the real and of history" (1);

(2) the emergence of the "dense body" of "the 'silent majorities'" or "the masses," for whom history is meaningless or beside the point—their only function is the refusal of meaning (3–4);[5]

(3) meaning and liberty, which were once historical, have been traded in for mere consumer comforts and empty leisure—the Disneyfication of everything (118 and *passim*);

(4) if history means the dialectic in the Hegelian-Marxist sense, it no longer exists because "capital has cannibalized all negativity," eliminating—"parodistically," at least—all contradiction (52);

(5) if history is a linear sequence of events "each engendering the other by cause and effect" (7), it has vanished because time is no longer (if it ever was) linear, or anyway we can no longer be sure that it is linear;

(6) for some mysterious or at least unspecified reason, "at some point in the 1980s, history took a turn in the opposite direction" so that now, if it runs at all, it runs "in reverse" (10–13);

(7) if it hasn't been dissipated through the "centrifugal expansion of communication" and therefore lost in the infinity of meaningless "news" and televised chatter, then it has either been "deep-frozen" or incinerated in "the concentration camps" (29);

(8) because the media and the masses both operate by a logic or illogic of their own having nothing to do with either human or divine agency, there can be no such thing as meaningful history ("No one is

responsible. It is all an effect of the infernal cycle of credibility"—whatever that may be: faith? [57]);

(9) anyway, if history has involved the struggle to create order, coherence, or goodness in the world, it has always already been doomed to failure by something like original sin—what Baudrillard calls "the transparence of Evil" (47);

(10) but there is no such thing as original sin because there is no God and therefore no absolute categories of good and evil to give meaning to history or human experience ("God, for his part, if he exists, does not believe in his existence" [92]);

(11) "in the concentration camps . . . it was death that was exterminated," though perhaps history has ended because "we" are already dead (98–99);

(12) but history cannot end because "history itself has become interminable" (116);

(13) and anyway history no longer exists because causality and causes have vanished—"nothing exists now but effects" (117).

At the end of his essay, Baudrillard offers the final apocalyptic scoop that he has brought back from his tour of history's illusory endings: "The illusion of our history opens on to *the greatly more radical illusion of the world*" (122; his emphasis).

Baudrillard presents his contradictory ideas about "the end of history" like so many prophetic headlines (the news of the news to come, so to speak) perhaps in imitation of his Canadian mentor, Marshall McLuhan, who in The *Gutenberg Galaxy* included such headlines as: "Schizophrenia May Be a Necessary Consequence of Literacy," and: "Heidegger Surf-Boards along on the Electronic Wave as Triumphantly as Descartes Rode the Mechanical Wave" (22, 248). For Baudrillard, too, postmodernist theory takes the simulacral form of the evening news with its regular doses of "information as catastrophe" (56). This is not to say that Baudrillard isn't wittily parodying or satirizing something-or-other: perhaps the evening news, perhaps *posthistoire* theory, perhaps himself. For all their incoherence, his claims about history are best read as ironic, often sharply observant aphorisms on a Wildean or Nietzschean model. For example:

The ironic thing about the end, is that communism should have collapsed exactly as Marx had foreseen for capitalism, with the same suddenness.... The fact that he got the victor wrong in no way detracts from the exactness of Marx's analysis; it merely adds the objective irony which was lacking.... It is as though some evil genie had substituted the one for the other—communism for capitalism—at the last moment.... An admirable division of labour: Capital has done communism's work and communism has died in Capital's place. (51–52)

Later in his essay, Baudrillard has this to say about racism, difference, and computers:

The problem of Frankenstein... is that he has no Other and craves otherness. This is the problem of racism. But our computers also crave otherness. They are autistic, bachelor machines: the source of their suffering and the cause of their vengeance is the fiercely tautological nature of their own language. (109)

These passages are representative of the postmodern theorist as satirist. In a hyperreal or virtual world where only simulations matter, irony or, perhaps, what Peter Sloterdijk has called "cynical reason" takes the place of evidence and logic. Social and cultural theory becomes, as it were, virtual theory, just as illusory and Disneyfied as everything else.

Much of Baudrillard's willful incoherence arises because he makes no distinction between historiography and historical reality. He seems often to be talking only at the level of the text or the signifier. From a poststructuralist angle, perhaps this makes sense: just as for Derrida there is "nothing beyond the text," so for Baudrillard there is nothing beyond simulation. "The fact that we are leaving history to move into the realm of simulation is merely a consequence of the fact that history itself has always, deep down, been an immense simulation model" (7). Baudrillard declares that it has become impossible to write coherent narratives about the past because they are swamped or somehow rendered incoherent by the mass media, "the news" (6); moreover, all narratives, since signifiers supposedly only refer to other signifiers, have always already been simulations, illusions, or fictions.

In relation to all explanatory and philosophical models of the past, Lyotard has famously defined "postmodern" as "incredulity toward metanarratives" (*Condition*, xxiv). The grand, totalizing systems—Christianity, Hegelianism, Marxism, Liberalism, Comtean Positivism, Social Darwinism, Imperialism, Fascism/Nazism—have all been contradicted by recent events. Lyotard includes in the wreckage the items that Fukuyama attempts to rescue: Hegel's "universal history" combined with liberal political and economic faith in progress. Of course Lyotard must adopt a meta-narrational stance in order to judge past metanarratives to be defunct, a performative contradiction that he himself recognizes ("Universal," xxiii–xxv). But as with Baudrillard, and precisely because he sees himself as operating within a hermetically sealed system of signification (that is, within "the prison-house of language") it remains uncertain whether Lyotard is making claims about historical reality in the form of an actual "postmodern condition," or instead only about how historical reality can or cannot be apprehended and represented.

Baudrillard and Lyotard both belong in the company of *posthistoire* intellectuals whom Niethammer analyzes. Niethammer mentions Lyotard only in footnotes, but he has more to say, mostly negative, about Baudrillard (see especially 28–30). Yet for neither Baudrillard nor Lyotard is it clear whether they are proclaiming or predicting "the end of history" or only the end of coherent ways of understanding history. For both, history in the sense of historiography has ended because it is no longer possible to explain the past (except, perhaps, minimally, in the form of micronarratives or of ironizing aphorisms). Their versions of postmodernist theory therefore also point to what they see as the collapse or bankruptcy of the Enlightenment project of modernity. But what seems especially to have collapsed isn't modernity in the form of capitalism; rather, it is modernity in the form of social-critical theories and utopianisms based upon Enlightenment rationality. When Lyotard speaks of the "defaillancy of modernity" ("Universal," 319), he doesn't appear to be thinking of capitalism, though he is thinking of liberal as well as Marxist theories of universal progress. In this regard, Derrida's insistence, no matter how qualified by poststructuralist "hauntology," on the continued relevance of the "problematics" of "the Marxist tradition" is clearly antithetical to the irrationalism and perhaps nihilism involved in postmodernist theory à la Baudrillard and Lyotard. According to Christopher Norris, "Derrida has been at some pains to dissociate his project from the kind of irrationalist or nihilist outlook which takes it for granted—in Baudrillard's manner—that truth and reason are obsolete values, overtaken by...postmodern 'hyper-reality'" (*Uncritical Theory*, 17). (This is one of the reasons why it is inaccurate to identify postmodernism with poststructuralism.)

"The loss of the modern we" is, for Lyotard ("Universal," 319), virtually the end of social critique because it is the end of philosophy—an ending also announced by some neopragmatists such as Richard Rorty in the American context—presumably including an end even to the forms of postmodernist theory like Lyotard's. In my view, however, postmodernist and/or neopragmatist skepticism, even when couched in terms of a seemingly satiric irony or cynical reason like Baudrillard's, isn't nearly skeptical enough about capitalism. "One measure of postmodernism's retrograde stance," writes Norris, "is the way that its proponents have...consigned the whole legacy of critical-emancipatory thought to the dustbin of outworn 'Enlightenment' ideas" (196). On one level, Fukuyama's resurrection of the Hegelian metanarrative obviously conflicts with the postmodern thesis of the bankruptcy of metanarratives. But on another, whether history ends because of the triumph of liberalism-capitalism or because of the demise of metanarratives carries the same meaning: the affirmation of the economic-political-social status quo, if not as the best of all possible worlds, then as the only possible world. The neo-Hegelian Fukuyama can hardly be charged with attacking the Enlightenment "legacy of critical-emancipatory thought." But his "end of history" thesis leads in the same direction as do Baudrillard's and Lyotard's projects, to the rejection of those versions of "critical-emancipatory thought" (above all, of Marxism) that have, in both the past and the present, opposed capitalism and its liberal-ideological underwritings that see no need to regulate or reform, much less abolish, the regime of the same. Both Fukuyama and Baudrillard, whether wittingly or not, express what Nietzsche excoriated as the "admiration for 'the power of history'" which in practice transforms every moment into a naked admiration for success and leads to an idolatry of the factual" (*Untimely Meditations*, 105).[6] Perhaps the wild "Indians" who attack Fukuyama's wagon train of history are just such critical intellectuals as Marx, Nietzsche, and their descendants, present-day Marxists, feminists, environmentalists, and so on. Meanwhile, westward ho go the wagons, headed for Disneyland.

For Baudrillard and Lyotard as well as for Fukuyama, capitalism seems to be the new idealism—*credo quia absurdum*—sublime, transcendent, unopposed and unopposable. At best, critique for Baudrillard has degenerated into cynical reason's self-mockery. The "postmodern sublime" comes to mean capitalism without opposition and without limits (although even Adam Smith understood that it had limits). Irony permits Baudrillard an ambivalence through which he seems, like Lyotard, simultaneously to celebrate and to mourn the inexorable forward march or forced march of transnational capitalism. And Fukuyama has his moments of doubt and even pessimism (see Callinicos, 37). Moreover, ironic ambivalence seems philosophically and perhaps even politically preferable to the nonironic, quasi-religious faith in the powers-that-be that Fukuyama expresses in his more recent contribution to capitalist theodicy, *Trust: The Social Virtues and the Creation of Prosperity* (for the religious dimension of his argument, see especially the final chapter, "The Spiritualization of Economic Life").[7]

Even if one has lost faith in the eternal progress promised by capitalism, if one has also lost faith in critical metanarratives such as Marxism, capitalism must appear either triumphant, as it does to Fukuyama, or mysteriously purgatorial and knowable only through its effects, as it does to Baudrillard. Like God (whether or not He exists), capitalism is, from their postcritical perspectives, too big and too triumphant to criticize or oppose. At the same time, capitalism becomes all things to all people—an effect evident in Baudrillard's 1986 travelogue *Amerique*, for instance, according to which America is simultaneously an "achieved utopia" and "an anti-utopia that is being achieved" (97)—"the anti-utopia of unreason, of deterritorialization, of the indeterminacy of language and of the subject, of the neutralization of all values, of the death of culture" (97). Here Baudrillard clearly echoes such *posthistoire* pessimists as Adorno and Jünger. Perhaps Baudrillard's most recent works, including *The Illusion of the End*, are best read as trendy, McLuhanesque popularizations and, to some extent, cheering-ups of *posthistoire* pessimism, just as Fukuyama's *The End of History and the Last Man* can be read as a cheery popularization of Hegel and Kojève, the "good news" of the end of the bad infinity of history.

197

Given the quasi-theological implications both of postmodernism à la Baudrillard and of *posthistoire* theory à la Fukuyama, it seems appropriate to invoke *Angels in America*. Tony Kushner's play brilliantly expresses the mood of the contemporary United States and perhaps other Western societies, their borders and authority increasingly overridden and overwritten by transnational capitalism, that no longer believe in their manifest destinies. Not only is faith in the nation-state waning, but so is the oppositional power of critique once centered in Marxism. In place of a once-sustaining nationalism, what has emerged is an hysterical, neoconservative and neofascist drumbeating and warmongering, as in the Gulf and the Falklands Wars.[8] And in place of radical critique with an influential purchase on the world, what has emerged is theoretical skepticism and endless, academic refinements of that skepticism: poststructuralisms, postmodernisms, neopragmatisms, together with cynical reason or irony like that involved in the very idea of angelic visitations to AIDS-plagued America.

Certainly Baudrillard's postmodern America is similar to Kushner's: at once angelic and damned, a dystopian "achieved utopia." We mourn as we celebrate, or vice versa. Kushner's version of heaven is "a City Much Like San Francisco"—though San Francisco after the Big Bang, the 1906 earthquake or perhaps a postmodern one, a demolished, anachronistic heaven where a bunch of underemployed, dysfunctional angels sit around in their council room wondering what on earth's going to happen next, and trying to learn what on earth is literally happening by listening to the news on a beat-up 1940s radio. Just before it goes silent, this "dim, crackly" device, "in very poor repair," brings the angels the bad news of Chernobyl.

The angels are, of course, neoconservatives, only a little more backward in their unblinking anachronism than the various right-wing politicos named in the play: Roy Cohn, Nixon, Reagan, George Bush Sr., Gingrich, and others. They understand neither change nor history. But as Prior Walter, dying of AIDS while rejecting his prophet's role, tells the assembled angelic host, humans aren't going to change—or rather, they *are* going to change, constantly and yet unpredictably, for better or worse, something that the neocon angels can't fathom: "We're not rocks," says Prior in his most prophetic moment; "progress, migration, motion is . . . modernity. It's *animate*, it's what living things do. We desire. Even if all we desire is stillness, it's still desire *for*. Even if we go faster than we should. We can't *wait*. And wait for what?" (2:132)

Prior's affirmation of modernity as the outcome of an inevitable drive to change for change's sake seems to affirm, with Fukuyama, the relentless technological, scientific, economic, imperialist, westernizing forces that now dominate the globe more thoroughly than when there were colonial empires. But, Kushner appears to wonder, who does the transnational, capitalist world system—the New World disorder—benefit? And who does what Boris Kargarlitsky calls "the mirage of modernization" impair, damage, destroy? These questions demand forms of social and economic critique that postmodernist theory does not provide, but that versions of Marxism once did and still can provide. At the start of "Perestroika," the title of part 2 of Kushner's play, Aleksii Antedilluvianovich Prelapsarianov, "the oldest Bolshevik in the world," speaks from a podium before an enormous red flag inside the Kremlin. This Procrustean conservative, near-relative of Ross Perot, rails against the liberal reforms that have transmogrified communism and the Soviet Union into their postmodern antitheses:

> And what have you to offer now, children of this Theory [i.e., Marxist-Leninism]? What have you to offer in its place? Market Incentives? American Cheeseburgers? Watered-down Bukharinite stopgap makeshift Capitalism!... Pygmy children of a gigantic race! (14)

The oldest Bolshevik in the world may be "totally blind," but he surely has a point. Is Russia better off now that it's got McDonald's and its own version of the Mafia? Is the former Yugoslavia better off now that it's got free-market capitalism, civil war, and ethnic cleansing? And is America better off than it was, say, in 1900, now that it's got its AIDS epidemic, its neo-Nazi "patriot" militias, its despicable sons of Roy Cohn, its deforested mountains and toxic deserts, its hysterical sightings of angels and UFOs? Not to mention those cheeseburgers again: when will the cattle supply, the grasslands, the wetlands, the rain forests, the oceans, and the safe air supply run out? The classical economists, ideological champions of capitalism and industrialism, expressed clear-sighted anxieties, at least, about the limits set by nature on untrammeled economic "progress." But their neoconservative descendants, including Fukuyama, sweep those anxieties aside with declarations of "trust," the miracle-working powers of techno-science, and the ultimate beneficence of a transnational capitalism that, as George Brockway says, is "fundamentally irresponsible" because it respects "no boundaries other than the bottom line" (242).

In Kushner's play, even heaven—or San Francisco—is a city in ruins. The angels themselves, moreover, may be only Disneyfied simulations, dimwit bureaucrats (either Democrats or Republicans—does it matter?), or even just the crumbling, pigeon-daubed statues guarding waterless foun-tains in the urban deserts of postmodern America. But in the wake of *pere-stroika* and the disintegration of eastern Europe, Marx needs to be rescued from the mounting ruins *both* of "official" Marxism *and* of transnational capitalism, just as Adam Smith, Tom Paine, Thomas Malthus, and John Stuart Mill need to be rescued from the falsifications of neoconservative apologists for late capitalism and "the postmodern condition." Meanwhile, "in the global ecology of capital today, the privilege of the few requires the misery of the many" (Anderson, 353). The gap between living standards in the First and the Third Worlds is accelerating, not shrinking, and ditto for the gap between rich and poor in the First World. "But even with such stag-gering inequality," writes Anderson, the growing wealth of the wealthy is only buying more trouble: "The ozone layer is being rapidly depleted, tem-peratures are rising sharply, nuclear waste is accumulating, forests are being decimated, myriad species wiped out. This is a scene where Hegel's spirit . . . is lost. Fukuyama has nothing to say about it" (353).

One hopes, however, that the next generation of university-trained cit-izens (of all countries), leaders, intellectuals, and experts will have a lot to say about it. I don't expect that Shakespeare or English professors will be in the forefront of what will have to be a huge, collective rescue effort. Yet per-haps the global spread of the English language, today nearly a *lingua franca* for all educated people around the world, will help—though this is, no doubt, a minor point, a relic or after-effect of the recent success and then ruination of the British Empire. In any case, if the negative trends listed by Perry Anderson are to be reversed, the only conceivable way will be through social planning on a global scale. It remains to be seen whether that planning can happen through democratic processes of world federal-ism and international law, or whether (as seems more likely) it will be imposed in oligarchic, perhaps totalitarian fashion—if it happens at all. But if such planning does not occur, the results, I believe, are bound to be catastrophic, leading, for the entire planet, not to the "stationary state" that Adam Smith considered "dull," but to the "declining" one he called "melancholy." Or worse: instead of *Angels in America, Robocop* or *Mad Max.* Despite the retreat of the threat of nuclear holocaust, and despite the alleged triumph of political liberalism and "free market" (transnational corporate) capitalism, the way history and humanity are likely to end soon will be through catastrophes bred by that triumph. Rather than the "end of history" in the sense either of goal or of grand finale, what the temporary, extremely hazardous success of transnational capitalism reveals is the "power of history" which, as Nietzsche declared, always brings in its wake a clamorous retinue of Panglosses, eager worshipers and ideologues of whatever reality or hyperreality, no matter how destructive, that power produces. "If the snake sheds his skin before a new skin is ready," says the Last Bolshevik, "naked he will be in the world, prey to the forces of chaos.... Have you, my little serpents, a new skin?" (Kushner, 2:14).

Sir Francis Bacon, who some have contended was Shakespeare, or at least the author of Shakespeare's plays, would have answered the Last Bolshevik's question in the affirmative. But, then, unlike the Shakespeare who wrote *Hamlet* and *King Lear,* Bacon was an optimist: a believer in the positive effects of science and of human ability to overcome all difficulties. According to Bacon, in his essay "Of Studies,"

> Histories make men wise; poets, witty; the mathematics, subtile; natural philosophy, deep; moral, grave; logic and rhetoric, able to contend.

Let's hope so.

Notes

Chapter 1

1. I call Kernan's *Death of Literature* "modern" rather than "postmodern," to indicate in part its neoconservative bent. A postmodern account would be more apt to celebrate the demise of literature as traditionally construed. Cultural and literary modernisms in general tended to be based on a hierarchical dichotomy between high and mass culture. In English departments today this dichotomy is often played out between proponents of "the canon" and various academic "radicals" seeking to expand, pluralize, deconstruct, or reject "the canon" altogether. On the literary canon in general and what has been happening to it since the 1960s, see, for instance, Paul Lauter, *Canons and Contexts.*

Chapter 2

1. I wrote most of this essay some time ago. More recently, Woody, the brother of Congressman Dan Burton, decided it was time to close down the Kinsey Sex Institute on my campus, because (he has somehow decided) Kinsey was a pedophile and sex maniac. Fortunately, he hasn't succeeded.
2. Of course, there are many reasons for public resentment against higher education in general. See Wilson, 25.
3. I was once on a panel discussing unions and collective bargaining for faculty. One of the participants was an economist who presented a version of his "stochastic" research, which told him that if faculty were given higher salaries and were protected in other ways by unionization, their "productivity" would decline. A lot depended, it seemed, on the significance of "stochastic."
4. Mario DiGangi, who has since taken a position at another university, published *The Homoerotics of Early Modern Drama* in 1997.

Chapter 3

1. This was in the early 1970s; Bloom's *Closing of the American Mind* appeared in 1987.
2. I was operating under what Richard Miller calls "the teacher's fallacy," which "imbues teachers with [the illusion of] an almost magical power . . . to transform the objects of instruction into whatever the teacher pleases"—something like Prospero's magic, only unreal (24).

3. On the more or less utopian aspects of college and university teaching in all fields, see James Axtell, *The Pleasures of Academe.*

4. After all, Jameson continues to be a Marxist and "socialist," with all these terms imply in relation to utopianism.

5. For the "end of history" thesis, see chapter 9.

6. In *The Aesthetic Dimension*, Herbert Marcuse says much the same when he writes:

> Art breaks open a dimension in which human beings, nature, and things no longer stand under the law of the ... reality principle. Subjects and objects encounter the appearance of that autonomy which is denied them in their society. (72)

Marcuse adds: "The autonomy of art reflects the unfreedom of individuals in the unfree society. If people were free, then art would be the form and expression of their freedom" (72).

7. I have in mind Michaels's *The Gold Standard and the Logic of Naturalism.*

8. Richard Miller writes of both faculty and students "being trapped by the fanciful notion that learning occurs only under conditions of absolute freedom." Moreover, all parties to general conflicts about pedagogy "imagine an alternative, free space where a different kind of learning and teaching might go on; and in more cases than not, this utopian space is deployed to justify the speaker's own nonperformance or political ineffectiveness in the fallen world of the academy" (7). I would add that, like Miller and everyone else I've ever encountered in a position of authority in education, I belong to this "fallen world."

9. Compare Richard Miller: "The trafficking in ... utopian visions is a time-honored academic pastime ... [but] the academy ... is ... a bureaucratic institution for sifting, sorting, and credentialing the otherwise undifferentiated masses" (22).

10. For a summary of the various national surveys and statistics, see Axtell, 5–8.

11. Among the major research universities, it takes a major threat to a major academic privilege to make unionizing a realistic option. I am thinking of the impact that the threat to end tenure had on faculty at the University of Minnesota in 1995–96. They did not finally unionize or go on strike, because the administration backed down.

12. Because the dean has only belatedly authorized the search, the initial list of a couple hundred candidates has dwindled to three, and the committee cannot decide whether to toss out the two men and go with the remaining candidate, a woman, on the grounds of gender equity, or to toss out just one of the men because he's a poet and also teaches modern literature, areas covered by Gracie, one of the committee members. When Gracie mentions that the department already has a poet (herself), Devereaux pretends not to know who that poet is. Gracie smacks him with her notebook, the loose end of the metal spiral snags one of his nostrils, and the meeting ends with a bit of comic bloodshed, if not exactly a blood sacrifice.

13. Nelson and Watt are talking about "academic departments" in general, and not just English.
14. On the "homology" between the academic hierarchy and social classes, see Pierre Bourdieu, *Homo Academicus* (53–54 and passim).
15. The teaching of writing (composition) is typically seen as the lowest of the low—that is, the most dystopian of tasks—though it also provides English departments with huge enrollments.
16. Ohmann also says: "The critical force of literary culture must have played some role in the personal-political lives of literature professors this past decade [the 1960s]. I admire the many teachers of literature who, like many poets, spoke out early against our government's conduct in Vietnam, and I would like to think that their humanistic training and practice helped them see and oppose injustice. But in our institutional efforts to preserve and transmit culture, I see only a denial of the critical spirit. Our computerized bibliographies, our fragmented 'fields,' our hundreds of literary journals and 30,000 books and articles [per year], our systems of information storage and retrieval, our survey courses and historical pigeonholes, our scramble for light loads and graduate seminars...our hierarchy of scholarly achievement, our jealous pursuit of social neutrality and political vacuity—in all this I see a retreat from criticism and a movement into more comfortable ways of life" (49).
17. To sample both sides of this ideological divide, one should read Roger Kimball's *Tenured Radicals* back to back with Cary Nelson's *Manifesto of a Tenured Radical*.
18. As I am writing these sentences, on the weekend of November 20–21, 1999, the media headlined the story of the collapse of the huge log pile that students were building and preparing to torch at Texas A&M University. Twelve students were killed and twenty-seven others injured. This obviously dangerous and ecologically wasteful ritual is one "Aggies" perform annually before the football game between their school and their archrival, the University of Texas. Only two days after this tragic accident, students, administrators, reporters, and even parents of the deceased rushed to the defense of the school and its ritual. According to the *Chicago Tribune*: "The decision to enroll at Texas A&M University can never be made lightly, for it means far more than choosing a school. It means choosing an identity.... Being an Aggie forever defines you. It confers a certain social standing, authorizes entry into a certain business network, and guarantees that despite the school's high academic reputation you will serve as the butt of withering jokes. (Why does it take two Aggies to eat a bowl of soup? One has to hold his hand under the fork to catch the drippings)" (4). Reading this tactless joke, I infer that the reporter was struggling for a way to say, without explicitly saying, "bonfire" is an incredibly stupid, wasteful ritual—like a lot of college rituals, of course, such as fraternity hazing. But also, there is little doubt of "bonfire's" interpellative power. The reporter, Karen Brandon, stresses the notion of "*choosing* an identity," and there seems little cause to question this emphasis: Aggies, who wear military uniforms, stand up throughout football games, and

believe in the legend of "the twelfth man," must on some level seek out such interpellative power. This is no more than to say that students and parents often select colleges or universities on the basis of the sort of "interpellation" they hope to receive—conservative, liberal, progressive, sectarian. Given the defense of "bonfire," a ritual which will no doubt continue, one can also wonder just what it would mean to try to teach "critical thinking" in such an atmosphere? I suspect the answer is, not much.

19. "The postmodern ethic...is at once a utopian dream about a harmonious planet and a dream about wholeness in which [the] various parts are allowed their autonomy" (Siebers, 7).

20. Vattimo writes: "The possible 'truth' of late-modern aesthetic experience is probably that of 'collectionism,' the fickleness of fashion and the museum. In the end it is the market itself, where objects circulate that have demythologized the reference to use value and have become pure exchange value—not necessarily monetary exchange alone, but also symbolic exchange, as status symbols and tokens of group recognition" (71). To "collectionism" one might compare canon formation and reformation.

21. Here I part company from Bill Readings, who seems to believe that "the posthistorical university" is today so entirely market driven that any pretense of "disciplinary grounding" is false and should be abandoned. But the disciplines including English have always had connections to the market (or the economy), precisely because they are more or less economically useful and productive. That fact of life does nothing to undermine disciplinarity, though of course it raises the question of how much influence economic pressures do, can, and should have on the disciplines—as in any of the debates around scientific research that is funded by corporations or that leads to immediate commercial production and profits for the researchers.

22. Richard Miller, summarizing Watkins, writes that the discipline "looks different depending on whether one focuses on the content of graduate education or the content of its members' work time" (35). Further, the real-and-imagined, multiple, reversible characteristics of heterotopias are facilitated by the logic of secular bureaucracies, both corporate and governmental. Although bureaucracies tend to be rigidly hierarchical and to follow often highly complex rules and regulations, the spaces they open or produce or oversee or govern or sell are frames for contents, rather than the contents themselves. Thus, even required courses for undergraduate majors in English are, in the major universities, relatively open frames for contents. A required course in British modernist literature, as ordinarily defined by departmental and university guidelines, asks a professor to teach literary works written between, say, 1900 and 1945, and may suggest that multiple genres and authors will be taught, but otherwise leaves open a wide range of choice for the teacher, who may herself leave open other choices for the students. Most professors understand what the canonical

expectations of "field coverage" are, but since they can't expect their students to read everything, can design syllabi within the larger parameters almost as they please.

23. "In general," Foucault says, "the heterotopic site is not freely accessible like a public place. Either the entry is compulsory, as in the case of entering a barracks or a prison, or else the individual has to submit to rites and purifications. To get in one must have a certain permission and make certain gestures" (26).

Chapter 4

1. The mix includes, in alphabetical but not exhaustive order, African-American, ethnic, and postcolonial theories; cultural studies; deconstruction; feminism; hermeneutics; Marxism; neopragmatism; the new historicism; phenomenology; postmodernism; poststructuralism; psychoanalysis; queer theory; reader-response theory; semiotics; and structuralism.

2. But in *Professing Literature*, Gerald Graff demonstrates that today's "conflicts" in the "theory wars" had their analogues, at least, throughout the history of the academic disciplining of English and American literary studies. Neoconservative and/or traditionalist narratives of decline and fall based on the prior "unity" provided by the New Criticism ignore or downplay the contentiousness with which it was at first greeted.

3. On the antithesis between philosophy and rhetoric, see Neel, and also the introduction and several of the essays in Mailloux. For various studies focused upon the relationship between rhetoric and ideology, see Kneupper.

4. The "linguistic turn" occurred earlier in philosophy, with the movement away from metaphysics to logical positivism and Wittgensteinian language analysis.

5. But in being based upon a politics, it is no different from older versions of canon formation, although this is something that the neoconservatives are loath to acknowledge; to do so would entail the recognition that all literary canons, along with all other cultural hierarchies, are ideological.

6. Neoconservatives like Roger Kimball believe "theory" is how "tenured radicals" (Marxists, feminists, deconstructionists, and so on) continue their 1960s project of politicizing the academy. But this narrow view misses the fact that literary criticism has always tended to become cultural and social criticism. The neoconservatives often cite Matthew Arnold, but *Culture and Anarchy* is an obvious case of a literary critic operating as a social critic.

7. Of course, not all versions of literary theory are overtly political, much less radical. And it is possible to be a quite traditional literary scholar, minus theory, while also being an ardent political radical and activist beyond and even within the academy.

8. As Groden and Kreisworth put it in their introduction, "The diverse, often apparently competing or incompatible approaches, perspectives, and modes of inquiry that flourish today under the generic label 'theory' have brought most

scholars to a welcome awareness of the importance of attending at least to methodological concerns in critical practice" (ix).

9. Nor do they contain entries under "literary theory." Makaryk's *Encyclopedia* has an entry for "critical theory," meaning the work of the Frankfurt Institute philosophers (Adorno et al.).

10. "Reading in de Man's definition always expresses a rhetoric of mourning" (Siebers, "Mourning," 363). Heidegger's claim that spirit or *Geist* entails "nostalgia for its own essence" could be rewritten: theory is nostalgia or mourning for a theoretical finality that it knows it cannot attain (Heidegger qtd. in Derrida, *Of Spirit*, 80).

11. Further, several recent publications whose titles announce the demise of theory simultaneously imply its miraculous rebirth. *The Wake of Deconstruction* (Barbara Johnson) and *After Poststructuralism* (Easterlin and Riebling), for example, are titles whose double meanings involve the now-familiar poststructuralist trope of the apocalyptic pun. Such-and-such is ending (history, for instance) but wait a minute... it is really just beginning, or anyway its aim or purpose or end has yet to be ascertained. "Rumors about the death of deconstruction," Barbara Johnson says, "have always already been exaggerated" (17).

12. Lacan insists that "there is no meta-language" (188), or in other words that there can be no theory about language (and therefore also about the unconscious, which "is structured like a language") that is not composed of words, those units of desire which, like Zeno's arrow, forever outrun themselves while never reaching their mark.

13. Eagleton sees de Man as offering "penetrating insights" into many subjects, but also as a key figure in the poststructuralist extension of Nietzsche's radical subversion of all forms of rationality and knowledge through which "rhetoric took its terrible revenge" by "contaminating" everything. This was a radicalism with depoliticizing effects. "In retreat from marketplace to study, politics to philology, social practice to semiotics, rhetoric was to end up as that vigorous demystifier of all ideology that itself provided the final ideological rationale for political inertia" (*Walter Benjamin*, 108).

14. According to Žižek: "Ideology is not a dreamlike illusion that we build to escape insupportable reality; in its basic dimension it is a fantasy-construction which serves as a support for our 'reality' itself.... The function of ideology is not to offer us a point of escape from our reality but to offer us the social reality itself as an escape from some traumatic, real kernel" (45).

15. In theorizing the relationship between ideology and rhetoric from a poststructuralist perspective, moreover, one must also take account of Lacan's insistence that "the unconscious is structured like a language," and also that it is only through interminable speaking or writing that desire and subjectivity make themselves known. From this perspective, either ideology and rhetoric are just different words for the same category of our unknowing alienation through or within language, or else ideology is the creature of rhetoric, perhaps a specific

and limited offshoot of the Symbolic Order or the language which speaks us more than the other way around.

16. Theories that assert the social constructedness of all forms of knowledge, culture, subjectivity, gender identity, and so forth can either take a deterministic direction, as in Althusser's theory of ideology, or an apparently antithetical direction, toward claims of at least partial human and even individual agency, as in Judith Butler's performance theory of gender.

17. Robbins's main example is feminist critic-theorists.

18. One objection to such a view is that many familiar utopian fantasies (Plato's *Republic*, More's *Utopia*, and so forth) dissolve social contradictions and differences by way of an identitary ruthlessness that seems totalitarian. Such utopias, in other words, are versions of ideology all over again. But "concrete utopias," as Ernst Bloch contends, inform every emancipatory movement, and these are not necessarily marked by false ideological or rhetorical closure. "The mistake of traditional thinking is that identity is taken for the goal," Adorno writes; instead, "nonidentity is the secret *telos* of identification. It is the part that can be salvaged" (*Negative Dialectics* 149). What Adorno has in mind involves a reconfiguration of utopian aspiration in terms of difference (or "nonidentity") rather than identity: "Utopia would be above identity and above contradiction; it would be a togetherness of diversity" (150). Compare Siebers on "heterotopias."

19. While from a psychoanalytic perspective, literature may be reducible to collective daydreams or wish fulfillments (the rhetoric and/or ideology of the unconscious), these daydreams are, as Ernst Bloch argues, a repository of utopian images. But this is quite different from saying that every literary work is or should be an explicit utopian fantasy. Reducing literature and the other arts to the straitjackets of traditional utopian fantasies (many of which can easily be read as dystopias) is an error directly related to its apparent opposite: the reduction of "the aesthetic dimension" to an affirmative, idealistic transcendence of politics and the social.

20. Partly through Nietzsche, partly through psychoanalysis, and partly through feminism, *desire* has been central in recent theoretical discourse. A theory of hope would have to distinguish it as at least potentially collective and rational, making for the common good, as opposed to individual and irrational. Besides older starting points in political theory and ethics, some of the ingredients of a theory of hope are evident in, for instance, Derrida's stress on Walter Benjamin's "weak messianism" in *Specters of Marx*, and Habermas's stress on "the ideal speech situation" in *Theory of Communicative Action*. See also Raymond Williams, *Resources of Hope*; Cornel West, *Prophetic Thought in Postmodern Times*; Ernst Bloch, *Das Prinzip Hoffnung*; and Tobin Siebers's *Heterotopia*.

21. There are various names for each of the ideologies corresponding to each mode of domination, but playing double roles of signification are the names of the modes themselves: logocentrism, patriarchy, racism, homophobia, imperialism. Capitalism is an economic mode of domination/production whose most

directly correspondent ideologies are: political conservatism and liberalism, economic free enterprise or free marketism, antiegalitarian rationalizations of social class hierarchies, and notions of value not based on labor.

Chapter 5

1. Thomas says: "In the general sense, I am a new historicist," but then, in the rest of the book, goes on to spell out his "specific disagreements with various practices of cultural poetics" or new historicism (5).
2. The naming and hence point of origin of the new historicism came in Greenblatt's introduction to a special issue of *Genre* in 1982. The topic of the issue was "The Forms of Power and the Power of Forms in the Renaissance."
3. A number of studies compare the two movements. See, for instance, John Brannigan, *New Historicism and Cultural Materialism*, and Kiernan Ryan's anthology, *New Historicism and Cultural Materialism: A Reader.*
4. Compare the statement about the shift away from Marxist "ideology critique" to Foucauldian "discourse analysis" in Gallagher and Greenblatt, *Practicing New Historicism*, 9.
5. Foucault offers a brilliant, charismatic, but ultimately contradictory model for reconstructing the past. Works like *Discipline and Punish* and *The History of Sexuality* are, in a sense, histories without history: "genealogies" which do not purport to reconstruct the past *wie es eigentlich gewesen*, but rather analyze texts that exist only in the present. This is not to say that the old historicism that Foucault subverts—the historicism that, following Leopold von Ranke, sought to reconstruct the past "as it actually happened"—is *less* contradictory than Foucauldian genealogy: in a sense, just the opposite, because Foucault sticks tenaciously to his nominalism and, hence, to one version of historical relativism. But histories influenced by Foucault are narratives woven out of present discourses that pertain to an irretrievable, ultimately unknowable past—narratives motivated by the historian's "will to knowledge" rather than grounded in any scientific or verifiable methodology that can produce "the truth."
6. Fish, however, likes to have it both ways—or perhaps all ways—at once. Despite his critique of the new historicism in *Professional Correctness* and elsewhere, it isn't much of a surprise to find him praising *Practicing New Historicism* in one of the blurbs on the cover of that book.
7. Fish's contexts include biographical, historical, religious, psychological, and publishing materials. These all have relevance to "Lycidas," of course, but are in no other sense "literary." In "Rethinking Intellectual History and Reading Texts," Dominick LaCapra, an historian who has repeatedly done the unprofessional thing (in Fish's view) by crossing over into literary criticism, offers a good analysis of the different kinds of contexts relevant to the interpretation of literary texts.
8. On the "postal politics" of poststructuralism and of Derridean postcards, see Bennington.

9. The new historicism is mentioned just twice in Victoria Bonnell and Lynn Hunt, eds., *Beyond the Cultural Turn: New Directions in the Study of Society and Culture*, an anthology of essays devoted to "the new cultural history."

10. For a related comparison, see Easthope, 119–123.

11. To put it mildly, Fish's contentions that the academic realm has no purchase whatsoever in the public realm of politics, and that literary critics can never be and should not pretend to be cultural and social critics, much less public intellectuals, is a puzzling position for the dean of a public university to take.

12. Jameson adds: "Jean-Joseph Goux's *Numismatiques* was still a 'contribution' to Marxist thinking; Marc Shell's pathbreaking books on money and coinage were already a good deal more neutral than that; while, in Michaels, 'money' is merely another 'text,' albeit a kind of final frontier and an arid zone into which humanists without his stamina are still generally reluctant to venture" (193). But in Michaels as in Greenblatt, what surfaces is "the ontological priority of explanations in terms of the self over all other levels" (198).

13. Like *Marvelous Possessions*, most of the essays in *Learning to Curse* open onto the terrain of cultural conflict and genocide that constitutes early American history.

14. I will continue to quote the text of "Towards a Poetics of Culture" as it appears in Veeser, *The New Historicism*.

15. The phrase "self-fashioning" comes from Greenblatt's *Renaissance Self-Fashioning*.

16. A version of the essay reappears in Thomas's *The New Historicism and Other Old Subjects*, the fullest account (and critique) to date of the new historicism.

17. But the argument of *Professional Correctness* is professionally incorrect, of course, in taking on at least the politics of academic, disciplinary border disputes. Despite declaiming against "interdisciplinary studies" in general, Fish signs on as a practitioner both of literary and of legal studies.

Chapter 6

1. See, for instance, Ashcroft, Griffiths, and Tiffin, *The Empire Writes Back*: "So the literatures of African countries, Australia, Bangladesh, Canada, Caribbean countries, India, Malaysia, Malta, New Zealand, Pakistan, Singapore...and Sri Lanka are all post-colonial.... The literature of the USA should also be placed in this category" (2).

2. See Spivak, "Can the Subaltern Speak?"

3. I participated in a conference titled "The Decolonization of Imagination" in 1991 in Amsterdam. Among the other participants was Ngũgĩ Wa Thiong'o, who had published *Decolonising the Mind* in 1988. A number of the papers from the conference are collected in Jan Nederveen Pieterse and Bhikhu Parekh, eds., *The Decolonization of Imagination: Culture, Knowledge and Power* (1995).

4. For a fuller account and critique of theories about "posthistory," see chapter 9.

5. The great worry on the part of the critics of multiculturalism is that if there is not a common culture to unify a nation-state, then that society is weakened, divisive, and without standards or values or traditions that all citizens can subscribe to. As David Theo Goldberg points out in the introduction to *Multiculturalism: A Critical Reader*:

> The motley crew who argue against multiculturalism...William Bennett, that philosopher-educator turned drug czar and now guardian of the nation's virtues,...William Buckley, Linda Chavez and Lynne Cheney, Arthur Schlesinger in his analysis of the "disuniting of America," Saul Bellow, Allan Bloom, and the like [all believe in] the sociopolitical and cultural necessity of homogeneity.

But in fact there is no and never has been such homogeneity, at least in the United States. "The *fact* of heterogeneity," Goldberg adds, "where it is acknowledged at all (by Schlesinger, for instance), is taken to necessitate the *aspiration* to a set of unifying, homogenizing ideals" (20; his italics). The normative standard, moreover, is always some version of the dominant, white, middle-class, majority culture, which makes the position of the opponents of multiculturalism logically similar to the position of white supremacists, or at any rate of whiteness, which if it weren't for everyone else's racial difference or color would be invisible and untroubled in its dominance. "The invisibility of whiteness as a racial position in white (which is to say dominant) discourse is of a piece with its ubiquity," writes Richard Dyer; today "to talk about race is to talk about all races except the white" (18). That is why Dyer among others insists that whiteness needs to be foregrounded, analyzed, and taught as a racialized and racializing category.

6. A partial solution to the main weakness in particularism is Gayatri Spivak's tactic of "strategic essentialism." See, for instance, *The Post-Colonial Critic*, 11–12.

7. One name for that means of distinction is Enlightenment rationality; perhaps one way to avoid the pitfall of Eurocentricism that that idea entails is Gianni Vattimo's postmodernist concept of "weak reason," or possibly Jürgen Habermas's ideal of "communicative reason."

8. The two British Marxist historians Gilroy names are E. P. Thompson and Eric Hobsbawm. His alignment of Thompson with a version of "Little Englandism" is perhaps more reasonable than his treatment of Hobsbawm in the same terms. For one thing, Hobsbawm's major achievement is a multivolume treatment of European history over the last two centuries, including the European impact on the rest of the world (i.e., European war, slavery, imperialism, finance, etc.). For another, like Gilroy himself, Hobsbawm has been insistent that nationalisms and national identities are unstable social and cultural constructions and "invented traditions."

Chapter 7

1. Among the participants (not including moderators) were Nancy Armstrong, Michael Awkward, Seyla Benhabib, David Bromwich, John Frow, T. Jackson Lears, Marjorie Perloff—a mixed lot, to say the least.

2. These speakers seemed all to have just read Richard Rorty's *Achieving Our Country*, in which Rorty sets up a straw-man "multiculturalist" Left to mow down (Rorty, 100).

3. Paying tribute to Leavis while rejecting his elitism, Williams declared that he and the other founders of cultural studies "wanted . . . a democratic culture, and did not believe that it could be achieved by . . . a Leavisite 'minority'" ("Future," 171).

4. Like some other political terms including "liberalism" and "conservatism," "populism" is baggy, difficult to pin down to any one definition. "Marxism" has the advantage of being more specific. In all of its variations, however, from the nineteenth-century American Populists to the "authoritarian populism" of Thatcherism, the p-word shares with the l-word the assumption that political legitimacy does or should inhere in ordinary citizens or the common people. It sometimes, but not always, also shares with Marxism the assumption that such legitimacy can only be fully realized through some form of egalitarian economic justice or redistribution of wealth. And yet populism involves an "appeal to the people and not to classes" (Laclau, 147). Its antithesis seems often to be nothing more specific than "elitism," and it can take both right-wing and left-wing forms (Bell, Trautman). Apart from these assumptions and valences, the various populisms from the nineteenth century down to the present have been vague on details. So, too, with the pop cultural populism that Mulhern, McGuigan, and other critics of it find in much cultural studies work today. It isn't so much a politics, or even a form of cultural theory, as a reaffirmation both that "culture is ordinary" and that what ordinary people like or consume is just as valuable and probably more pleasurable as what cultural elitists think ordinary people should like or consume.

5. Noting that by the end of the 1980s one major issue for cultural studies "was the future of Marxism," McRobbie writes:

> Lyotard's critique of the meta-narratives of history coincided with the emergence of the post-colonialist . . . subject who could not find a comfortable space of identity. . . within the Marxist class analysis. . . . This [also] coincided with the demise of the so-called Marxist regimes and the . . . fragmentation of the working classes of the western world as . . . industrial labour gave way to the service sector. . . and to forms of identity. . . not constructed around work. . . : the body, sexuality. . . ethnicity. . . nationality, style, image . . . subculture. (5–6)

In this sense, the falling away from Marxism that constitutes cultural studies has at least one point of origin within Marxism, in the Frankfurt School analysis of "the dialectic of Enlightenment." British cultural studies has never been much influenced by Adorno and Horkheimer, but after the Soviet invasion of Hungary in 1956 there was a repudiation of Stalinism by a number of British Marxists, precursor of the migration, post–May 1968, of various French intellectuals from Marxism into poststructuralism. Next came the impact of Althusser's structuralist Marxism, with Gramscian hegemony theory soon arriving to rescue cultural studies, if not from the economism of an older Marxism, then from what E. P. Thompson, for one, saw as the machinic rigidity of Althusser's ideas.

6. To cite just one example, in his essay "Art and Fortune," included in *The Liberal Imagination*, Trilling claims that "the real basis of the novel" has historically been "the tension between a middle class and an aristocracy which brings manners into observable relief as the living representative of ideals" (252). In the same essay, he also cites Marx on the "indecent power" of money "to reproduce" itself, as if, Marx says, "love were working in its body" (250).

7. McGuigan shows how some cultural studies populists have even turned to corporate marketing research as epistemologically more valid than Marxist ideology critique (116–122).

8. For Hall's idea of "articulation," much praised though underexplained by some practitioners of cultural studies, see "The Theory and Method of Articulation in Cultural Studies" by Jennifer Daryl Slack and "On Postmodernism and Articulation: An Interview with Stuart Hall" by Lawrence Grossberg in Morley and Chen, eds., *Stuart Hall: Critical Dialogues in Cultural Studies*.

9. This is what Joseph Litvak means when, at the end of *Strange Gourmets*, he condemns "the pluralistic consensus, the happy law of *chacun à son goût*, now operative in cultural studies" (149). McGuigan rightly distinguishes cultural populism, which tends to fall into a bland sociologism because it refuses to pass critical judgment on popular or mass cultural artefacts, and the "non-populist" "appropriation of popular cultural artefacts as 'art,'" as in "*Screen* theory" (116).

10. McGuigan contends that the academic influence of cultural populism has dealt cultural elitism "a fatal blow: opening up the range of 'texts' worthy of study (from grand opera to soap opera...), evincing humility towards popular tastes and installing the active audience at the centre of the picture. None of this is *unpolitical*. It challenges the traditional academic politics of the humanities" (80).

11. On the academic bourgeoisie and "*academica mediocritas*," see Pierre Bourdieu, *The State Nobility*, 24–25.

12. One of my favorite examples of this "new kind of superficiality" comes from the title essay of Michael Rogin's *Ronald Reagan the Movie*. While still governor of California, Reagan "refused to visit a mental hospital to see the effects of his cuts in state aid." It was then suggested to him by a psychiatrist that he "was under strain," to which Reagan replied: "'If I get on that couch, it will be to take a nap.'" Rogin notes that the future president's "affability...seems to exclude the investigator.... He seems to have fulfilled Freud's lament...that Americans have no unconscious" (10). Reagan possessed, in other words, no "ditch of truth" to be plumbed by "depth analysis."

Chapter 8

1. "Critical thinking," Robins and Webster observe, is "the most common transferable skill currently sought after in higher education." Writing about Britain, they

note: "We suspect that it is difficult to find any degree programme in the country that does not profess to develop 'critical thought'" (198). As the importance of older, content-based ideas—culture, the liberal arts—wane, skill-based goals are taking their place, partly in response to "informatics" and the general pressure from the high-tech industries for people with "flexible" skills.

2. The authors of *Thinking* also offer this interesting improvement on or "adaptation" of Shakespeare: "We are such stuff as thoughts are made on."

3. http://www.iuinfo.indiana.edu/ocm/informakit/infopres.htm

4. This is a standard definition. Compare the one in *International Encyclopedia of Information and Library Science*: "Informatics is now often used as a synonym for information technology," but it also means "the rational and systematic application of information technology to economic, social and political development" (Feather and Sturges, 176). In *How We Became Posthuman*, Katherine Hayles gives the term a more broadly social, historical, and even biological emphasis: "I take *informatics* to mean the technologies of information as well as the biological, social, linguistic, and cultural changes that initiate, accompany, and complicate their development" (28).

5. For these and related developments, see David Noble, "Digital Diploma Mills," and also Nelson and Watt, 114–120.

6. Anyone at my university who thinks there is no such threat might recall that the first so-called superprofessor hired through special dispensation from our president's office was a French mathematician, whose six-figure salary was one of the highest among our faculty at the time. To lure this mathematician to our campus (on just a half-time basis, as it turned out), the university also purchased an Alliant computer that cost five times as much as our new colleague's salary. The superprofessor needed the computer to do the complex computations that he could not do himself, no doubt more because of lack of time than lack of brainpower.

7. As David Noble notes in "Digital Diploma Mills": "At York University [in Toronto], untenured faculty have been required to put their courses on video, CD-ROM, or the Internet or lose their job. They have then been hired to teach their own now-automated course at a fraction of their former compensation" (6).

8. In their 1949 *The Mathematical Theory of Communication*, Claude Shannon and Warren Weaver declared: "The word *information*, in this theory, is used in a special sense that must not be confused with its ordinary usage. In particular, information must not be confused with meaning. In fact, two messages, one of which is heavily loaded with meaning and the other of which is pure nonsense, can be exactly equivalent, from the present viewpoint, as regards information" (99). See also Hayles, 51–57.

9. One of the ways that some academics have tried to salvage culture in the traditional sense has been to reduce it to information, which is tantamount to reducing it to "holes in paper." Most famously, there was E. D. Hirsch's *Cultural Literacy*, about which Readings writes:

Hirsch presents cultural identity as if it were not historical tradition but simply an aggregate of necessary facts, a formulation that incidentally favors the production of standardized tests.... For the contents of the textbook do not give access, as they were once supposed to do, to a culture of knowledge (a way of thinking and talking, a way of *being*).

Hirsch's version of "culture as 'what every American should know,'" *Readings* says, is no different from any other quick-fix, how-to, trivial pursuits book, "ready to take its place on the self-help shelves in the local drug and bookstore" (86).

10. The acceleration of upgrading is also, of course, the acceleration of the trashing of machines, often almost brand-new. This is planned obsolescence with a vengeance, and one of the ways in which the high-tech industries are ecologically damaging. For some of the other ways in which these supposedly "clean" industries are ravaging the environment, see, for instance, Aaron Sachs, "Virtual Ecology."

11. Many of these machines and new technological capacities are on exhibit in works by scientists, including Rawlins. See also Neil Gershenfeld's *When Things Start to Think*.

12. McLuhan, writes Katherine Hayles, emphasized "that electronic media are capable of bringing about a reconfiguration so extensive as to change the nature of 'man'" (34).

13. *Data Trash* is coauthored by Michael A. Weinstein, but I take its main design and ideas to be Kroker's, because these ideas appear in Kroker's many other works on postmodernity. Kroker's (or is it Weinstein's?) dismissive treatment of McLuhan in this text should be compared to the highly favorable account of McLuhan as a "Catholic humanist" in Kroker's *Technology and the Canadian Mind*.

14. Baudrillard cites McLuhan as an important forerunner of his own ideas in several places, including *Simulations* (54, 99, 103, 123). Douglas Kellner analyzes the influence of McLuhan on Baudrillard in detail, though he too recycles the notion that McLuhan is straightforwardly optimistic about the media and their effects: "While McLuhan and the ideologues of the post-industrial society celebrate the new media and information technologies as purely progressive forces, with purely (or largely) beneficial results, Baudrillard sees them as producing predominantly, if not completely, baleful results" (206). See also the entire chapter, "Media, Simulations, and the End of the Social" (Kellner, 60–92).

15. For some of the "unintended consequences" of technology, see Edward Tenner, *Why Things Bite Back.*

16. This is less true of Kroker than of Baudrillard and Virilio. Though in *Technology and the Canadian Mind*, Kroker treats McLuhan as a basically optimistic "Catholic humanist," there is nothing simpleminded about the optimism: "No less critical than [George] Grant of the human fate in technological society, McLuhan's imagination seeks a way out of our present predicament by recovering a highly ambivalent attitude towards the *objects* of technostructure" (58).

216

McLuhan, Kroker adds, "was therapist to a population mesmerized, and thus paralyzed, by the charisma of technology" (54). In the preface to the reprint of part of this chapter in *Digital Delirium*, Kroker writes: "McLuhan was never the technotopian that contemporary technophiles like to portray" (89).

17. Besides Hayles, see also Haraway, "Manifesto for Cyborgs"; Chris Hables Gray, ed., *The Cyborg Handbook*; and Sherry Turkle, *Life on the Screen: Identity in the Age of the Internet.*

Chapter 9

1. Niethammer points out that *Posthistoire*, though it "sounds like a French neologism, does not actually exist in French—and in German the addition of the article '*das*' makes it all the more conspicuous. In both languages, history as a collective singular is as feminine as its muse, Clio; apparently that is why *das Posthistoire* had to become a neuter noun in German," coined by Arnold Gehlen in the 1950s (2, 10).

2. Mill states that, because of diminishing returns in agriculture and the tendency of the rate of profits to fall in other forms of productivity, economic expansion leads inevitably to the limits beyond which lies "the stationary state" (2:734–735). The four factors that can prevent progress from turning into its opposite are commercial crises, through which excess capital is destroyed; improvements in production, so long as these lead to maintaining or raising profits rather than the wages of labor; the importing of cheap goods and materials from other countries; and the investment of capital abroad, whether in colonies or in other countries (2:741–746).

3. The 1987 best-seller *The Closing of the American Mind*, by Fukuyama's mentor, Allan Bloom, is a recent addition to the *posthistoire* canon. It is also noteworthy that Bloom edited the English translation of Kojève's lectures, *Introduction to the Reading of Hegel* (1969). Callinicos confuses Allan with Harold Bloom.

4. Callinicos offers an interesting comparison of Fukuyama with Paul Kennedy's *The Rise and Fall of the Great Powers* (1988), which also belongs to the end (or at least decline) of the nation-state genre. Kennedy sets "America's relative economic decline in the postwar era in the context of a long-run historical cycle in which Great Powers tend to undermine their economic bases by over-reaching themselves militarily, while Fukuyama by contrast apparently endorsed Ronald Reagan's prophecy that 'the best is yet to come' for the United States" (Callinicos, 5).

5. In *In the Shadow of the Silent Majorities*, Baudrillard says that the masses equal the refusal or "abyss of meaning" and "the end of the social" (6–10).

6. Quoting this passage from Nietzsche's anti-Hegelian "On the Uses and Disadvantages of History for Life," Callinicos points to the unwitting irony in Fukuyama's adoption of the "last man" theme from *Thus Spake Zarathustra*. Nietzsche was at least as hostile to all versions of the ratification of the present social formation as the end (or goal) of history as was Marx (Callinicos, 10, 33–34).

7. In *Trust*, Fukuyama doesn't directly defend religion, or even religion plus capitalism. Instead, he identifies something called "social capital" (that is, "trust" or, in more familiar economic language, credit, which is not too different from grace and which, he claims, has characterized "traditional societies," including those "Confucian" Asian ones that seem now to have a postmodern leg up on the United States. But the ethical values that Fukuyama somewhat fuzzily identifies with "social capital" have been the main themes of socialism: community, equality, justice, coupled with democracy and individual liberty. Rather than grant any credit to the socialist tradition and Marx, Fukuyama would just as soon combine capitalism and feudalism.

8. According to Raymond Williams, "It is not because the British people are excessively nationalist and self-confident that you got the absurd jingoism of the Falklands episode. It is because the real national self-identification and self-confidence…have gone, that a certain artificial, frenetic, from-the-top, imagery of a nation can be injected" (*Resources*, 164).

Bibliography

Adorno, Theodor. *Negative Dialectics*. Trans. E. B. Ashton. New York: Continuum, 1973.

———. *Aesthetic Theory*. Trans. Robert Hullot-Kentor. Minneapolis: U of Minnesota P, 1997.

Adorno, Theodor, and Max Horkheimer. *Dialectic of Enlightenment*. Trans. John Cumming. New York: Seabury, 1972.

Ahmad, Aijaz. *In Theory: Classes, Nations, Literatures*. London: Verso Books, 1992.

Althusser, Louis. "Ideology and Ideological State Apparatuses." *Lenin and Philosophy and Other Essays*. Trans. Ben Brewster. New York and London: Monthly Review Press, 1971.

Altvater, Elmar, Kurt Hübner, Jochen Lorentzen, and Raúl Rojas, eds. *The Poverty of Nations: A Guide to the Debt Crisis from Argentina to Zaire*. Trans. Terry Bond. London: Zed Books, 1991.

Anderson, Perry. "The Ends of History." *A Zone of Engagement*. London: Verso, 1992. 279–375.

Anzaldúa, Gloria. *Borderlands/La Frontera: The New Mestiza*. San Francisco: Aunt Lute Books, 1987.

Aronowitz, Stanley. *The Crisis in Historical Materialism: Class, Politics, and Culture in Marxist Theory*. Minneapolis: U of Minnesota P, 1990.

Asante, Molefi Kete. "Multiculturalism: An Exchange." In *Debating P.C.*, ed. Paul Berman. 299–311.

Ashcroft, Bill, Gareth Griffiths, and Helen Tiffin, eds. *The Empire Writes Back: Theory and Practice in Post-Colonial Literatures*. London and New York: Routledge, 1989.

Auletta, Ken. *The Underclass*. Rev. ed. Woodstock, NY: Overlook Press, 1999.

Axtell, James. *The Pleasures of Academe: A Celebration and Defense of Higher Education*. Lincoln: U of Nebraska P, 1998.

Bailey, Peter. *Popular Culture and Performance in the Victorian City*. Cambridge: Cambridge UP, 1998.

Baker, Houston A., Jr. "Introduction." *Narrative of the Life of Frederick Douglass, An American Slave*. Harmondsworth: Penguin, 1982.

Barnet, Richard J., and John Cavanagh. *Global Dreams: Imperial Corporations and the New World Order*. New York: Simon and Schuster, 1994.

Barthes, Roland. *Mythologies.* Trans. Annette Lavers. New York: Hill and Wang, 1972.

Baudrillard, Jean. *America.* Trans. Chris Turner. London: Verso, 1989.

———. *The Illusion of the End.* Trans. Chris Turner. Standford, CA: Stanford UP, 1994.

———. *In the Shadow of the Silent Majorities ... or the End of the Social.* Trans. Paul Foss, Paul Patton, and John Johnson. New York: Semiotext(e), 1983.

———. "The Masses: The Implosion of the Social in the Media." In *Jean Baudrillard: Selected Writings,* ed. Mark Poster. Stanford, CA: Stanford UP, 1988. 207–219.

Bauman, Zygmunt. "Universities: Old, New and Different." In *The Postmodern University? Contested Visions of Higher Education in Society,* ed. Anthony Smith and Frank Webster. 17–26.

Bell, Daniel. *The Coming of Post-Industrial Society.* New York: Basic Books, 1973.

———. *The End of Ideology.* Glencoe, IL: Free Press, 1960.

Bell, Jeffrey. *Populism and Elitism.* Washington, DC: Regnery Gateway, 1992.

Bennington, Geoffrey. "Postal Politics and the Institution of the Nation." In *Nation and Narration,* ed. Homi K. Bhabha. 121–137.

Berlant, Lauren, and Michael Warner. "Introduction to 'Critical Multiculturalism'" and "Critical Multiculturalism." In *Multiculturalism: A Critical Reader,* ed. David Theo Goldberg. 107–139.

Berman, Paul, ed. *Debating P.C.: The Controversy over Political Correctness on College Campuses.* New York: Dell, 1992.

Bhabha, Homi K., ed. *Nation and Narration.* London and New York: Routledge, 1990.

Bloch, Ernst. *Das Prinzip Hoffnung.* Frankfurt: Suhrkamp Verlag, 1959.

———. *The Utopian Function of Art and Literature: Selected Essays.* Trans. Jack Zipes and Frank Mecklenburg. Cambridge, MA: MIT Press, 1988.

Bloom, Allan. *The Closing of the American Mind: How Higher Education Has Failed Democracy and Impoverished the Souls of Today's Students.* New York: Simon and Schuster, 1987.

Boahen, A. Adu. *African Perspectives on Colonialism.* Baltimore: Johns Hopkins UP, 1987.

Bonnell, Victoria E., and Lynn Hunt, eds. *Beyond the Cultural Turn: New Directions in the Study of Society and Culture.* Berkeley: U of California P, 1999.

Bourdieu, Pierre. *Distinction: A Social Critique of the Judgment of Taste.* Cambridge, MA: Harvard UP, 1984.

———. *Homo Academicus.* Trans. Peter Collier. Stanford, CA: Stanford UP, 1998.

———. *The State Nobility: Elite Schools in the Field of Power.* Trans. Lauretta C. Clough. Stanford, CA: Stanford UP, 1996.

Brandon, Karen. "Bonfire Tragedy Brings Tight-Knit School Even Closer." *Chicago Tribune.* 21 November 1999: 1:4.

Brannigan, John. *New Historicism and Cultural Materialism.* New York: St. Martin's, 1998.

Brantlinger, Ellen. *The Politics of Social Class in Secondary School.* New York: Teachers College Press, 1993.

Brantlinger, Patrick. "Cultural Studies versus the New Historicism." In *English Studies/Cultural Studies: Institutionalizing Dissent,* ed. Isaiah Smithson and Nancy Ruff. Urbana: U of Illinois P, 1994: 43–58.

———. *Bread and Circuses: Theories of Mass Culture as Social Decay.* Ithaca, NY: Cornell UP, 1983.

———. *Crusoe's Footprints: Cultural Studies in Britain and America.* New York and London: Routledge, 1990.

Brenkman, John. *Culture and Domination.* Ithaca, NY: Cornell UP, 1987.

Brockway, George P. *The End of Economic Man.* New York: Norton, 1995.

Bromwich, David. *Politics by Other Means: Higher Education and Group Thinking.* New Haven, CT: Yale UP, 1992.

Brooks, Cleanth, and Austin Warren. *Understanding Poetry.* New York: Holt, 1947.

Brown, Lester, Michael Renner, and Christopher Flavin. *Vital Signs 1997: The Environmental Trends that Are Shaping Our Future.* New York: Norton, 1997.

Brubach, Holly. "Luxe Populi." *The New York Times Magazine.* 12 July 1998: 23–29, 38–39, 52, 56–59.

Brundage, Slim. *From Bughouse Square to the Beat Generation: Selected Ravings of Slim Brundage.* Chicago: Charles H. Kerr, 1997.

Butler, Judith. "Marxism and the Merely Cultural." *New Left Review* 227 (January/February 1998): 33–44.

Callinicos, Alex. *Theories and Narratives: Reflections on the Philosophy of History.* Durham, NC: Duke UP, 1995.

Carey, James W., and John Quirk. "The Mythos of the Electronic Revolution." *Communication as Culture: Essays on Media and Society.* Boston: Unwin Hyman, 1989: 113–141.

Carroll, David, ed. *The States of 'Theory': History, Art, and Critical Discourse.* New York: Columbia UP, 1990.

Chow, Rey. *Writing Diaspora: Tactics of Intervention in Contemporary Cultural Studies.* Bloomington: Indiana UP, 1993.

Cohen, Ralph, ed. *The Future of Literacy Theory.* New York: Routledge, 1989.

Crewe, Jonathan. "Toward Uncritical Practice." In *Against Theory,* ed. W. J. T. Mitchell. 53–64.

Davies, Laurence. "At Play in the Fields of Our Ford: Utopian Dystopianism in Atwood, Huxley, and Zamyatin." In *Transformations of Utopia: Changing Views of the Perfect Society,* ed. George Slusser et al. New York: AMS Press, 1999. 205–214.

DeBord, Guy. *Society of the Spectacle.* Detroit: Red and Black, 1977.

Delacampagne, Christian. "Racism and the West: From Praxis to Logos." In *Anatomy of Racism,* ed. David Theo Goldberg. Minneapolis: U of Minnesota P, 1990. 83–88.

DeLillo, Don. *White Noise.* New York: Penguin, 1986.

De Man, Paul. *The Resistance to Theory.* Minneapolis: U of Minnesota P, 1986.

Derrida, Jacques. "Différance." *Margins of Philosophy.* Trans. Alan Bass. Chicago: U of Chicago P, 1982. 3–27.

———. *Of Spirit: Heidegger and the Question*. Trans. Geoffrey Bennington and Rachel Bowlby. Chicago: U of Chicago P, 1991.

———. "Some Statements and Truisms about Neo-Logisms, Newisms, Postisms, Parasitisms, and Other Small Seismisms." In *States of "Theory"*, ed. David Carroll. 63–94.

———. *Specters of Marx: The State of the Debt, the Work of Mourning, and the New International*. Trans. Peggy Kamuf. New York and London: Routledge, 1994.

———. "Structure, Sign, and Play in the Discourse of the Human Sciences." In *The Structuralist Controversy*, ed. Richard Macksey and Eugenio Donato. 247–265.

DiGangi, Mario. *The Homoerotics of Early Modern Drama*. Cambridge: Cambridge UP, 1997.

Dirlik, Arif. *The Postcolonial Aura: Third World Criticism in the Age of Global Capitalism*. Boulder, CO: Westview Press, 1997.

Dollimore, Jonathan, and Alan Sinfield, eds. *Political Shakespeare: New Essays on Cultural Materialism*. Ithaca, NY: Cornell University Press, 1985.

Dorfman, Ariel, and Armand Mattelart. *How to Read Donald Duck: Imperialist Ideology in the Disney Comic*. Trans. David Kunzle. New York: International General, 1984.

Douglas, Mary. *Natural Symbols: Explorations in Cosmology*. New York: Pantheon, 1982.

D'Souza, Dinesh. *The End of Racism: Principles for a Multicultural Society*. New York: Free Press, 1995.

Dworkin, Dennis L., and Leslie G. Roman, eds. *Views beyond the Border Country: Raymond Williams and Cultural Politics*. London and New York: Routledge, 1993.

Dyer, Richard. *White*. London and New York: Routledge, 1997.

Eagleton, Terry. *The Ideology of the Aesthetic*. Oxford: Basil Blackwell, 1990.

———. *Literary Theory: An Introduction*. Minneapolis: U of Minnesota P, 1983.

———. *The Significance of Theory*. Oxford: Basil Blackwell, 1990.

———. *Walter Benjamin: or Towards a Revolutionary Criticism*. London: Verso Books, 1981.

Easterlin, Nancy, and Barbara Riebling, eds. *After Poststructuralism: Interdisciplinarity and Literary Theory*. Evanston, IL: Northwestern UP, 1993.

Easthope, Anthony, *Literary into Cultural Studies*. London: Routledge, 1991.

Engell, James, and David Perkins, eds. *Teaching Literature: What Is Needed Now*. Cambridge, MA: Harvard UP, 1988.

Enzensberger, Hans Magnus. "Ways of Walking: A Postscript to Utopia." In *After the Fall: The Failure of Communism and the Future of Socialism*, ed. Robin Blackburn. London: Verso Books, 1991. 18–24.

Fanon, Frantz. *The Wretched of the Earth*. Trans. Constance Farrington. New York: Grove, 1991.

Feather, John, and Paul Sturgis, eds. *International Encyclopedia of Information and Library Science*. London and New York: Routledge, 1997.

Fineman, Joel. "The History of the Anecdote: Fiction and Fiction." In *The New Historicism*, ed. H. Aram Veeser. 49-76.

Fish, Stanley. "Commentary: The Young and the Restless." In *The New Historicism*, ed. H. Aram Veeser. 303–316.

———. *Professional Correctness: Literary Studies and Political Change*. Cambridge, MA: Harvard UP, 1995.

Foucault, Michel. "Nietzche, Genealogy, History." *Language, Counter-Memory, Practice*. Trans. Donald Bouchard and Sherry Simon. Ithaca, NY: Cornell UP. 1977: 139–164.

———. "Of Other Spaces." *diacritics* (spring 1986): 22–27.

———. *Power/Knowledge: Selected Interviews and Other Writings, 1972–1977*. Ed. Colin Gordon. New York: Pantheon Books, 1980.

———. "What Is an Author?" *Language, Counter-Memory, Practice*. 113–138.

Francis, David R. "A Widening Rich-Poor Gap Gets Wider Political Play." *Christian Science Monitor* 91:211 (27 September, 1999): 16.

Freire, Paulo. *Pedagogy of the Oppressed*. New York: Seabury, 1968.

Frith, Simon. "The Good, the Bad, and the Indifferent: Defending Popular Culture from the Populists." *diacritics* 21:4 (winter 1991): 102–115.

Frye, Northrop. *Anatomy of Criticism*. New York: Atheneum, 1966.

———. *The Secular Scripture: A Study of the Structure of Romance*. Cambridge, MA: Harvard UP, 1976.

Fukuyama, Francis. *The End of History and the Last Man*. New York: Avon Books, 1993.

———. *Trust: The Social Virtues and the Creation of Prosperity*. New York: The Free Press, 1995.

Gallagher, Catherine. "Marxism and the New Historicism." In *The New Historicism*, ed. H. Aram Veeser. 37–48.

Gallagher, Catherine, and Stephen Greenblatt. *Practicing New Historicism*. Chicago: U of Chicago P, 2000.

Gates, Henry Louis, Jr. *Loose Canons: Notes on the Culture Wars*. Oxford: Oxford UP, 1992.

Gell, Michael, and Peter Cochrane. "Learning and Education in an Information Society." In *Information and Communication Technologies: Visions and Realities*, ed. William H. Dutton. Oxford: Oxford UP, 1996. 249–263.

Gershenfeld, Neil. *When Things Start to Think*. New York: Henry Holt, 1999.

Gilbert, Sandra, and Susan Gubar, eds. *The Norton Anthology of Literature by Women*. New York: W.W. Norton, 1996.

Gilroy, Paul. *The Black Atlantic: Modernity and Double Consciousness*. Cambridge, MA: Harvard UP, 1993.

Glazer, Nathan. *We Are All Multiculturalists Now*. Cambridge, MA: Harvard UP, 1997.

Gleick, James. *Faster: The Acceleration of Just about Everything*. New York: Pantheon, 1999.

Goldberg, David Theo, ed. *Multiculturalism: A Critical Reader*. Oxford: Blackwell, 1994.

Graff, Gerald. *Professing Literature: An Institutional History.* Chicago: U of Chicago P, 1987.

Graham, Gordon. *The Internet://A Philosophical Inquiry.* London and New York: Routledge, 1999.

Gray, Chris Hables, ed. *The Cyborg Handbook.* New York and London: Routledge, 1995.

Greenblatt, Stephen J. "Introduction." *Genre* 13 (1982): 1–6.

———. *Learning to Curse: Essays in Early Modern Culture.* New York and London: Routledge, 1990.

———. *Marvelous Possessions: The Wonder of the New World.* Chicago: University of Chicago Press, 1991.

———. *Renaissance Self-Fashioning: From More to Shakespeare.* Chicago: U of Chicago P, 1980.

———. "Towards a Poetics of Culture." In *The New Historicism*, ed. H. Aram Veeser. 1–14.

Groden, Michael, and Martin Kreisworth, eds. *The Johns Hopkins Guide to Literary Theory and Criticism.* Baltimore: Johns Hopkins UP, 1994.

Gronow, Jukka. *The Sociology of Taste.* New York and London: Routledge, 1997.

Guéhenno, Jean-Marie. *The End of the Nation-State.* Trans. Victoria Elliott. Minneapolis: University of Minnesota Press, 1995.

Guillory, John. *Cultural Capital: The Problem of Literary Canon Formation.* Chicago: U of Chicago P, 1993.

Habermas, Jürgen. "Modernity—An Incomplete Project." In *The Anti-Aesthetic: Essays on Postmodern Culture*, ed. Hal Foster. Seattle: Bay Press, 1983. 3–15.

———. *The Philosophical Discourse of Modernity.* Cambridge, MA: MIT Press, 1987.

———. *The Theory of Communicative Action.* 2 vols. Trans. Thomas McCarthy. Boston: Beacon Press, 1984, 1987.

Hall, Stuart. "Cultural Studies and Its Theoretical Legacies." In *Stuart Hall*, ed. David Morley and Kuan-Hsing Chen. London: Routledge. 262–275.

———. "The Formation of a Diasporic Intellectual." In *Stuart Hall*, ed. David Morley and Kuan-Hsing Chen. 484–503.

———. "When Was 'The Post-Colonial'? Thinking at the Limit." In *The Post-Colonial Question: Common Skies, Divided Horizons*, ed. Iain Chambers and Linda Curti. New York: Routledge, 1996. 242–260.

Haraway, Donna. "A Cyborg Manifesto." *Simians, Cyborgs, and Women: The Reinvention of Nature.* New York: Routledge, 1991. 127–148.

Harvey, David. *The Condition of Postmodernity.* Oxford: Blackwell, 1989.

Haskins, Charles Homer. *The Rise of Universities.* Ithaca, NY: Cornell UP, 1957.

Hawthorn, Jeremy. *A Glossary of Contemporary Literary Theory.* 2nd ed. London: Edward Arnold, 1994.

Hayles, N. Katherine. *How We Became Posthuman: Virtual Bodies in Cybernetics, Literature, and Informatics.* Chicago: U of Chicago P, 1999.

Heath, Rebecca Piirto. "The New Working Class." *American Demographics* 20:1 (January 1998): 51–55.

Hebdige, Dick. *Subculture: The Meaning of Style.* London: Methuen, 1979.

———. *Hiding in the Light: On Images and Things.* London and New York: Routledge, 1988.

Hegel, Georg Wilhelm Friedrich. *The Philosophy of History.* Trans. J. Sibree. New York: Dover, 1956.

Herron, Jerry. *Universities and the Myth of Cultural Decline.* Detroit: Wayne State UP, 1988.

Holquist, Michael. "The Politics of Representation." In *Allegory and Representation,* ed. Stephen Greenblatt. Baltimore: Johns Hopkins UP, 1981. 163–183.

Hughes, H. Stuart. *History as Art and as Science: Twin Vistas on the Past.* New York: Harper and Row, 1964.

Huyssen, Andreas. *The Great Divide: Modernism, Mass Culture, Postmodernism.* Bloomington: Indiana UP, 1986.

Jacoby, Russell. *The Last Intellectuals: American Culture in the Age of Academe.* New York: Basic Books, 1987.

———. "Marginal Returns: The Trouble with Post-colonial Theory." *Lingua Franca* (September/October 1995): 30–37.

Jameson, Fredric. "Marx's Purloined Letter." *New Left Review* 209 (January/February 1995): 75–109.

———. *Postmodernism: or, The Cultural Logic of Late Capitalism.* Durham: Duke UP, 1992.

———. *The Seeds of Time.* New York: Columbia UP, 1994.

Jay, Martin. *Adorno.* Cambridge, MA: Harvard UP, 1984.

Johnson, Barbara. *The Wake of Deconstruction.* Cambridge, MA: Blackwell, 1994.

Johnson, Richard. "What Is Cultural Studies Anyway?" *Social Text* 6:1 (1987): 38–80.

Kant, Immanuel. *The Conflict of the Faculties.* Trans. Mary J. Gregor. Lincoln: U of Nebraska P, 1992.

Kaplan, Amy, and Donald Pease, eds. *Cultures of United States Imperialism.* Durham, NC: Duke UP, 1993.

Kargarlitsky, Boris. *The Mirage of Modernization.* New York: Monthly Review Press, 1995.

Kellner, Douglas. *Jean Baudrillard: From Marxism to Postmodernism and Beyond.* Stanford, CA: Stanford UP, 1989.

Kernan, Alvin. *The Death of Literature.* New Haven, CT: Yale UP, 1990.

Kerr, Clark. *The Uses of the University.* New York: Harper and Row, 1966.

Kimball, Roger. *Tenured Radicals: How Politics Has Corrupted Our Higher Education.* New York: Harper and Row, 1990.

Kirby, Gary, and Jeffrey Goodpaster, eds. *Thinking.* 2d ed. Upper Saddle River, NJ: Prentice Hall, 1999.

Knapp, Steven, and Walter Benn Michaels. "Against Theory." In *Against Theory,* ed. W. J. T. Mitchell. 11–30.

Kneupper, Charles, ed. *Rhetoric and Ideology: Compositions and Criticisms of Power.* Arlington, TX: Rhetoric Society of America, 1989.

Kozol, Jonathan. *Savage Inequalities.* New York: Crown, 1991.

Kroker, Arthur. *Technology and the Canadian Mind: Innis/McLuhan/Grant.* New York: St. Martin's, 1985.

Kroker, Arthur, and Michael A. Weinstein. *Data Trash: The Theory of the Virtual Class.* New York: St. Martin's, 1994.

Kumar, Amitava, ed. *Class Issues: Pedagogy, Cultural Studies, and the Public Sphere.* New York: New York UP, 1997.

Kurzweil, Ray. *The Age of Spiritual Machines.* New York and London: Penguin, 1999.

Kushner, Tony. *Angels in America: A Gay Fantasia on National Themes.* 2 vols. New York: Theatre Communications Group, 1992–93.

Lacan, Jacques. "Of Structure as an Inmixing of an Otherness Prerequisite to Any Subject Whatever." In *The Structuralist Controversy*, ed. Richard Macksey and Eugenio Donato. 186–195.

LaCapra, Dominick. "Rethinking Intellectual History and Reading Texts." *Rethinking Intellectual History: Texts Contexts Language.* Ithaca, NY: Cornell UP, 1983. 23–71.

———. "The University in Ruins?" *Critical Inquiry* 25 (autumn 1998): 32–55.

Laclau, Ernesto. *Politics and Ideology in Marxist Theory: Capitalism—Fascism—Populism.* London: New Left Books, 1977.

Latour, Bruno. *We Have Never Been Modern.* Trans. Catherine Porter. Cambridge, MA: Harvard UP, 1993.

Lauter, Paul. *Canons and Contexts.* New York and Oxford: Oxford UP, 1991.

———, et al., eds. *The Heath Anthology of American Literature.* 2 vols., 2d ed. Lexington, MA: D.C. Heath, 1994.

Lehman, David. *Signs of the Times: Deconstruction and the Fall of Paul de Man.* New York: Poseidon, 1991.

Lem, Stanislaw. *The Futurological Congress.* Trans. Michael Kandel. New York: Avon Books, 1974.

Lentricchia, Frank. "Foucault's Legacy: A New Historicism?" In *The New Historicism*, ed. H. Aram Veeser. 231–242.

———. "Last Will and Testament of an Ex-Literary Critic." *Lingua Franca* (September/October 1996.): 59–67.

Levine, Lawrence. *Highbrow/Lowbrow: The Emergence of Cultural Hierarchy in America.* Cambridge, MA: Harvard UP, 1988.

Lipsitz, George. "Class and Consciousness: Teaching about Social Class in Public Universities." In *Class Issues*, ed. Amitava Kumar. 9–21.

Litvak, Joseph. *Strange Gourmets: Sophistication, Theory, and the Novel.* Durham, NC: Duke UP, 1997.

Loomba, Ania. *Colonialism/Postcolonialism.* New York: Routledge, 1998.

Lyotard, Jean-François. 1979. *The Postmodern Condition: A Report on Knowledge.* Trans. Geoff Bennington and Brian Massumi. Minneapolis: U of Minnesota P, 1984.

———. "Universal History and Cultural Differences." In *The Lyotard Reader*, ed. Andrew Benjamin. Oxford: Blackwell, 1989. 314–323.

Macksey, Richard, and Eugenio Donato, eds. *The Structuralist Controversy: The Languages of Criticism and the Sciences of Man.* Baltimore: Johns Hopkins UP, 1972.

McChesney, Robert, Ellen Meiksins Wood, and John Bellamy Foster, eds. *Capitalism and the Information Age: The Political Economy of the Global Communication Revolution.* New York: Monthly Review Press, 1998.

McClintock, Anne. *Imperial Leather: Race, Gender and Sexuality in the Colonial Contest.* New York and London: Routledge, 1995.

McGuigan, Jim. *Cultural Populism.* New York: Routledge, 1992.

McLuhan, Marshall. *The Gutenberg Galaxy: The Making of Typographic Man.* Toronto: U of Toronto P, 1962.

——. *Understanding Media: The Extensions of Man.* New York: McGraw-Hill, 1965.

McRobbie, Angela. *Postmodernism and Popular Culture.* New York: Routledge, 1994.

Mailloux, Steven, ed. *Rhetoric, Sophism, Pragmatism.* Cambridge: Cambridge UP, 1995.

Makaryk, Irena R., ed. *Encyclopedia of Contemporary Literary Theory.* Toronto: University of Toronto Press, 1993.

Marcuse, Herbert. *The Aesthetic Dimension: Toward a Critique of Marxist Aesthetics.* Boston: Beacon, 1978.

Marx, Karl, and Friedrich Engels. *The Marx-Engels Reader,* ed. Robert C. Tucker. New York: W.W. Norton, 1978.

Michaels, Walter Benn. *The Gold Standard and the Logic of Naturalism: American Literature at the Turn of the Century.* Berkeley: U of California P, 1987.

Mill, John Stuart. *Principles of Political Economy.* (Vols. 2 and 3 of *Collected Works.*) Toronto: U of Toronto P, 1965.

Miller, D. A. *The Novel and the Police.* Berkeley: U of California P, 1988.

Miller, Richard. *As If Learning Mattered: Reforming Higher Education.* Ithaca, NY: Cornell UP, 1998.

Mitchell, W. J. T., ed. *Against Theory: Literary Studies and the New Pragmatism.* Chicago: University of Chicago Press, 1985.

Miyoshi, Masao. "A Borderless World? From Colonialism to Transnationalism and the Decline of the Nation-State." *Critical Inquiry* 19:4 (summer 1993): 726–751.

Moore-Gilbert, Bart. *Postcolonial Theory: Contexts, Practices, Politics.* London: Verso, 1997.

Morley, David, and Kuan-Hsing Chen, eds. *Stuart Hall: Critical Dialogues in Cultural Studies.* London: Routledge, 1996.

Mulhern, Francis. "The Politics of Cultural Studies." In *In Defense of History: Marxism and the Postmodern Agenda,* ed. Ellen Meiksins Wood and John Bellamy Foster. New York: Monthly Review P, 1997. 43–50.

Neel, Jasper. *Plato, Derrida, and Writing.* Carbondale: Southern Illinois UP, 1988.

Nelson, Cary. *Manifesto of a Tenured Radical.* New York: New York UP, 1997.

Nelson, Cary, and Stephen Watt. *Academic Keywords: A Devil's Dictionary for Higher Education.* New York and London: Routledge, 1999.

Ngugi wa Thiong'o. *Decolonising the Mind: The Politics of Language in African Literature*. London: James Currey/Heinemann, 1988.

Niethammer, Lutz. *Posthistoire: Has History Come to an End?* Trans. Patrick Camiller. London: Verso, 1992.

Nietzsche, Friedrich. *Beyond Good and Evil*. Trans. Walter Kaufmann. New York: Vintage Books, 1966.

———. *Untimely Meditations*. Trans. R. J. Hollingdale. Cambridge: Cambridge UP, 1983.

Nkrumah, Kwame. *Neo-Colonialism: The Last Stage of Imperialism*. London: Nelson, 1965.

Noble, David. "Digital Diploma Mills: The Automation of Higher Education." Parts I and II. *October* 86 (fall 1998): 107–130.

Norris, Christopher. *Uncritical Theory: Postmodernism, Intellectuals, and the Gulf War*. Amherst: U of Massachusetts P, 1992.

———. *What's Wrong With Postmodernism? Critical Theory and the Ends of Philosophy*. Baltimore: Johns Hopkins UP, 1990.

Ohmann, Richard. *English in America: A Radical View of the Profession*. New York: Oxford UP, 1976.

Orr, Leonard. *A Dictionary of Critical Theory*. New York: Greenwood Press, 1991.

Parker, William Riley. "Where Do English Departments Come From?" *College English* 28:5 (February 1967): 339–351.

Pecora, Vincent. *Households of the Soul*. Baltimore and London: Johns Hopkins University Press, 1997.

Pelikan, Jaroslav. *The Idea of the University: A Reexamination*. New Haven, CT: Yale UP, 1992.

Perlstein, Rick. "Criticism versus Citizenship." *The Nation* 261:21 (18 December 1995): 792–797.

Pieterse, Jan Nederveen, and Bhikhu Parekh, eds. *The Decolonization of Imagination: Culture, Knowledge and Power*. London: Zed Books, 1995.

Pollitt, Katha. "Race and Gender and Class, Oh My!" *The Nation*. 8 June 1998: 9.

Postman, Neil. *Technopoly: The Surrender of Culture to Technology*. New York: Vintage Books, 1993.

Project on Disney. *Inside the Mouse: Work and Play at Disney World*. Durham, NC: Duke UP, 1995.

Ravitch, Diane. "Multiculturalism: E Pluribus Plures." In *Debating P.C.*, ed. Paul Berman. 271–298.

Rawlins, Gregory. *Slaves of the Machine: The Quickening of Computer Technology*. Cambridge, MA: MIT P, 1997.

Readings, Bill. *The University in Ruins*. Cambridge, MA: Harvard UP, 1997.

Robbins, Bruce. "Oppositional Professionals: Theory and the Narratives of Professionalization." In *Consequences of Theory*, ed. Jonathan Arac and Barbara Johnson. Baltimore: Johns Hopkins UP, 1991. 1–21.

———. "The Return to Literature." In *Class Issues: Pedagogy, Cultural Studies, and the Public Sphere*, ed. Amitava Kumar. New York: NYUP, 1997. 22-32.

Robins, Kevin, and Frank Webster. *Times of the Technoculture: From the Information Society to the Virtual Life*. London and New York: Routledge, 1999.

Rogin, Michael. *Ronald Reagan the Movie: And Other Episodes in Political Demonology*. Berkeley: U of California P, 1987.

Rorty, Richard. *Achieving Our Country: Leftist Thought in Twentieth-Century America*. Cambridge, MA: Harvard UP, 1998.

Rosenthal, Raymond, ed. *McLuhan: Pro and Con*. Baltimore: Penguin, 1968.

Roszak, Theodore. *The Cult of Information: The Folklore of Computers and the True Art of Thinking*. New York: Pantheon, 1986.

Rushdie, Salman. "Hobson-Jobson." *Imaginary Homelands: Essays and Criticism 1981–1991*. London: Penguin, 1992. 81–83.

Russo, Richard. *Straight Man*. New York: Vintage Books, 1997.

Ryan, Kiernan, ed. *New Historicism and Cultural Materialism: A Reader*. London: Arnold, 1996.

Ryan, Michael. *Marxism and Deconstruction*. Baltimore: Johns Hopkins UP, 1982.

Ryecroft, Charles. *The Innocence of Dreams: A New Approach to the Study of Dreams*. New York: Pantheon Books, 1979.

Sachs, Aaron. "Virtual Ecology: A Brief Environmental History of Silicon Valley." *World Watch* 12:1 (January/February 1999): 12–21.

Said, Edward. *Culture and Imperialism*. New York: Alfred A. Knopf, 1993.

———. "Narrative, Geography and Interpretation." *New Left Review* 180 (1990): 81–97.

———. *Orientalism*. New York: Vintage Books, 1978.

———. "Orientalism Reconsidered." *Race and Class* 27:2 (1985): 1–15.

———. "Representing the Colonized: Anthropology's Interlocutors." *Critical Inquiry* 15 (winter, 1989): 205–225.

———. *The World, the Text, and the Critic*. Cambridge, MA: Harvard UP, 1983.

Sale, Kirkpatrick. *Rebels against the Future: The Luddites and Their War on the Industrial Revolution*. Reading, MA: Addison-Wesley, 1995.

Schlesinger, Arthur M., Jr. *The Disuniting of America*. New York: Norton, 1992.

Shannon, Claude, and Warren Weaver. *The Mathematical Theory of Communication*. Urbana: U of Illinois P, 1949.

Shenk, David. *Data Smog: Surviving the Information Glut*. New York: HarperCollins, 1997.

Siebers, Tobin, ed. *Heterotopia: Postmodern Utopia and the Body Politic*. Ann Arbor: U of Michigan P, 1994.

———. "Mourning Becomes Paul de Man." In *Responses: On Paul de Man's Wartime Journalism*, ed. Werner Hamacher, Neil Hertz, and Thomas Keenan. Lincoln: U of Nebraska P, 1989. 363–367.

Simpson, David. "Raymond Williams: Feeling for Structures, Voicing 'History.'" *Social Text* 30 (1992): 9-26.

———, ed. *Subject to History: Ideology, Class, Gender*. Ithaca: Cornell UP, 1991.

Smith, Adam. *The Wealth of Nations*. New York: Modern Library, 1965.

Smith, Anthony, and Frank Webster, eds. *The Postmodern University? Contested Visions of Higher Education in Society*. Buckingham: Open UP, 1997.

Snow, C. P. *The Two Cultures and a Second Look*. New York: New American Library, 1964.

Soja, Edward W. *Thirdspace: Journeys to Los Angeles and Other Real-and-Imagined Places*. London: Blackwell, 1996.

Spivak, Gayatri. "Can the Subaltern Speak?" In *Marxism and the Interpretation of Culture*, eds. Cary Nelson and Lawrence Grossberg. Urbana: U of Illinois P, 1988. 271–313.

———. *The Post-Colonial Critic: Interviews, Strategies, Dialogues*. Ed. Sarah Harasym. New York and London: Routledge, 1990.

Stallybrass, Peter, and Allon White. *The Politics and Poetics of Transgression*. Ithaca, NY: Cornell UP, 1986.

Taylor, Charles. "The Politics of Recognition." In *Multiculturalism: A Critical Reader*, ed. David Theo Goldberg. 75–106.

Tenner, Edward. *Why Things Bite Back: Technology and the Revenge of Unintended Consequences*. New York: Alfred A. Knopf, 1996.

Thomas, Brook. *The New Historicism and Other Old-Fashioned Topics*. Princeton: Princeton University Press, 1991.

Thurow, Lester C. *The Zero-Sum Society: Distribution and the Possibilities for Economic Change*. New York: Basic Books, 1980.

Tillyard, E. M. W. *The Elizabethan World Picture*. New York: Vintage Books, 1961.

Trumpbour, John, ed. *How Harvard Rules: Reason in the Service of Empire*. Boston, MA: South End Press, 1989.

Turkle, Sherry. *Life on the Screen: Identity in the Age of the Internet*. New York: Simon & Schuster, 1995.

Vattimo, Gianni. *The Transparent Society*. Oxford: Blackwell, Polity Press, 1992.

Veblen, Thorstein. *The Higher Learning in America: A Memorandum on the Conduct of Universities by Businessmen*. New York: B. W. Huebsch, 1918.

Veeser, H. Aram, ed. *The New Historicism*. New York and London: Routledge, 1989.

———. *The New Historicism Reader*. New York and London: Routledge, 1994.

Vendler, Helen. "What We Have Loved." In *Teaching Literature*, ed. James Engell and David Perkins. 13–25.

Vicinus, Martha. *Independent Women: Work and Community for Single Women, 1850–1920*. Chicago: U of Chicago P, 1985.

Virilio, Paul. *The Art of the Motor*. Trans. Julie Rose. Minneapolis: U of Minnesota P, 1995.

———. *Open Sky*. Trans. Julie Rose. London: Verso, 1997.

———. *Pure War*. Trans. Mark Polizzotti. New York: Semiotext(e), 1983.

———. *Speed and Politics*. Trans. Mark Polizzotti. New York: Semiotext(e), 1986.

———. *The Virilio Reader*. Ed. James Der Derian. London: Blackwell, 1998.

Viswanathan, Gauri. "Raymond Williams and British Colonialism: The Limits of Metropolitan Cultural Theory." In *Border Country*, ed. Dennis Dworkin and Leslie Roman. 217–230.

Watkins, Evan. *Work Time: English Departments and the Circulation of Cultural Value*. Stanford, CA: Stanford UP, 1989.

Webster, Frank. *Theories of the Information Society.* New York and London: Routledge, 1995.

Wellek, René, and Austin Warren. *The Theory of Literature.* New York: Harcourt, Brace, 1955.

Wersig, Gernot. "Information Theory." In *International Encyclopedia of Information and Library Science,* ed. John Feather and Paul Sturges. London and New York: Routledge, 1997. 220–227.

West, Cornel. *Prophetic Thought in Postmodern Times.* Monroe, ME: Common Courage Press, 1993.

Williams, Raymond. "Base and Superstructure in Marxist Cultural Theory." *Problems in Materialism and Culture.* London: Verso, 1980. 31–49.

———. *Marxism and Literature.* Oxford: Oxford UP, 1977.

———. "Means of Communication as Means of Production." *Problems in Materialism and Culture.* London: Verso. 50–63.

———. *Problems in Materialism and Culture.* London: Verso, 1980.

———. *Resources of Hope.* London: Verso, 1989.

Wilson, John K. *The Myth of Political Correctness: The Conservative Attack on Higher Education.* Durham, NC: Duke UP, 1997.

Wood, Ellen Meiksins. *The Retreat from Class: A New "True" Socialism.* London: Verso, 1986.

Worrumarra, Banjo. "Pigeon Story." In *Paperbark: A Collection of Black Australian Writings,* ed. Jack Davis, Stephen Muecke, Mudrooroo Narogin, and Adam Shoemaker. St. Lucia: U of Queensland P, 1990. 158–163.

Young, Robert. *White Mythologies: Writing History and the West.* London and New York: Routledge, 1990.

Zavarzadeh, Mas'ud, and Donald Morton. *Theory as Resistance: Politics and Culture after (Post)structuralism.* New York: Guilford, 1994.

Žižek, Slavoj. "Multiculturalism, Or, the Cultural Logic of Multinational Capitalism." *New Left Review* 225 (September/October 1997): 28–51.

———. *The Sublime Object of Ideology.* London: Verso, 1989.

Index